GOD'S MIRACLES

THE COVER DESIGN: the background
on the cover is taken from cloth
designed and woven in Indonesia.

GOD'S MIRACLES:
INDONESIAN
CHURCH GROWTH

Ebbie C. Smith

William Carey Library

South Pasadena, California

International Standard Book Number: 0-87808-302-2
Library of Congress Catalog Number: 78-132010

Published by the William Carey Library
533 Hermosa Street
South Pasadena, Calif.   91030
Telephone 213-682-2047

PRINTED IN THE UNITED STATES OF AMERICA

Contents

Figures

Acknowledgments

Few are the projects any one person can alone conclude.
This general principle is doubly true concerning this book.
Acknowledgments must be directed to many different sources.

First, to the faculty and students of the School of
World Mission and Institute of Church Growth, I owe a debt of
gratitude for the many influences, insights, and encouragements
during the course of the study leading to this work.
Especially to Dr. Donald A. McGavran with whom the author
tabernacled weekly for several months during the preparation
and from whom many suggestions, corrections and directions were
taken. Dr. Ralph Winter, also of the faculty of the School of
World Mission, has aided immeasurably in the preparation of the
manuscript for publication.

Secondly, the library staff at Fuller Theological
Seminary has proved helpful beyond the call of duty. Not only
have they made available the full facilities of their own
shelves, but they have been tireless in securing materials from
other libraries. Mr. Roy Shearer rendered noble aid in the
area of library research.

Thirdly, not enough can be said about my family and
their help. They gave aid and comfort without which the study
could not have been concluded. The two younger children, Robin
and Rianna did all in their power to get the job done. Roger
helped with compiling data and reading of the final manuscript.
To Randy, I am indebted for the maps, for proof reading and for
helping with the index. My wife, Donna, in addition to all a
wife usually does in such a project, has edited, encouraged,
corrected and typed both the draft and the final copy. No
author has ever owed so much to his family.

Fourth, several others have rendered noble assistance.
Roger Knox helped in the preparation of some of the graphs.
Several interested parties have aided financially, both in the
conclusion of the period of study and the preparation of the
printed book. In particular, we think of the Mission Trust

Fund of the Broadway Baptist Church, Houston, Texas and the First Baptist Church, Conroe, Texas.

Last, but not least, to the Indonesian Baptist Mission at whose request the study was undertaken.

To these and all others who had a part--we express our sincere appreciation.

Abbreviations

IRM   International Review of Missions

CMA   Christian and Missionary Alliance

CGB   Church Growth Bulletin

VOC   Dutch East India Company
            (Vereenigde Oostindische Compagnie)

GMIM   Minahasan Evangelical Christian Church

RMG   Rhenish Missionary Society

NGZV   Netherlands Reformed Church
            (Nederlands Gereformeerde Aendingsvereenining)

NZG   Netherlands Missionary Society

TEAM   The Evangelical Alliance Mission

UFM   Unevangelized Fields Mission, Inc.

RBMU   Regions Beyond Missionary Union

ABMS   Australian Baptist Missionary Society

DGI   Dewan Geredja Indonesia
            (Indonesian Council of Churches

Introduction

Few regions have seen more remarkable church growth
than has the Republic of Indonesia. One stands in awe of what
the Holy Spirit has accomplished in these widespread islands.
The marvelous stories of the Batak Churches in northern Sumatra
tell of the development of three separate Churches with member-
ships of 819,000, 85,000 and 65,000. These accounts rank with
God's mightiest deeds. The island of Nias, just off Sumatra's
northwest coast, experienced one of the most productive
revivals in Christian history--a revival that has resulted in a
Church of 225,000 members. Some of the truly noble servants of
God have labored in Indonesia--men like Ludwig Nommenson,
Gottlob Bruckner, Jabez Carey, Joseph Kam, Riedel and Schwarz.
Great chapters have been written by lay Christians, both
European and Indonesian. People movements, such as took place
in Minahasa, have resulted in areas that are predominantly
Christian. No other area already under the sway of Islam has
experienced anything like the church growth seen in Central and
East Java.

Not all the miracles of church growth in Indonesia were
written in the past. Since the upheaval of 1965, when the
Indonesian Communist Party was defeated in its attempt to seize
power, unusual responsiveness has been experienced among some
of the peoples of Indonesia. The Karo Batak Church doubled its
membership in two years, reaching 65,000 in 1967. Thousands
were baptized in East and Central Java during the same period.
The Church on the island of Timor, under the stimulus of a
tremendous spiritual awakening, baptized 200,000 into its
fellowship in 1965 and 1966. Southern Baptists on Java and
Sumatra saw their membership triple by 1969.

The only term for such blessings is miracle. The works
of God in Indonesia are among his mightiest deeds. Therefore,
this study is entitled, "God's Miracles: Indonesian Church
Growth." It tells of God's mighty deeds in Indonesia.

The present book naturally divides into three parts.
The first two chapters consider the historical and ethnological

background of the islands of Indonesia. They deal with the
political and church history of the region, the peoples (ethnic
units) who live in the islands and their religions. Church
growth can be understood only in direct relation to the
historical factors that have shaped the peoples and the
ethnological and religious factors that have influenced their
culture.

The second part of the study is contained in the rather
lengthy chapter three which discusses some of the major Churches
of Indonesia. No attempt is made to cover all the Churches of
Indonesia. Those Churches that show revealing insights into
church growth and are inspiring accounts of missionary service
by either European or Indonesian evangelists are included.
Some of God's mightiest miracles are reviewed. The chapter
should introduce these fine Christian groups to English readers,
who presently, I am afraid, know altogether too little of the
miracles God has wrought on these islands.

No apology is offered for the third part of the study
which concerns the advance of the churches associated with the
Indonesian Baptist Mission of the Southern Baptist Convention.
These pages are penned with a practical purpose. In 1969 the
Indonesian Baptist Mission planned a church growth survey for
the seventeen year old mission. To provide the background for
this survey, the author was asked to study at the School of
World Mission and Institute of Church Growth, Fuller Theological
Seminary, Pasadena, California. This work is the library
research project necessary for any complete survey.

The present project is then a research in progress. It
attempts to supply the Mission and the survey team with the
historical, ethnological and analytical material needed for the
survey. While it is preliminary, the study is not written as
by a spectator. It purposely reveals the writer's convictions,
biased opinions, prejudices and conclusions. It is designed to
be cross-examined. The conclusions regarding the Baptist
Churches should be thoroughly tested, evaluated, confirmed,
rejected or restated as the survey reveals further insight. It
will be equally instructive to note those areas in which the
survey disproves the conclusions stated herein as to see those
conclusions that are substantiated. The overall purpose of the
last three chapters is to aid the Baptist Churches and missionaries to take a thorough, dispassionate, critical and objective
look at the work they have been doing.

The reason for the extensive discussion of the Baptist
Churches is therefore obvious. These churches are discussed,
not because they are more important than others, but to provide
background for a survey that will have the purpose of aiding
the churches to better carry out their mandate to disciple the
peoples of Indonesia. The history of the Mission, an analysis
of the growth of the churches and a final chapter on
recommendations complete this section.

Several technical matters should be mentioned. First, for readers unacquainted with the geography of Indonesia, it is suggested that attention be directed to the map included at the end of this introduction. Likewise, several maps showing the location of the major ethnic groups in Indonesia are included in chapter two and should be consulted. Graphs of growth are given for several of the Churches. The graph for every Church is not included but only those that reveal some exciting aspect of church growth. Some Churches were not depicted on a graph due to insufficient data. The graphs in chapter three are all constructed on the same scale to give some idea of relative size of the Churches discussed. At times the study mentions "growth rate per decade." This is a technique to show relative growth rates. The growth per decade is found by finding the average growth per year and multiplying by ten. For example, a Church that grew from 1,200 to 2,100 in eight years would show an average growth of 112.5 per year of 1,125 per decade growth rate. The technique is used for comparison.

This project is primarily a library research. Letters and questionnaires were employed to add information about Churches and local congregations. While the letters provided highly valuable facts and insights, the bulk of the material came from books, periodicals and other library sources.

Several books not available to English readers were most profitably used. Th. Muller-Kruger's Sedjarah Geredja di Indonesia (Church History in Indonesia), Badan Penerbitan Kristen, 1959, is a wonderfully complete and knowledgeable account of the history of Christianity in the islands. Someone would do English readers a favor by translating this important work.

The author is indebted also to Hendrik Kraemer's Agama Islam (Islamic Religion), Badan Penerbitan Kristen, 1952. This is a fine treatment of Islam in general and Indonesian Islam in particular. The fine article by Tanutama on "Geredja Isa Almasih" (The Church of Jesus the Messiah) was most helpful in considering this important Church. Finally, the author's own, Perkembangan Geredja-Geredja Baptis (The Development of the Baptist Churches) has been of limited usefulness in preparing this work.

This book is presented with the prayer that it will, in addition to preparing for a survey and introducing some of God's greatest miracles, stimulate thinking on mission methods, strategy and church growth. If these pages illicit a response and in any way aid in advancing the Kingdom of our Lord, they will have achieved their purpose. It is anticipated that the work will be received in the same spirit in which it is given and therefore, will be used in furthering the Will of our Lord.

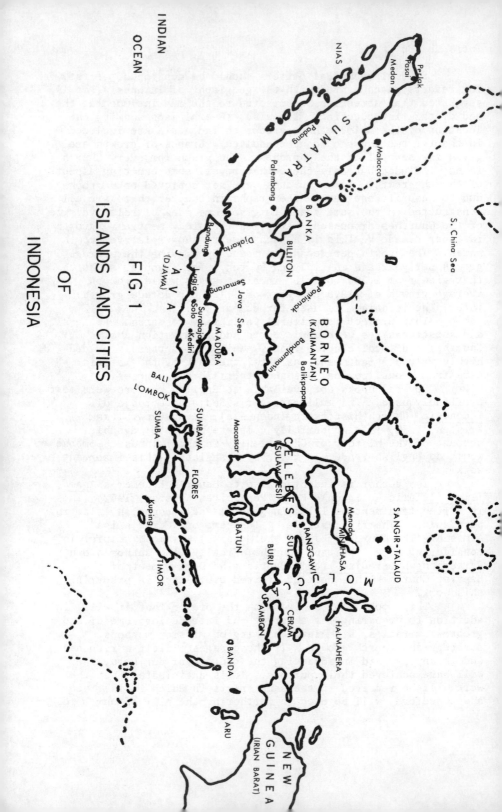

FIG. 1

ISLANDS AND CITIES

OF

INDONESIA

1

The Political and Church
History of Indonesia

The three thousand islands stretched for over three
thousand miles along the equator between the mainland of
Southeast Asia and Australia, formerly the Netherlands East
Indies, since 1945 have been known as the Republic of Indonesia
(Department of State, 1969:1). No more appropriate motto could
have been devised for Indonesia than "Diversity Becoming Unity"
(Bhinneka Tunggal Ika). A unified people using primarily the
national language, Bahasa Indonesia, is being fused from over
three hundred ethnic groups who speak more than two hundred
fifty regional languages (H. Geertz, 1963:24).
  The area of some islands is but a few square miles while
Borneo (Kalimantan) and New Guinea (Irian Barat) are among the
world's largest islands (D. Smith, 1961:9). Indonesia boasts
many highly educated citizens (over sixty percent of its people
are literate), but at the same time, some in West New Guinea
have progressed but little beyond stone age culture (Department
of State, 1969:1). Economic adaptations run from seminomadic,
shifting cultivators to wet rice farmers and on to modern manu-
facturers (H. Geertz, 1963:24). Religious persuasions include most of the world's religions. Around eighty-five percent embrace Islam, but Buddhism, Hinduism and Christianity
as well as various indigenous religions are represented (Fisher,
1964:250-251). The animistic base of Indonesian religion has
never been eradicated with the result that many, if not most,
are still animists at heart (Kennedy, 1943:106). Within this
mosaic Southern Baptists have served since 1951.

INTRODUCTION

Geographical factors such as volcanic mountains, extended coast lines and tropical jungles have influenced both
the history and development of Indonesian culture and church
growth. Indonesia's coast line, one of the longest in the
world, has allowed an ease of contact between the coastal peoples
while the inland peoples have been more isolated, cut off as

1

they were by tropical forests and land masses (H. Geertz, 1963: 25).

The geographical variations have given rise to three different types of Indonesian societies: the trade-oriented, strongly Islamic coastal peoples; the Hinduized inland peoples and the animistic tribal groups of the mountainous interiors H. Geertz, 1963:25-30). The location and nature of many of the islands, such as the Moluccas, Java and Sumatra, resulted in their earlier contact with the outside world and thereby with Hinduism, Islam and Christianity. Other islands, Borneo, parts of the Central Celebes, New Guinea and other interior areas, being off the main trade routes, have remained more re- mote and animistically oriented (cf. Fisher, 1964:221). The meaning of these geographical factors to church growth is apparent. The most spectacular church growth has been real- ized among the more isolated peoples.

Indonesia's 115,000,000 people constitute the world's fifth largest population (Department of State, 1969:1). This population makes church growth imperative. Population is in- creasing at between 2.4 and 2.5 percent per year. In 1961 ex- perts were surprised that the census revealed 97.8 million people. The Central Bureau of Statistics estimated the pop- ulation at 109,592,000 in 1966 and 112,000,000 in 1968. Such expanding population of necessity puts a strain on the economy which is growing at only 1.57 percent and has not been able to keep pace with the increasing population (Cooley, 1968: 10).

Indonesia's population problem is intensified by its imbalance in distribution. An estimated 64.5 percent of Indonesia's millions are concentrated on Java and Madura which comprise only around seven percent of the land total. The population density on these two islands is twenty-one times that of the rest of Indonesia (Cooley, 1968:11). Presently the population of Java is in the neighborhood of seventy-five million with a density of over 1,020 people per square mile.

The density of the population of Central and East Java can be explained on natural grounds. Arid winds from Australia result in lessening of rainfall during certain months giving an opportunity for water control and soil conservation not enjoyed in many parts of Indonesia. The volcanic topsoil being thus conserved, the Javanese have been able to fully employ the valuable minerals and perennial fertility (Cady, 1964:9, 10). Thus, it is not by accident that Java has been the center for some of the greatest Indonesian civilizations and the focal point of its population (Vlekke, 1943:xiv).

To attempt to alleviate the crowding on Java the **govern-** ment in recent years has instituted a program of transmigration and resettlement to the under populated regions of Sumatra and Borneo (Wertheim, 1965:182-209).

These resettlement areas must receive close attention from
Christian groups. History has indicated that displaced peoples
who intend to remain in the new area are usually ripe for
change, including religion. Although much has been accomplished through these programs, as well as by spontaneous movements
from Java and Madura, transmigration in itself can only alleviate the pressure but can never solve the problem of overcrowd-
ing on Java (Pelzer, 1963:23).

The islands of the Indonesian archipelago have exerted
an influence on world history far out of keeping with their
size. Their story is associated with such names as Marco Polo,
Kublai Khan, Magellan, Sir Francis Xavier and other voyagers
of the age of discovery (D. Smith, 1963:10). It was partly
to reach these islands that Prince Henry the Navigator financed
the navigation adventures of the fifteenth century. These adventures resulted in circumnavigating the Cape of Good Hope by
1488 and Vasco da Gama's voyage to India by 1497. The way to
the East (and the Indies) without having to force the way
through the Islamic Ottoman Empire was now open to Europeans
(Latourette, 1965:163). It was to these "Spice Islands" that
Columbus sailed in 1492 when his voyage was rudely interrupted
by a previously unknown continent (Department of State, 1969:
1)

The Indonesian islands were the seat of great empires
that flourished before 1000 A.D. The Srivijaya Empire was
well established by 500 and the Sailendra Rulers in Java had
attained advanced civilizations before the 700s. Thus, the
islands of Indonesia had developed a rather advanced civilization in a period when Europeans were being characterized by
names such as barbarian and vandal.

Indonesia's extensive resources naturally constituted
a prize for the powers engaged in World War II. Since independence the names of Indonesian leaders such as Sukarno, Hatta,
Nasution and Soeharto have become familiar to people the world
over. Church growth has been no stranger in the matrix of
historical phenomena that makes up the complex story of
Indonesia.

PREHISTORIC INDONESIA

Prehistoric man left his footprints in Indonesia's
volcanic soil at least 600,000 years ago. Fossil remains,
"Homo Modjokertensis", dating from the early plestocence age,
were found near the East Java city of Modjokerto. The
"Pithecanthropos erectus", discovered in 1890 was thought to
have lived some 300,000 years ago. Eleven skulls found in
Central Java near Solo (Homo Solensis) were judged to be some
40,000 years old (Vlekke, 1943:3,4). The Wadjak skulls were
thought to be of late or even post-pleistocene age and related
to proto-australoid man. The contention that "Homo

Modjokertensis" and "Pithecanthropus" resemble "Sinanthropus"
(Peking Man) has been refuted by authorities (Hall, 1964:5).
It is extremely doubtful that modern Indonesians descended from
these prehistoric races (Vlekke, 1943:3).

Modern Indonesians descended from peoples who migrated
into the islands in four waves. The earliest of these, the
Australoid, was characterized by coarse features, beetling
brows and hairy bodies. Traits of these people can still be
detected in areas near Australia. In addition, two branches
of Negroid peoples lived on the islands in ancient times. One
branch, which has disappeared from Indonesia except in the extreme eastern islands, migrated beyond New Guinea to the
Solomons, Fijis and New Caledonia. The other Negroid branch,
the Negrito or dwarf Negro, is still found in sections of
eastern Sumatra, Timor, Alor and some mountainous regions of
New Guinea (Kennedy, 1943; 5, 6).

Another archaic stratum of Indonesian population, the
Veddoid, is found in relatively pure form among the Vedds of
Ceylon. While secluded peoples in Indonesia such as the Gajo
of northern Sumatra, the Bodha of Lombok and the Kubu of the
jungles of eastern Sumatra show more marked Veddoid traits
than other Indonesians, the Veddoid strain is widely represented. Before the Malay invasions most of Indonesia was likely
inhabited by Veddoid tribes, interspersed by small groups of
Negrito stock (Kennedy, 1937:286-287).

Two waves of Malay peoples forced these earlier peoples
deeper into the jungles and mountains. The first wave, the
Proto-Malays, originated from southern China from where they
migrated into Indo-China, Thailand and then to the archipelago.
The Proto-Malays were the ancestors of the Malay-Polynesian
who spread from Madagascar to the eastern Pacific (Vlekke, 1943:
5). They are mostly found in the interior districts of Java,
Sumatra, Borneo and the Celebes as well as in the chain of
islands from Bali to Timor (Kennedy, 1943:5).

The Deutro-Malay peoples, showing a more Mongoloid nature,
pushed into the islands about three hundred years before Christ.
They are thought to have brought iron culture to the islands
(Vlekke, 1943:5). The Deutro-Malays pushed the Proto-Malays
back into the interior regions and seized the coastal regions
for themselves (Kennedy, 1943:5).

These early races have mixed until now it is difficult
to distinguish between the strains. The situation is further
confused in that linguistic differences do not always follow
the racial divisions (Vlekke, 1943:5, 6). Thus, from the times
of the early migrations the diversity of the peoples of
Indonesia has progressed toward a unity.

INDIANIZATION AND THE EARLY EMPIRES 500-1000

The Indian Influence

The earliest Indonesian political institutions above the village level were formed by local leaders who combined village and clan groups into larger, more stable communities. Commercial contacts with India acquainted Indonesians with Indian social and political concepts which embodied a centralized, hierarchial political organization under a sacred king. Such a cultural vehicle for the legitimization and extension of their authority appealed to Indonesian princes (Van Niel, 1963;272).

The exact way in which Indian influences reached the Indonesian archipelago is disputed (Bosch, 1961:1). Authorities agree that the coming of Indianization was peaceful and non-political and was easily assimilated into the indigenous traditions (Cady, 1964:41). Disagreement prevails concerning the means of Indianization.

Some historians contend that colonies of Indian merchants migrated to Indonesia, intermarried with local people and thereby transmitted Indian culture. Communities influenced by these merchants sought Brahman priests to serve in performing magical rites (Cady, 1964:41). The French historian, Georges Coedes, characterized the Indonesians as the passive recipients of Indian culture. He contended that the Indonesian society was an Indian superstructure erected on the old indigenous substratum (Hall, 1964:21). Over a period of time, according to this theory, intermarriage and the teachings of Brahman priests completed the merger of Hindu religion with local cults and the transmission of Indian literature, legal codes and governmental forms (Cady, 1964:41-42).

The Dutch scholar, J. C. Van Leur, insists that Indian merchants could not have transmitted the philosophical Indian religious and civil ideas. Since most of the traders were from lower social groups and their crews often slaves, it "...was impossible for such people to have been administrators of ritual, magical consecration and disseminators of rationalistic, bureaucratic, written scholarship and wisdom." Van Leur continues that the process was essentially the summoning to Indonesia of Brahman priests and other court artificers for the purpose of establishing Hindu rites for Indonesian courts (Van Leur, 1955:98-103). Van Leur is supported in this view by another authority, Wertheim, who contends that the Indian influences entered through a comparatively small number of influential Indian Brahmans who lent political support to Javanese rulers by providing them with a kind of investiture and genealogic confirmation of membership in a high caste. These priests acted as advisers in affairs of government and things sacred (Wertheim, 1956:237-238).

Buddhism entered Indonesia through a more popular

transfer. Buddhist pilgrims came to Indonesia as missionaries.
They would appear at Indonesian courts, preach their law, con-
vert the ruler and his family and found an order of monks.
Often they stimulated a stream of devotees to India where a
Buddhist monestary was established for Indonesians around 860.
The Buddhists returned to promote Buddhist teaching and phil-
osophy (Hall, 1964;20-21).

Indianization, both Hindu and Buddhist, was basically
added to the existing Indonesian culture which became infused
with Indian philosophy (Bosch, 1961:20). Indonesian adat
(customary) law remained unimpaired in authority and influence
(Wertheim, 1956:240-241). Van der Kroef correctly notes that
the Buddhist monument, Borobudur, reflects the Hindu architecture but that many items included in the carving are
Javanese both in origin and execution (Van der Kroef, 1951:
17-30).

Hindu and Buddhist influences materially influenced the
developing Indonesian way of life. Indian influences consolidated the emergence of political units, providing both organizational techniques and religious sanctions for Indonesian
leaders (Legge, 1964:35,36). Java and Bali were most deeply
influenced by Indianization but Sumatra, Borneo and the
Celebes did not remain uneffected. Areas further to the east
received relatively less Indian influence (Woodman, 1955:133).

The Early Empires

When the Chinese Funan Empire began to disintegrate
around 500 A.D., the first great Indonesian empire, the
Srivijaya, rose to power in the area of modern Palembang
Hall, 1964:41). By 670 the Srivijaya Empire had become an
important center of Buddhist learning and within a few years
extended its rule over much of Sumatra, the western tip of
Java, a small section of West Borneo and sections of the
Malay peninsula (Cady, 1964:62-69).

The Srivijaya Empire persisted for six centuries even
though it paid little attention to agricultural matters. It
lived a parasitic life connected with the stream of commerce.
Longevity and wealth not withstanding, the empire made few
durable contributions. This empire lacked the essential
economic base, the disciplined labor supply and the cultural
solidarity required for creative achievement in literature,
art and architecture (Cady, 1964:70).

The second Indonesian empire, the Sailendra, centered
in Central Java where its first ruler, Sanjaya, came to power
around 732. The language of the empire was Sanskrit and the
religion was Shivaism, a type of Brahmanism. The temples
whose ruins are found on the Dien Plateau were dedicated to
Shiva, indicating an origin in southern India (Bengal).
Sanjaya's successor apparently not only belonged to a different

dynasty but professed a new creed (Buddhism) and used a
different script (Vlekke, 1943:21-22). Apparently the Buddhist
Sailendras drove the Sanjaya dynasty from Central Java and with
it their Saivite religion (Hall, 1964:46).

The Buddhist Sailendras created the religious monuments
on the Kedu plain in Central Java. These eighth and ninth
century edifices marked a high point in Javanese architectural
and artistic achievement. Borobudur, the greatest of the
monuments, was built between 760 and 860. The Javanese sculptors adapted the Indian motifs to their own uses (Van Niel,
1963:273).

The Hindu Shivaitic Kingdom still persisted in East
Java and with the decline of the Buddhist Sailendras returned
to Central Java. The Hindu religious complex near Prambanan
contains a statue of Durga, the goddess who is one of the
personifications of Devi, the consort of Shiva. The monuments
are called "Lara Djonggrant" or the slender maiden (Vlekke,
1943:24-28).

After around 930 King Sindok moved the center of Hindu
power back to East Java near the Brantas River where he maintained the empire of Mataram. The Mataram Empire persisted
until 1222 (Van Niel, 1963:274). The move resulted in the
eventual weakening of Hinduism and the culture definitely and
progressively became more Javanese and less Hindu (Vlekke,
1943:29).

A powerful king in East Java, King Dharmavamsa (985-
1006) extended his rule over Bali and parts of Borneo.
Dharmavamsa's attack on the Srivijaya failed because
Srivijaya employed Malay vassals. Srivijaya mounted a counter
attack and reduced the Mataram Kingdom to chaos (Hall, 1964:
57). For some years there was no real authority in Java,
but after Srivijaya was defeated by the Cholas from India in
1025, King Airlangga from Bali established rule over most of
East Java (Vlekke, 1943:36,37).

Airlangga divided his kingdom between his two sons
around 1045. One son established the kingdom of Kadiri that
was succeeded by the kingdom of Singhasari. The last king
of Singhasari completed the assimilation of Sivaism and
Buddhism bringing into play the worship of Siva-Buddha (United
States Army Handbook, 1964:30). So complete was the syncretism
that the two religions were brought into the same building,
the lower floor dedicated to Shiva and the upper to Buddha
(Vlekke, 1943:44).

The Senghasari Kingdom earned the ire of the Mongol
leader, Kublai Khan, who in 1292 sent a thousand ships and
twenty thousand men on a punishing mission to Java. Before
this mission reached Java, Jayakatawang, the Prince of Kadiri
murdered King Kertanegara and forced the crown prince, Vijaya,
to flee to Madura. Vijaya joined Khan in the mission which
defeated Jayakatawang after which Vijaya ambushed the Khan's

army and on the strength of his victory returned to the throne
(Cady, 1964:140). Thus, the only real result of the Khan ex-
pedition was to return to power the son of the man they had
come to punish (Vlekke, 1943:51).

Vijaya founded the Majapahit Kingdom around 1293. This
kingdom began a final decline with the death of Vijaya's grand-
son, Hayam Wuruk in 1389. Events leading to this situation
brought to the scene one of the greatest Indonesian statesmen,
Gadjah Mada. Gadjah Mada rose to power never before held by a
minister. Until his death in 1364 he was the real ruler of
the Majapahit Kingdom (Hall, 1964:80-81).

Gadjah Mada almost attained his goal of subjugating all
of Indonesia (United States Army Handbook, 1964:31). Religious-
ly there was further progress toward an indigenous Javanese
standard. The death of Gadjah Mada brought to an end the
ideal of Nusantara (all of Indonesia). Islam was already reaching the shores of northern Sumatra and the visit of Marco Polo
foretold the advent of European powers who would be soon visiting the waters and lands of Indonesia. The period of Indianization and the great empires was coming to an end.

THE COMING OF ISLAM AND CHRISTIANITY 1000-1600

The next period, extremely important from the viewpoint
of church growth, witnessed the coming of Islam and Christianity.
Trade was a major yet not exclusive factor for the unequal
struggle of the two religions in the archipelago. By an irony
of history, the needs of a prosperous Europe, the Crusades and
the Mongol invasions combined to implement the spread of Islam
over the Far East, including Indonesia (Schrieke, 1966:12).
Thus, at a time when Constantinople had fallen and the Turks
were threatening Europe, their co-religionists were pressuring
the Javanese Empire of Madjapahit (Cole, 1945:244).

The Earliest Moslem Strongholds

The earliest reliable report of Islam in Indonesia is
contained in Marco Polo's journal which reported that the city
of Perlak on Sumatra had been won to Moslem laws and religion
by "Saracene" merchants. The nearby kingdom of Samudra was
converted soon after Perlak. A Malay tradition places the
conversion of the king of Samudra to Islam at around 1270-1275
(Djajadiningrat, 1958:375-376). Obviously Moslem principalities existed in northern Sumatra as early as the thirteenth
century (Benda, 1958:9).

Islam reached the islands, perhaps as early as the
tenth century, but did not gain great strength until the
coming of the Moslem merchants from Gujerat, India (United
States Army Handbook, 1964:229). The real impetus of Islamic
expansion came from the city of Malacca on the coast of the

Malay peninsula (Fisher, 1964:249). The Sailendra Prince,
Parameswara, fleeing from the war with the Majapahit Javanese,
settled in the small fishing village of Malacca. He accepted
Islam around 1414. Primarily to strengthen his position along
the trade routes he took this step. From Malacca, Islam spread
across Indonesia (Cady, 1964:166, 167).

Factors in the Spread of Islam

By the latter part of the fifteenth century, Javanese
converts to Islam had risen to positions of political leadership in cities along the north coast of Java. Towns such as
Ngampel (Surabaja), Benang, Gresik, Tuban, Djapara and
Tjeribon had Moslem rulers. The first of these Moslem cities
on Java, Demak, founded by Raden Patah in 1518, provided Islam
a base from which it spread easily along the north coast but
met opposition in the more Hinduized interior regions (Berg,
1932:250). Leaders from these towns known as wali, served as
Moslem missionaries. Their stories are told in the traditional Javanese epic, Babad Tanah Djawi. The wali owed their power
to the Majapahit Kingdom but justified their renunciation of
loyalty to Majapahit by the appeal to the superior authority
of Islam (Jay, 1963:6)

Several factors stimulated the Moslem advance into
Indonesia. First, Islam penetrated Indonesia along family
lines and by peaceful means. The Moslems followed the plan
first of exterior mission, to make the people Islamic in name
and if possible bring them under Moslem rule. According to
the plan, later the Islamic faith could infuse all of life
(Berg, 1932:251). Moreover, Islam traveled along family lines
with the wives of Moslem traders becoming Moslem and often
extended to the families of the wives. The children of these
unions were educated as Moslems and enhanced the peaceful
spread of Islam (Djajadiniagrat, 1958:375-376).

Secondly, Islam reached Indonesia at a time when Hindu
religion was declining and indigenous cultural and religious
life was reviving. There was a tendency toward change, even
in strongly Hindu East Java. The Sundanese Princes in West
Java, with their antagonism toward the East Java Majapahit
Kingdom, welcomed Islam. The unstable conditions that existed,
advanced the religion of the Prophet (Nieuwenhiujze, 1958:
35-36).

In the third place, Indonesian society, especially in
the rural regions, had been influenced by the Hindu caste
system. The lower castes welcomed the Islamic doctrine of
the equality of men in the ummat Islam, the Community of
Islam. Any view that lent dignity to the common man would have
had great appeal to the lower classes who chaffed under ideas
of caste and second class citizenship (Nieuwenhiujze, 1958:35).

Islam reached Indonesia with its doctrine of equality at a time
when this doctrine was most attractive to large segments of
Indonesian society.

Fourthly, Islam's spread was enhanced by its concessions
to the old customs. Many Hindu court habits persisted even
though they were intolerable to basic Islam. The literature
remained soaked in Hinduism, the wajang plays were inseparably
connected with Hindu epics and the music, dance and other
elements in ancient culture remined little changed (Berg, 1932:
252). A case in point would be the persistence of the matri-
linial social structure among the Minangkabau of West Sumatra
who adopted the Moslem religion.

A strong factor in Moslem advance was the arrival of
the Portuguese in 1497 (Van Leur, 1955:113). The struggle between Islam and Christianity had already been joined in Europe.
The Portuguese came to Indonesia partly for trade and partly
to oppose Islam. Knowing this, the Moslems pressed their advantage in the years before the Portuguese became strong enough
to be any real competition (Schrieke, 1957:232-237). By cutting
off contact with India, the Europeans stimulated the contact
with Arabia and more orthodox Islam. This contact led to the
creation of a "Jawi" colony in Mecca where many Indonesians
studied and returned to Indonesia as teachers who moved
Indonesian Islam to a more orthodox position (Berg, 1932:257-
260). Eventually, both in the Portuguese and later in the
Dutch periods, adherence to Islam included opposition to
Europeans. Thus, the Europeans themselves stimulated the
spread of Islam (Kraemer, 1958:114-115). At any rate, even
when Malacca fell to the Portuguese in 1511 the Crescent was
already ahead of the Cross and it has never relinquished its
lead (Schrieke, 1957:237).

The Portuguese Intrusion 1511-1610

The Portuguese goals of attaining the monopoly on the
spice trade as well as opposing the Moslems could best be attained from the city of Malacca (Cady, 1964:172). Therefore,
when Alfonso de Albuquerque replaced the less aggressive
Francisco de Almeida, one of his first efforts, after securing
the Indian territories, was an attack on Malacca. Capturing
Malacca on August 19, 1511, Albuquerque immediately began the
construction of a fort (Vlekke, 1943:74,75). He built the
fortress with materials from a razed mosque and the tombs from
Moslem sultans, thereby further alienating the Moslems (Cady,
1964:176).

The Portuguese attempted to establish their monopoly on
the spice trade. Spices could be sold in Europe at a profit
of over 2500 percent (Vlekke, 1943:75). To obtain this monopoly, the Portuguese had to drive out the Javanese traders and
police the sea routes between Indonesia and Arabia. The task

was made more difficult by the fact that many islanders had
been recently won to Islam (Hall, 1964;219).

An abortive attempt of the Javanese princes to retake
Malacca in 1513 resulted in the decimation of the Javanese
fleet (Cady, 1964:178). Even weakened, Javanese antagonism
forced the Portuguese to use the northern route by way of north
Borneo to reach the spice islands. The Spanish intrusion in
the Moluccas (Halmahera and Ambon) also constituted a problem
to the Portuguese. The Spanish withdrew in 1530 but reappeared
in 1542 and 1570. The Portuguese maintained a fort at Ternate
until 1574 when their own folly resulted in their expulsion
(Cady, 1964:184).

Inefficient administration, faulty and often foolhardy
relations with the residents and a purely commercial outlook
all combined to defeat the Portuguese in Indonesia. Growing
hatred of the Portuguese was based largely on their abuse of
power and disregard for the people (Cady, 1964:172). They
contributed little or nothing to the development of the
Indonesian economy or culture. They were essentially parasitic
and limited their trade to spices and luxury goods (Van Leur,
1955:117-119, 159-166). So great was the cruelty of the
Portuguese that St. Francis Xavier once wrote that knowledge
of Portuguese in the Moluccas was restricted to the conjugation
of the verb <u>rapio</u>, in which they showed "...an amazing capacity
for inventing new tenses and participles" (Hall, 1964:222).

Eventually, the resources of the Portuguese proved too
small to hold the islands against their many foes. The coming
of the English, in the person of Sir Francis Drake in 1578,
and the Dutch shortly thereafter spelled the end of Portuguese
suzanerity. After 1610 control passed to the Dutch who were
not motivated by crusading concerns. Although they held
Malacca until 1641, the day of the Portuguese had passed (Cady,
1964:173).

The Beginnings of Christianity

Recognizing Islam as a major factor mitigating against
their commercial interests, the Portuguese turned to an attempt
to convert the non-Moslem territories to Christianity (Hall,
1964:222-223). While the commercial interests had only worldly
reasons for the mission, the missionaries served from sincere
motives and accomplished growth. Portuguese mission work began
as early as 1537 in the Moluccas. When the Jesuit, St. Francis
Xavier, reached Ambon in 1546, he found congregations already
in existence (Cooley, 1966:343). The Portuguese Catholics
established churches in the Moluccas, in Minahasa, in
Sangir-Talaud and in Halmahera (Muller-Kruger, 1959:74,86,96).
Churches were planted in Solor, Flores and Timor during these
early years as well (Cooley, 1968:40). In these areas where
the Portuguese began evangelistic efforts in the 1530s are

today found some of Indonesia's strongest churches.

THE DUTCH COMPANY PERIOD 1610-1811

The seventeenth century saw three powers competing for control in Indonesia. The Mataram Kingdom, founded by the legendary Senapati, had been consolidated under Sultan Agung (1613-1645) and had extended its control over most of East Java, parts of Borneo and into West Java (Hall, 1964:260-261). Mataram was opposed by the merchant center of Bantam which controlled much of the trading in spices and pepper (Van Niel, 1963:280). The Dutch, through the Dutch East India Company, made up the third and eventually the dominant element in the power struggle.

The Formation and Acts of the Dutch East India Company 1602-1795

European developments such as the defeat of the Spanish Armada in 1588 and the policy of Philip II of Spain denying the Dutch access to the spice trade out of Lisbon, stimulated Dutch ascendancy in the Indies. Dutch vessels undertook numerous voyages such as that of Cornelius de Houtman in 1595. Houtman was received warmly in most places but his unnecessarily cruel actions in East Java and Madura alienated many of the Indonesians (Vlekke, 1943:92-94). Houtman's actions help explain the contemporary anti-Christian feeling of the Madurese today.

In 1602, to overcome the intense competition between Dutch investors, the United Company was established and granted a charter to exclusive rights to trade, shipping, and the exercise of authority in the territory of Indonesia (Van Leur, 1955:176,177). The United East India Company, Vereenigde Oostindische Compagnie or VOC, became the instrument by which the Netherlands tried to exclude European rivals from Indonesian trade. The VOC continued until 1795 when its failure brought the Dutch government into direct control (Legge, 1964:67).

Continuing friction with the British and the leaders of Bantam led the Dutch Governor, Jan Pieterzoon Coen, to center Dutch commercial activity in the city of Jacatra which he renamed Batavia (modern Djakarta). Coen proceeded to sabotage the British interests in Indonesia. After the Dutch, in 1623 executed two-thirds of the workers of a British factory in Ambon (called the "Massacre of Ambonia") for alleged conspiracy, all pretense of cooperation vanished (Cady, 1964:207). Actually only about eight people were killed but it gave the British a pretext for leaving the Moluccas with dignity, saying their position was hopeless (Vlekke, 1943:124-125). Even so, British trade continued at Japara (north Java) until 1652 and at Macassar until 1667 (Cady, 1964:207).

Coen còntinued to consolidate Dutch holdings in Indonesia. Ruthlessly he extended Dutch control over the Moluccas and Banda before his death in 1629 (Cady, 1964:215). Interestingly, the Dutch historian, W. R. Wertheim, remarked on the subjugation of Banda that it was effected by "not too gentle means" rather than "ruthlessly" as used by the American Cady (Wertheim, 1956:47). The defeat of Sultan Agung in 1629 further strengthened the Dutch position. By 1660 the Dutch were controlling large segments of the archipelago but were only partially successful in Sumatra and Borneo. A foothold was obtained in Padang around 1650. Domination of Sumatra was far from realized (Wertheim, 1956:47-48). Finally, Macassar was subjugated by Speelman around 1667 (Cady, 1964:220). Much of the expansion of the VOC resulted from the work of Dieman who had sought a new home in the Indies after having gone bankrupt in Holland (Vlekke, 1943:129). By 1750 the VOC had consolidated its power over Java and many of the outer islands (Werthiem, 1956:48). Thus, from Batavia the Dutch established a powerful commercial empire with no ideas of crusading, missionary zeal or romantic adventure. The Dutch established a strictly commercial venture that paid great dividends (Cady, 1964:221).

The VOC used the policy of indirect rule in administering the Indies. They dealt with the chiefs, who using their traditional authority, forced the people to surrender a considerable portion of their produce (Wertheim, 1956:48). This policy, known as the Preanger system, was introduced in 1723 (Van Niel, 1963:282). The traditional scheme of vassalage continued, except now, the vassal princes of the powerful overlords paid homage to the VOC officials. These officials came to occupy positions almost as maharadjas in the Indies. The VOC accepted the role of feudal lords to insure their monopoly of trade in the archipelago (Kennedy, 1942:40).

By 1780 the VOC was bankrupt, the Dutch government had revolked its charter, assumed its assets and debts and taken authority in the Indies. Debate as to whether to employ the existing policy or to move to the laissez-faire concept in vogue in Europe was never completely resolved. The debate did not concern what was better for the Indonesians but what would be more profitable for Holland. The new Governor General, H. W. Daendels, introduced the policy of imposing Dutch ideas of government and administration on the Indonesians. The concept of sovereignty was extended to include ownership rights over all the lands of Java (Van Niel, 1963:282-283). The implementation of these policies was interrupted when the islands passed to British domination in 1811.

The Church During the Company Period 1602-1795

Under the Dutch Company Christianity was dominated by

the Reformed Church. The Reformed Church, with VOC backing,
took over the Portuguese Catholic congregations. The company
commissioned pastors to serve churches that were primarily
for the Dutch employees. Scant attention was given to the
Indonesian Christians inherited from the Catholics (Cooley,
1968:40-41). The VOC was more interested in exploiting than
converting. All outside attempts of evangelistic work were
frustrated by the VOC's edict that no religion would be practiced except the Dutch Reformed Church (Ponder, n.d.:94).

The VOC made as little attempt to expand the Church as
they did to shepherd the Indonesian Christians. They refused
the Church any freedom, giving no voice to Indonesian Christians. The Church was forced into the mold of the Church in
Holland. All business sessions and most worship services were
not only in the Dutch language but in forms entirely foreign
to Indonesians. It was an imported church totally unsuitable
for the Indonesian people. Only ordained pastors were allowed
to preach although some "guru indjil" (gospel teachers) were
allowed to read sermons. Restrictions were placed on the
ordinances of the Lord's Supper and baptism (Muller-Kruger,
1959:34-41). Clearly the Church was not even trying to reach
the indigenous people. ✓

The policy of the VOC had more serious consequences on
Java than elsewhere. For two hundred years the Dutch Church
existed solely for European Christians, making not the slightest effort to reach the Javanese. In fact, such effort was
avoided in the fear that evangelism among the Javanese might
have economic consequences (Bentley-Taylor, 1967:16,17).

One achievement of the Church during the Company period
was the publication of the New Testament in the Malay language
in 1733 (Cooley, 1968:41). This achievement was tarnished by
a regrettable delay. Leydekker and P. van der Vorm finished
a Malay translation of the Bible that was printed in 1723 but
was not distributed for ten years. The delay resulted from
questions raised by Ds. Valentijn, who desired his own translation rather than Leydekker's be used. Finally, the governors
of the VOC approved Leydekker's translation and it was distributed, but ten valuable years had been lost (Muller-Kruger,
1959:36-37).

In spite of the ineptness of the mission methods used
during the Company period, church growth did take place and
four of the existing churches of Indonesia trace their early
history to this period. The Moluccan Protestant Church (Geredja
Protestan Maluku), the oldest evangelical church in Asia, was
built on the Portuguese Catholic churches (Muller-Kruger, 1959:
74-75). Today this church boasts a membership of 380,000
(Cooley, 1968:52-53).

The Timor Evangelical Christian Church (Geredja Masehi
Indjili Timor) received its first Dutch pastor in 1612 but no
continuous ministry was available to build on the Catholic

foundation until 1670 (Muller-Kruger, 1959:119-120). Although development was hindered because of defective shepherding, the Timor church was awakened by a spiritual movement in 1964 when over 200,000 people were baptized. The Church's membership reached over 650,000 in 1967 (Cooley, 1968:6-7).

One of the largest and potentially strongest churches in Indonesia, the Minahasa Evangelical Christian Church (Geredja Masehi Indjili Minahasa) was also built on the Catholic foundations. However, by 1588 the small group of believers left by the Catholic, Magelhaes, had almost vanished. An agreement between the Dutch and the Sultan of Ternate (a strong Moslem) in 1607 placed Minahasa under the Moslem's power. Providentially, the agreement was never implemented and Minahasa escaped the Moslem net. The first Dutch pastor visited Minahasa in 1675 (Muller-Kruger, 1959:93). Today, nearly 600,000 of the 700,000 people in Minahasa are Christian (Cooley, 1968:55).

Christianity also became entrenched in the Sangir-Talaud Islands during the VOC period where both Portuguese and Spanish influences were in evidence in early years. The Dutch assumed responsibility in 1677 and tried to serve the islands with pastors from Menado and teachers from Ambon (Muller-Kruger, 1959:105-106). The churches in the area today are in great need of leadership.

Thus, even with the islands dominated by the Dutch East India Company which was seeking only commercial gain, the Church was planted and grew. The history of inadequate shepherding was indeed unfortunate. The period of British intrusion brought a new direction to mission work in Indonesia in the persons of the British Baptists from Serampore and missionaries of the London Missionary Society.

THE PERIOD OF BRITISH INTRUSION 1811-1819

During the closing days of Dutch rule in 1811, the policies of Daendels antagonized almost everyone. His policies both robbed the Javanese leaders of their self-respect and also failed to produce profits (Vlekke, 1943:229-237). When the British seized power in Indonesia in order to consolidate and defend their position in India during the Napoleonic Wars (Van Niel, 1963:283), thirty year old Thomas Stamford Raffles became the Governor of Indonesia. Already proficient in the Malay language, Raffles instituted what he hoped would be a humanitarian administration (Hall, 1964:449). Raffles' policies actually brought about further difficulties with the Indonesian leaders (Cady, 1964:318). Raffles did bring about a more progressive attitude on the part of both Indonesians and Europeans living in the Indies (Nance, 1969:14).

Raffles became an authority on Indonesian life and archaeology. One of his innovations was a land tax system patterned partially on the British system in India. This

policy held that the land belonged to the ruler who had the
right to collect rent on it in accordance with its productive
capacity. The Dutch continued this policy after the islands
were returned to their control in 1816 (Van Niel, 1963:283).
Raffles' friendship with the Baptist missionaries in India
opened the door for the Baptists to enter the Indies in 1813.

     The first British Baptist missionary to reach Indonesia,
William Robinson, came with instructions to consider himself
a missionary to the Javanese. No other missionary to Indonesia
had ever received such instructions. He was joined not only by
other Baptists, such as James Riley and Thomas Trowt, but also
three missionaries from the London Missionary Society, John
Supper, Gottlob Bruckner and Joseph Kam. By 1816 Robinson had
baptized forty British soldiers but had realized little response
from the Indonesian population (Payne, 1945:30-32). In December 1813, Jabez Carey, the third son of William Carey, arrived
in Ambon and began a notable ministry. Carey made unusual
progress with the Malay language and was given responsibilities
in several schools.

     Thomas Trowt and Gottlob Bruckner arrived in Semarang
within a period of three weeks. Bruckner became discouraged
because of the spiritual laxness of the Dutch church of which
he had become pastor (Muller-Kruger, 1959:161). Friendship
with Trowt, study and discouragement with the church, combined
to lead Bruckner to resign from the London Missionary Society
and become a Baptist in April, 1816. Bruckner was adopted by
the British Baptist Mission from England. Thanks to his German
origin, Bruckner was able to continue his ministry after other
Baptists were forced to leave when the Indies passed back into
Dutch control (Nance, 1969:17). The difficulty of direct
evangelism led Bruckner to concentrate on translation and
writing, producing tracts and finally a Javanese translation
of the New Testament (Muller-Kruger, 1959:161).

     Bruckner's tracts and Bible translations in Javanese
were of great influence. An early Christian community traces
its first contact with Christianity to Bruckner's Javanese
translation of the Gospel of Mark (Bentley-Taylor, 1967:70).
One of the earliest known Chinese converts in Indonesia came
also as a result of a tract by Bruckner (Lie, 1953:107). More
important still, Bruckner's work and encouragement to the
Dutch missionaries stimulated them to mission work among the
Javanese (Payne, 1945:79,89). British Baptists also served
on Sumatra, even making contact with the Bataks who later
were blessed with one of the strongest Christian movements in
all Asia (Nance, 1969:18).

     Despite this good beginning, the British Baptists were
not destined to serve long on the islands. Post-Napoleonic
conditions in Europe brought about the return of the islands
to Holland in 1816 (Van Niel, 1963:283). The British (with
the exception of Bruckner) were forced to leave.

THE DEVELOPMENT OF DUTCH RULE 1816-1940

"The history of Dutch rule in Indonesia from 1830 to
1920 affords a demonstration of economic imperialism at or
near its technical best" (Cady, 1964:378). The first Dutch
Governor inadvertently not only lost money, but led to the
Java War of 1825. Part of the problem involved falling coffee
prices, but also Van der Capellen's policies caused great dissatisfaction (Vlekke, 1943:265). The confused policy resulted
in the government's abrogation of land rental contracts. The
infuriated Javanese noblemen sought the leadership of
Diponegoro, a prince from Jogjakarta. The guerrilla war,taking
the form of an Islamic "holy war", lasted four years (Van Niel,
1963:283-284).

The devastation of large areas of Java as an aftermath
of the war intensified the problem of falling profits. In
1830 Governor van den Bosch assumed the governorship and instituted the so-called "cultivation system" (Cultuurstelsel)
(Van Niel, 1963:284). This policy brought fabulously productive years for the Netherlands government. It involved
using Indonesian leaders to force production of products for
the European market. The Dutch exploited the religious regard
of the Indonesian village for traditional chieftains. The
Dutch officials and the adat law chiefs were more or less
allied against the Moslem scribes and the exploited people.
Almost the entire population of Java was involved by the Dutch
rulers in agreements made with a few thousand chiefs, each of
whom profited personally from the arrangement (Nieuwenhuijze,
1958:41-42). The profits of the culture system amounted to
some 900 million guilders over a forty-five year period. The
Dutch debt was paid and the Netherlands National railways were
built with the profits (Cady, 1964:363).

The cultivation system did not advantage the Javanese
people. It led to a breakdown in their traditional ways.
Traditional cohesion was lost and much of the Javanese sense
of values destroyed. In addition, the Indonesians were forced
to trade for expensive Dutch products. It is said the Javanese
paid an estimated forty million guilders more for Dutch cloth
than cheaper British cloth would have cost (Cady, 1964:361-363).

The Dutch were forced into several wars against dissident
factions, usually Moslem, who resented the culture system. In
the Padris Wars in the Minangkabau territory, the Dutch took
the side of the adat chiefs against the more zealous Islamic
groups. This war was not concluded until 1837. The Dutch did
not, because of treaty obligations with the British, intervene
in the struggle between traditional and Islamic elements in
Atjeh (Van Niel, 1963:286-287). The Dutch were also forced to
put down a violent rebellion in south Borneo (Wertheim, 1956:
54).

During this period the Dutch slowly consolidated their

control over the islands. Most of Java, the Padang areas of
Sumatra, the Pontianak and Banjarmasin areas of Borneo, the
Macassar and Minahasa regions of Celebes, Halmahera, the
Moluccas, Flores, Timor and Sumba all were controlled by 1816.
Central Borneo was controlled in 1900 but the Central Celebes
was not passified until 1907. Atjeh was not fully controlled
until 1903 (Cady, 1964:357-369). From the headquarters in Java,
the Dutch controlled most of Indonesia by 1900.

The culture system was opposed by Dutch liberals as
well as by Indonesians. A principal defender of the Indonesians
was W. R. van Hoevell, a churchman who had been expelled from
Holland for criticizing the government (Vlekke, 1943:285).
In 1860 the struggle against the cultivation system was furthered by the novel, Max Havelaar, written by Edward Deuwes Dekker
under the pseudonym "Multatuli" (Much Have I Suffered). This
novel tells the story of a Dutch official who was expelled for
defending the Javanese against the culture system and stirred
up wide sympathy for the liberal campaign against the culture
system (Hall, 1964:543).

The Cultivation System was abolished and the Ethical
Policy instituted in 1870 with the passing of the Agrarian and
Sugar Laws. These laws were designed to protect Javanese
peasants against Western enterprise by limiting the land-owning
rights of non-Indonesians. The liberal policy which lasted
from 1870 to about 1900 was a period of economic expansion (Van
Niel, 1963:288-289).

The Ethical Policy brought an increase in mission schools
and other activity. In time there arose a feeling that the
connection of Church and government was too close. In 1932
the request was made for separation but the separation was not
effected until 1935. Even so, when the Japanese entered in
1942, there were still eighty-one European and 347 Indonesian
ministers on the civil service payroll (Vandenbosch, 1942:43-
46).

In an attempt to satisfy the legitimate grievances
against Dutch policy, the Peoples Council or Volksraad, was
approved in 1916 and the policy of forced labor outlawed in
1917. But the leisurely timetable of the Ethical Policy could
not keep pace with the continuing demands of the various protest movements. "In the crucial test of the beneficence of
their rule, the Dutch failed, not apparently from any malicious
design or from hypocrisy, but rather because the system which
they developed was so completely alien to Indonesian experience
and desires" (Cady, 1964:3760378). This observation has
immediate meaning to church planters.

Between 1900 and 1940 various reform movements came to
life. In 1900 Raden Adjeng Kartini began the movement for
women's rights including education. An organization of
Indonesian intellectuals and officials called Budi Utomo (High
Endeavor) sought to reinforce cultural patterns. This

organization took its inspiration from the Indian poet, Rabindranth', and to some extent from Mahatma Gandhi (Hall, 1964:708). The conservative Budi Utomo movement gave way to a more radical Indische Partij (Indies Party) led by E. F. E. Eouwes Dekker, a grandnephew of "Multatuli". This party, founded in 1912, openly advocated independence for the colony (Van Niel, 1963:293).

The Sarekat Islam party was formed around 1900 mainly by Sumatran and Arab merchants seeking to use Islamic sentiment against their Chinese rivals (Cady, 1964:376). Sarekat Islam, at first largely non-political, gained mass support due mainly to its religious basis (Van Niel, 1963:293-294). More and more the party came under radical and more political influences (Wertheim, 1956:59).

Sarekat Islam was infiltrated by Marxists who split to form the Indonesian Communist Party or PKI in 1920 (Van Niel, 1963:295). This was the first Communist Party founded in Asia (Brackman, 1963:3). The government's stronger measures against the Communists led to open rebellions in Java in 1926 and West Sumatra in 1927. Both were defeated and the Communist leaders exiled to New Guinea (Wertheim, 1956:61).

Another deviation from Sarekat Islam, the Muhammadijah Party, founded in 1912, gained strength. It was a reformist Islamic movement. Muhammadijah founded schools, clinics and benevolent groups and pressed for a purer Islam. In 1926 the more conservative Islamic faction formed their own association, the Nahdatul Ulama (Van Niel, 1963:295).

The weakening of Sarekat Islam and the socialist movements paved the way for the founding of the Nationalist Party (Partai Nasional Indonesia) by Ir. (engineer) Sukarno. Sukarno and other leaders, Mohammed Hatta, Tjipto Mangunkusumo and Sultan Sjahrir were interned by the Dutch authorities as a result of their revolutionary activities (Wertheim, 1956:61).

Between 1816 and 1940 some of history's most inspiring stories of church growth were recorded in Indonesia. Twenty-four of the thirty-five churches associated with the Indonesian Council of Churches mark their beginnings from this period (Cooley, 1968:6,7). Space will allow the mention of but a few of these inspiring stories of God's working in the archipelago.

The Batak Church, which began among the Toba Bataks in 1861, resulted from the ministry of the Rhenish Mission Society from Germany. Led by Ludwig Nommensen, "the Apostle of the Bataks", the Church among the Bataks became one of the notable people movements of modern missionary history (Muller-Kruger, 1959:180-186). By 1968 the Church counted over 819,000 members (Cooley, 1968:6-7). It is rightly said that the Batak Church "...belongs to the finest results of missionary activity in modern times" (Kraemer, 1958:43).

Not only among the Toba Bataks but among the Simalungun

Bataks and on Nias Island the Lord gave increase to the churches aided by the Rhenish Missionary Society. The Church among the Simalungun Bataks in 1968 numbered 85,257. The Nias Church, under the impetus of a spiritual awakening that began in 1915, has grown to a membership of over 220,000 (Cooley, 1968:6-7, 70-71)

The history of the Karo Batak Church brings to light regrettable factors, regarding missionary methods. The Church was started at the insistence of Dutch plantation owners who hoped that by civilizing the people through Christianity they would fit better into the commercial set up. The Netherlands Missionary Society in 1890 sent H. C. Kruyt, who brought with him four Minahasan evangelists. The use of evangelists from Minahasa when the Toba Bataks were only a few miles away, the extensive use of schools (which were later closed), the failure to translate the Bible into the Karo Batak language until the 1930s, all point to defective missionary strategy. Little wonder that the Church numbered only 5000 after fifty years of mission work (Muller-Kruger, 1959:199). The greatest growth in the Karo Batak Church occurred after the events of the Communist coup attempt in 1965. The Church which in 1965 numbered around 30,000 members more than doubled to 65,000 in 1967 (IRM, 1968:17).

Other miracles of church growth were experienced between 1816-1940. In the Central Celebes Albert C. Kruyt and N. Adriani witnessed one of history's most inspiring people movements. The two missionaries began studying both the language and the culture of the Toradja peoples. They presented the Gospel in ways understandable to primitive animists and in forms compatible to their culture (Kruyt, 1924:267-274). Realizing the Toradjas were a collective rather than an individualistic culture, the missionaries understood they would naturally come to Christ as clans, villages and families. In 1909 180 persons were baptized (Muller-Kruger, 1959:113-114), beginning a people movement that by 1968 reached 126,467 members (Cooley, 1968:81). In addition two other churches have developed among other Toradja peoples in the Central Celebes and number 185,000 and 40,000 members respectively (Cooley, 1968:6-7).

The Churches on Java began during this period. The Dutch, as noted, for over two hundred years made no attempt to evangelize the Javanese people. When evangelistic efforts began, they were due to Christian laymen rather than missionaries. Equally, if not more important were Indonesians such as Paulus Tosari, Sadrach, Abisai and Paulus Khow Tek San who labored to plant churches years before the first Dutch missionaries came (cf. Bentley-Taylor, 1967:80-82). Even after the missionaries did arrive to evangelize the Javanese, they refused to build on the indigenous foundations of these pioneers. The missionaries felt that the highly Javanized version of

Christianity had gone too far and therefore rejected it
(Muller-Kruger, 1959:141-142).

The Churches on Java have not grown as have those in
Batakland, Minahasa, Nias, Toradja or the Moluccas. Those
Churches all grew among basically animistic peoples. No other
Church among peoples already under the sway of Islam can
approximate the growth of the Churches on Java. The response
on Java, even before 1965 must be attributed in part to the
particular kind of Javanese found in Central and East Java
where Islam has been tempered by strong Hindu-Buddhist and
animistic elements.

However, since the Protestant Church of East Java could
count but 62,890 members in 1964, after over one hundred years,
the growth could not be counted as spectacular (Cooley, 1968:
90). The real growth in Java came only after the events of
1965 (to be related later) when in a two year period the East
Java Church received 24,456 new members (IRM, 1968:18). Other
Churches have experienced comparable growth.

This is but an incomplete picture of church growth between 1816-1940. It does however demonstrate that God was
working and churches were being planted during these crucial
years. The 1940s brought World War II and new problems for
Indonesia and the Churches. The war years and the Japanese
occupation form the material for the next section of this
chapter.

THE JAPANESE OCCUPATION 1940-1945

Dissatisfaction with Dutch rule was such that some
Indonesians welcomed the Japanese occupation in 1942, feeling
their lot could be no worse and might be better. The Japanese
typhoon rushed into Indonesia, wiped out the entire Dutch
administrative apparatus, and replaced it with a Japanese
military administration assisted by an Indonesian officialdom.
The halfhearted Dutch defense lessened Dutch prestige (Kahin,
1958:493). The harshness of Japanese rule soon shattered such
high expectations but did not dispose most Indonesians to welcome the return of the Dutch (Wertheim, 1956:64).

The Japanese planned to win Moslem support in Indonesia.
This policy, almost a complete reversal of the Dutch, was
directed at the grass roots of Indonesian Islam. However, full
freedom for Islamic leaders was not actually part of the plan.
The Japanese planned to turn the Islamic movement into new
channels (Benda, 1958:107-109). They were but partially
successful in this attempt.

In spite of their policy, the Japanese were as ob-
structionist to Indonesian nationalism as the Dutch had been.
Their aim was only to incorporate the Indonesians into their
war effort (Wertheim, 1956:65). However, the intensity of
Japanese resistance to Indonesian nationalism varied over the

archipelago. Indonesia was divided into three occupation zones,
each with distinct administration. The authorities in Java
gave the nationalist movement wide latitude. The administration in Sumatra was inclined to give less freedom to the
nationalists. The Celebes, Borneo, the Moluccas and the
Lessor Sundas were under the Japanese Navy which followed a
severly repressive policy that allowed nationalists little
more freedom than had the Dutch (Kahin, 1958:494).

    Despite the repressions during this period, Indonesians
gained administrative experience both through legal and underground activities (Cooley, 1968:22). As the war went against
the Japanese they were forced to give more freedom to the
Indonesians, finally promising self-government. Nationalist
leaders such as Sukarno and Hatta were able to increase their
following and prepare for the eventual struggle with the Dutch.
The occupation was a definite stimulus to Indonesian nationalism (Wertheim, 1956:65-66). The use of the Malay language,
which became the base of the national language in the new
Republic was furthered as well (Kahin, 1958:494).

    In March 1945 the Japanese appointed a committee of some
sixty Indonesians (mostly from Java and Madura) and seven
Japanese to work out plans for the political and economic
organization of an independent Indonesia. Sukarno played a
major part in these meetings. A major difference of opinion
existed between Sukarno and the Islamic leaders who desired
an Islamic state. Sukarno was convinced that the undogmatic
character of Islam among many Indonesians and the important
non-Islamic minorities indicated the country should not become an Islamic state. His Pantjasila or five principles
(nationalism, humanitarianism, representative government,
social justice and belief in God) became the official
Indonesian national philosophy. Sukarno's plan called for the
unification of the entire archipelago, from Sumatra to Papua
(Kahin, 1958:496-497).

    By 1944, the general feeling for freedom had taken on
added strength. Two days after the Japanese surrender at the
insistence of militant youth groups, Sukarno and Hatta issued a
declaration of Indonesia's independence from Holland. This
was on August 17, 1945 (Van Niel, 1963:300-301). The freedom,
so quickly declared, was four years in being achieved.

    The Church suffered during the Japanese occupation. In
some areas the Japanese suspected the former closeness of the
Churches with Dutch interests and for this reason subjected
the Church to persecution. In East Java many pastors were
killed when they refused to betray their churches and their
people (Cooley, 1968:89). This period helped prepare the
Church for its part in the revolutionary struggle and helped
the churches become self-sufficient.

THE REVOLUTIONARY STRUGGLE 1945-1949

Sukarno became President and Hatta Vice-president of
the newly formed Republic. A constitution was promulgated,
based on a draft already prepared a week after independence
was declared. The constitution called for a republican form
of government and a cabinet elected by popular vote. Through
the efforts of well-known figures a multiparty arrangement was
introduced (Van Niel, 1963:301-302).

Clashes between the armed Indonesian militia (Peta)
and the Japanese forces broke out with the result that the
Indonesians gained control over key cities and supplies of
arms (Wertheim, 1956:680). In eastern Indonesia, where the
Japanese had not allowed the nationals to be armed and the
Australian troops moved quickly to occupy the territory, less
intense military activity was experienced. In Java, when the
British landed some six weeks after the end of the war, they
found a functioning revolutionary government and an effective
militia. Moreover, the republican government had solid backing
from the people. While the Indonesians were happy to have the
British accept the Japanese surrender and send the Japanese
home, they rejected the idea of the British handing the islands
back to the Dutch (Kahin, 1958:498). Heavy fighting resulted.
The British helped the Dutch reenter some of the port cities
but the Indonesian Army strengthened its position in the
interiors of Java. Sumatra also was mostly in the hands of
Indonesians who were largely fighting not directly against
the Dutch but against the feudal chiefs who had formerly ruled
by association with the Dutch (Wertheim, 1956:68).

After some months of fighting, Dutch and Indonesian
authorities signed an ambiguously worded document, the
Linggadjati Agreement, which provided for the protection of
Dutch economic interests and the Dutch recognition of the
Republic's authority over Java and Sumatra. The Dutch later
accused the Republic of violating the Linggadjati Agreement
and launched an all out attack. The United Nations forced
the Dutch to stop the aggression and sign the Renville Agreement
in January 1947. While the Renville Agreement gave the Dutch
control over the territories they had taken, it called for a
plebiscite which was certain to be won by the Republican government. Disregarding the agreement, the Dutch sought to set up
puppet or semipuppet governments on Java as they had done in
Borneo and the Celebes (Kahin, 1958:500).

The Dutch set up a cruel blockade against the Republican
government. The Western powers did not take measures to insure
that the Netherlands live up to its committments and for this
reason the Indonesians began to lean toward Russia and later
China for support. The Stalinist Communists laid plans to take
over the government and oust Sukarno and Hatta. However, before their preparations were complete, Indonesian Communists

in the Central Java city of Madiun triggered a revolt on
September to November 1948. This revolt was suppressed by
government troops after bitter fighting (Kahin, 1958:500).
After this defeat the Communists went underground and did
not reappear until 1950 (Van Niel, 1963:306).

Six weeks after the close of the war with the Communists
the weakened army of the Republic suffered an all out attack
from the Netherlands forces. Indonesian forces showed un-
expected resistance and by spring, 1949, it was clear the
Dutch could not crush them. Agreement was reached at the
Round Table Conference in The Hague in the summer of 1949
which recognized full independence for Indonesia. The Dutch
retained control over West New Guinea with the provision that
its status be decided during the coming year through negoti-
ations (Kahin, 1958:500-501). On August 17, 1950, on the fifth
anniversary of the proclamation of independence of the Republic,
the unitary state became a reality (Wertheim, 1956:71).

The Churches of Indonesia participated in and contributed to the drive for independence. In the process they
erased much of the prejudice against them that had arisen as
a result of their closeness to the Dutch. After the independence struggle, the Church was better recognized and accepted.
This acceptance has aided the modern ministry of the Church
(cf. Cooley, 1968:93).

FROM THE REPUBLIC TO GUIDED DEMOCRACY 1950-1965

The period of liberal parliamentary democracy lasted
from 1950 to July 1959 (Cooley, 1968:24-24). The leaders of
the new Republic were the revolutionay leaders. Sukarno became President and Hatta Prime Minister. Hatta formed a
cabinet that was replaced after only a short time. There
followed a quick succession of cabinets and Hatta returned to
the post of Vice-president (which he had held in 1948). Even
though nine different cabinets were active between 1950 and
1959 there was considerable continuity in the government
(Feith, 1963:312-313).

One of the cabinets that failed during this period, that
of Sukiman, failed on the day that Baptists were seeking a
final answer from the Department of Religion to their request
to enter Indonesia. In spite of the confusion in government
circles, the Southern Baptists were well received and assured
that visa applications for missionaries would be granted
(Nance, 1969:44). This is an interesting side light into the
changing government scene in Indonesian history.

Although President Sukarno remained a strong rallying
figure during these developing years, there was far from un-
animity. Three rebellions against the central government broke
out. In West Java, the Darul Islam (House of Islam or Islamic
State) movement sought a theocracy, exclusive application of

Shafiite precept throughout the state and urged in effect
a jihad (holy war) against all kafir--non-Moslems, especially
Marxists and secular minded nationalists (van der Kroef, 1962:
51). Darul Islam resorted to terrorist tactics and open
rebellion against government troops. While its ideal spread,
the terrorist tactics did not gain wide acceptance
(Nieuwenhuijze, 1958:175-177). The movement was arrested in
1962 at which time West Java was secured (Feith, 1963:541).

The other rebellions in Sumatra and in North Celebes
produced stalemates. These rebellions were based partly on
dissatisfaction within the army. The Sumatran rebellion was
secured rather quickly but the North Celebes (Permesta) rebellion continued for some years. Finally, the army of the
Celebes agreed to return to the fold without any decisive
military settlement (Feith, 1963:322ff).

Important to this exciting period of Indonesian history
was the election of 1955 which selected Indonesia's first
elected parliament. The National Party of Sukarno (Partai
Nationalis Indonesia, PNI) emerged from these elections with
the largest vote, 8,434,653 or 22.3 percent and forty-seven
seats. The rapidly gaining Communist Party (PKI) won 6,176,914
votes and thirty-nine seats. Of this total Communist vote,
88.6 percent came from Java and over seventy-five percent from
Central and East Java alone. The Communist surge was led by
D. N. Aidit, who had been for at least one year training in
Communist China and North Vietnam (Kahin, 1958:556-557).

Continued political and economic difficulties, augmented
by the rebellions noted, led to the establishment of "Guided
Democracy" in July 1959. President Sukarno went back to the
revolutionary constitution of 1945 and at length established
a political philosophy based on five ideals: the 1945 constitution, Indonesian Socialism, Guided Democracy, Guided
Economy, and Indonesian Personality. The first letters of
these five principles were combined to form an acronym, "USDEK."
Combined with a shortening of Political Manifesto to "Manipol",
a new creed was formed: "Manipol-USDEK" (Feith, 1963:367).

President Sukarno was the primary figure in Indonesian
history between 1959 and 1965. He led the successful campaign
to regain West New Guinea, gave impetus to the increasing
alignment of Indonesia with Communist China and instituted the
unsuccessful "confrontation" with Malasia (Cooley, 1968:240).
Sukarno eschewed genuine, painstaking, nation-building policies
for assaults on foreign windmills (such as mentioned above) and
prestige projects at home. He had himself declared President
for life. Of these years of rule by Sukarno it has been said,
"But whereas a decade of halfhearted efforts to make a parliamentary system work had ended in paralysis, prompting impatient
men to take action, the six years of presidential dictatorship
ended in economic bankruptcy and political tragedy" (Pauker,
1967a:2-3).

Sukarno did not hesitate to ban the Islamic Masjumi
Party in 1960 but steadfastly, in the name of national unity,
refused to honor the army's demand that he ban the ascending
Communist Party. Although most observers felt that Sukarno's
tactics involved a balancing of the military and the Communists,
Guy Pauker of the Rand Corporation, as early as 1964 had expressed the opinion that the President had reached an agreement
with the PKI by which the Communists supported him during his
lifetime in exchange for his help in their struggle to name
his successor (Pauker, 1967b:6).

It cannot be doubted that President Sukarno dominated
the Indonesian scene by keeping a measure of balance among the
various factions of Indonesian power. In this effort Sukarno
created "NASAKOM" which involved the fusing of nationalism,
religion and communism into a working relationship. This
eventually led to his fall. The attempted Communist coup of
1965 and its aftermath brought "Guided Democracy" to an end.

THE NEW ORDER 1965

On the night of September 30th and morning of October
1, 1965 an attempted Communist coup involved the capture and
execution of six generals of the Indonesian Army. A
Revolutionary Council of forty-five persons (Sukarno's name
was not among them) was presented as the new government of
Indonesia. The only response to the announcement was in
Central Java where in Semarang a Revolutionary Council was
established in the army headquarters and in Jogjakarta where
six army commanders were kidnapped and murdered (Thomson, 1968:
8).

By 8:30 p. m. on October first, General Suharto announced over Djakarta Radio that he had assumed command and
loyal troops were in control of the capital (Thomson, 1968:8-
9). As the PKI came more and more to be associated with the
events and atrocities of September 30th, a nation-wide purge
against the Communists began. Various estimates are made
concerning the numbers of people killed. Despite this national
tragedy, Sukarno continued to maneuver to regain political
power. However, the army was clearly gaining power and moving
toward domination of the Indonesian government (Pauker, 1967c:
9-11).

The Indonesian youth entered the picture and began to
agitate for a settlement of the situation. The organization
of university students, "KAMI" and the organization of high
school students, "KAPPI", took to the streets to demonstrate
against Sukarno and his regime. On March 11, 1966 Sukarno
signed an order empowering General Suharto "To take all steps
deemed necessary for the smooth functioning of the government
and the course of the revolution." Hidden in the language
of this pronouncement was the end of Sukarno's power. The

next day, General Suharto signed a directive in the name of
the President dissolving the PKI and all its affiliated organizations. On March 18th a new cabinet was formed while the
army arrested Foreign Minister Dr. Subandrio and fourteen other
ministers. Thus, the "Generation of 1966" had contributed
significantly to the end of Sukarno's dictatorship (Pauker,
1967b:1-16).

The administration of President Suharto demonstrates
wisdom in the very areas that former administrations fell short.
Economic policies designed to increase food production and curb
inflation have been instituted. The government is promoting
planned parenthood, a matter decried by previous administrations
(Pauker, 1968:5-7). The "confrontation" with Malasia was
brought to an end and Indonesia reentered the United Nations.
The new regime has shown significant progress toward solving
the problems facing the young nation (Cooley, 1968:25).

There has been a rapid increase in the Churches of
Indonesia as an aftermath of the Communist coup failure and
the resulting events of 1965 and 1966 (Tasdik, 1969:2).
Mention has been made of the more than doubling of the Karo
Batak Church in northern Sumatra, of the phenomenal increase
in the Church in Timor and the unusual increases in Central
and East Java. A recent field study of the increasing responsiveness has proved that many have entered Christianity
because of the failure of all other avenues of life. The
government suggestion (directive) that every Indonesian should
"have a religion" also had a part in bringing men and women
to the Churches (Tasdik, 1969:2-8).

The new responsiveness must be closely examined. The
increases in the Karo Batak area and the Timor awakening have
been sweeping primarily animistic peoples into the Churches.
Frank Cooley notes that some of the response in Central and
East Java has been realized among those who had for some time
believed but had been afraid to acknowledge their belief due
to Communist pressure. After the pressure was lifted, they
acknowledged their faith and became members of the Church
(Cooley, 1968:70).

The point is that no Islamic area has become responsive
that was not at least partially open before the events of 1965.
The Javanese have long been known as a different type of Islam
so the responsiveness in Java is not a new phenomenon. It is
inaccurate to suggest that Indonesia is turning to Christ.
There is a new responsiveness that is bringing thousands of
certain populations into the Church. The new responsiveness
must be seen in this light.

Conclusion

Historical and political factors have played important
roles both in general church growth in Indonesia and in Baptist

growth as well. However, political and historical factors
certainly are not the whole story. Social and ethnological
factors are equally important. More important still is the
action of the Holy Spirit. This chapter on history simply
shows the rich background of the country where Baptist advance
is taking place.

2

The Peoples and Religions of Indonesia

Church growth most successfully takes place among
peoples, that is, a tribe, clan, family or other ethnic entity
with strong feelings of solidarity. Only after careful analysis of the social structure can missionaries recognize the
corresponding centers of power and the direction and relative
forces of the various currents of communication (Luzbetak, 1970:
299). For this reason it is imperative that the ethnic realites
of Indonesian society be understood and that social structure
and religion be carefully considered by those persons engaged
in church planting.

ETHNIC DIVISIONS IN INDONESIA

Over 300 different ethnic groups make up Indonesian
society. Raymond Kennedy in one classification notes fifty-four
different ethnic units, but many of these should be sub-divided
(cf. H. Geertz, 1963:479). In another book Kennedy expands the
list to over 200 distinct groups (Kennedy, 1943:3). Wertheim
simplifies the classification to only twenty-two divisions
(Wertheim, 1956:25-26) but M. A. Jaspan in Daftar Sementara
dari Sukubangsa-bangsa di Indonesia (A Provisional List of the
Ethnic Groups in Indonesia) lists over 360 ethnic groups
(H. Geertz, 1963:479). The maps on the next three pages show
the locations of the major ethnic groups in Indonesia.
The complexity of the ethnic variation is demonstrated
in that the Toradja people include over thirty sub-groups,
speaking a number of different languages. Each of the six
major ethnic divisions of the peoples of Borneo can be divided
into at leave twelve sub-groups (United States Army Handbook,
1964:66-69). The crucial importance of the smaller divisions
is apparent in the history of missions. Correct mission strategy
recognizes that church growth generally takes place in some one
homogeneous unit. The Church must seek out those cultural units
of mankind in which harvesting is possible (McGavran, 1965a:
558-559). As McGavran states, Christian mission needs to

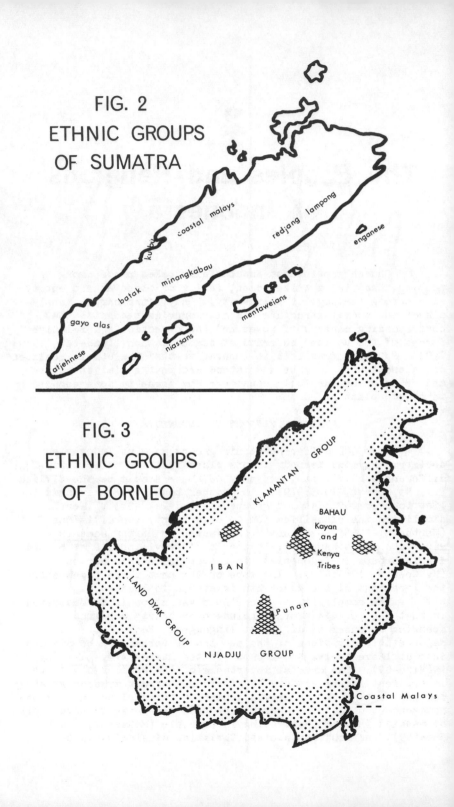

FIG. 2
ETHNIC GROUPS
OF SUMATRA

coastal malays
kubu
redjang lampong
enganese
batak
minangkabau
gayo alas
mentaweians
niassans
atjehnese

FIG. 3
ETHNIC GROUPS
OF BORNEO

KLAMANTAN GROUP
BAHAU
Kayan and Kenya Tribes
IBAN
LAND DYAK GROUP
Punan
NJADJU GROUP
Coastal Malays

FIG. 4 ETHNIC GROUPS
OF JAVA

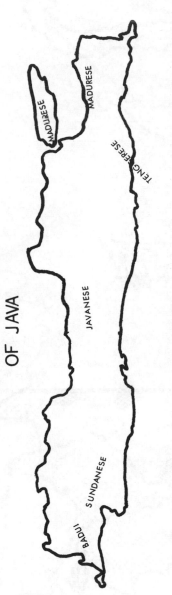

FIG.5 ETHNIC GROUPS OF LESSOR SUNDAS

FIG.6 ETHNIC GROUPS OF
CELEBES

MINAHASA – GORONTALO

LOINANG

TORADJA

mori

sadang

lcki

toala

macassarese

buginese

papuan

melanesians

w. dani

moni

kapauku uhuduni e. dani

FIG.7 ETHNIC GROUPS OF
NEW GUINEA

recognize that homogeneous populations are common and have enormous significance for church growth (McGavran, 1965b:72).

The ethnic mosaic of Indonesia reveals an incredible complexity. Sumatran patterns vary from the bilateral structure of the coastal Atjehnese and Malays to the patrilineal structure of the interior Atjehnese, Bataks, Goyo-alas, Niasans, Mentaweians and some of the Redjang-Lampung groups. In addition the Minangkabau and the Engganese are matrilineal (United States Army Handbook, 1964:78).

The Javanese employ a bilateral kinship system and put more emphasis on the nuclear than the extended family. The Madurese, while sharing the bilateral pattern have developed large extended families which may bring together as many as thirty persons. Joint property, shared work and the authority of the family head weld the Madurese extended family into a closed corporate entity whose claims overshadow the village ties. The Balinese likewise share the bilateral system but with a modified caste system which is the only pattern that approaches true caste in Indonesia (United States Army Handbook, 1964:83).

Among Indonesia's unsophisticated peoples even further variation is found. Tremendous variation among the Toradja peoples makes generalizations impossible. Many of these tribes however, have a corporate kinship pattern involving a village containing only those members related either by blood or marriage. The pattern is utrolateral (i.e. each person can choose to join either his father's or his mother's or his spouse's family group). Extended families jointly own property but the nuclear family owns its own storage barn, cooking hearth and other property. Some of the Toradja peoples require a high price for a bride as do the islanders of Nias (H. Geertz, 1963:72-73).

The unsophisticated peoples of Borneo, the Kayan and Kenya tribes of the Bahau people, build the famous long houses that are often hundreds of feet long. Some of these houses accommodate an entire sub-tribe (Kennedy, 1943:18). These long houses may house fifty or more families (United States Army Handbook, 1964:129). These peoples must claim the attention of the Church. Searching for a new religion, they are insulated from Islam by their diet of pork. People movements could easily develop in these long houses. The top priority in Indonesia today could be among the Kayan and Kenya tribes in Borneo.

In addition to the indigenous peoples, several groups of foreign minorities are represented in Indonesia. The largest group is the Europeans and Chinese. The Chinese form the more important division from the standpoint of church growth as around 2,500,000 Chinese now live in Indonesia. Almost one half live on Java and Madura but others are scattered over the entire archipelago. Even though most of the Chinese live on

Java, they form only about two percent of Java's population.
Smaller numbers of Chinese form higher percentages of the
populations in other regions. They make up around 4.4 percent
of the population in Sumatra and as high as nine percent in
Borneo. The highest concentration of Chinese are found in
West Borneo (20.5%), Billiton (25.2%), the Riau archipelago
(27.9%) and Bangka (32%). Chinese are also heavily concentrat-
ed along the east coast of Sumatra (Skinner, 1963:97-101). The
Churches should be active in trying to reach Chinese with
Chinese churches especially in these areas of concentration.

     The Chinese tend to concentrate in urban areas where
they engage in white collar work, trade and finance. On several occasions Chinese have been forced out of rural areas
by Indonesian law (United States Army Handbook, 1964:89-90).
Outside Java the Chinese show a greater tendency to live in
rural areas and in general have a greater influence but still
tend toward the financial trades (Skinner, 1963:101).

     Chinese in Indonesia are classified as those holding
or not holding Indonesian citizenship. Part of the Round
Table Agreement in 1949 gave to Indonesian-born Chinese
the right of choosing nationality, either Indonesian or
Chinese (Skinner, 1963:110). Another classification is based
on birth. China-born Chinese are called Totok and Chinese
born in Indonesia, Peranakan. The latter constitute roughly
seventy percent of the Chinese. Many Peranakan are exclusively
Indonesian speaking. Their families have been in Indonesia
for generations. While the status of the Peranakan is certainly better than the Totok, often all Chinese are the brunt of
discrimination and persecution (Cooley, 1968:99).

     Both the London Missionary Society and the British
Baptists worked among Chinese during the period of 1811-1815
but most early conversions resulted more from individual witnessing than from missionary work. For a long time Chinese
joined other believers in mixed congregations where they were
not always fully welcomed. Gradually Chinese Christians began
to form their own churches (Cooley, 1968:99). An interesting
fact is that the first Chinese congregation was formed in
Indramadu in 1858. Ang Boen Swie and his son led in the
formation of the congregation. Interestingly, the father had
been converted by reading a Javanese New Testament (Lie, 1953:
101). This New Testament was almost certain to have been the
work of Bruckner in Semarang.

SOCIAL STRUCTURE AND CHURCH GROWTH

     Indonesian social structure demonstrates the same
diversity as other features of the Indonesian picture. A
full treatment of Indonesian social structure would demand a
study of each ethnic unit and its regional variations. This
study will concentrate on Javanese social structure. Most of

the Southern Baptist work and growth is within the Javanese
sections of Central and East Java. The study of social structure will relate to how this information can aid church growth.

The Javanese, who occupy the central and eastern two
thirds of the island, numbered around fifty-one million people
in 1967 (Cooley, 1968:86). The extreme density among the
Javanese led Raymond Kennedy to declare the Javanese the world's
champion breeders (Kennedy, 1943:5). In 1967 about 0.35 percent of the Javanese were Protestant Christian, a percentage
figure far less than many of the outer islands (Cooley, 1968:
86).

Development of Javanese Social Structure

Early Indonesian society probably included no units
larger than the village and small tribal groups. Each community
was governed by a council of family heads, nominally led by
a senior chief who had largely advisory powers. This pattern,
going back to prehistoric times, persists in some outer islands. The spread of wet-rice agriculture on Java increased
food production and allowed increased population. The nec-
essities of irrigated farming required the adoption of a
settled community and cooperative work. This need resulted in
the formation of villages and subsequently, chiefs began to
acquire wealth and power as they assumed leadership of clusters
of neighboring villages (United States Army Handbook, 1964:
104-105).

The rapidly increasing power of these chiefs was augmented by the teaching and philosophy of the Hindu priests
from India. These priests authenticated the Indonesian
nobility's claim to power and rule. The Hindu influence, as
seen earlier, contributed to the empowering of the great
Javanese and Sumatran empires (cf. Van Leur, 1955:98-105).

The result was the development of three major social
strata (see chart page 36). At the top was a divinely ordained
ruler and hereditary nobility (ndara). They were found in
the four court centers of Central Java, Jogjakarta, Surakarta,
Mangkunegaran and Paku Alaman. Next was the administrative
officials, known as prijaji, who were recruited from the masses
to serve the sultan. Under these two groups, the wong tjiliq
or little people were representative of the masses (United
States Army Handbook, 1964:105).

In the villages the position of chief was not one of
authoritarian command but rather of primus inter pares. A
certain amount of basic democracy was inherent in primitive
Indonesian social structure. Important decisions were not
made by a single leader but by a council of elders or a meeting
of the villagers. A gulf existed between the noble families
and the common people. In addition there was a slave class,
which had resulted from war, debt or an offense against the

FIGURE 8

JAVANESE SOCIAL STRUCTURE

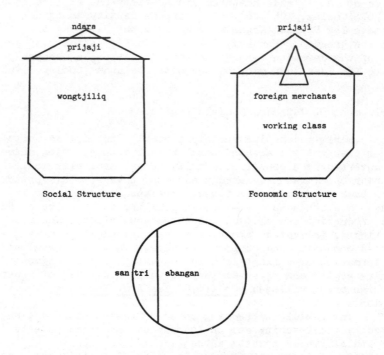

Social Structure

Economic Structure

RELIGIOUS STRUCTURE

Note: The first figure denotes the basic social stratification
of Javanese into the three basic groups, the ndara,
nobility, the prijaji, non-manual workers, wong tjiliq,
little people. The figure shows but few in the very
lowest strata (people like beggars, criminals, etc.).
The masses are from the little people with a small
minority above them in the two groups.
Economically, there is a larger group of very poor
people in the lowest strata with a majority in the
working classes. The higher economic groups are joined
by the foreign merchants (mostly Chinese) who for the
most part are on the same level as the prijaji.
Religious structure is divided roughly between the
smaller numbers of santri, the more devout Moslems and
the abangan, who more emphasize the animistic side of
Indonesian religious life.

adat (customary law). The nobility lived on the labor of the peasants and slaves, eschewed manual labor and maintained a strict endogamy which made it criminal for a noble woman to marry a commoner or a slave (Wertheim, 1956:116-117). The princely courts (Kratons) were centers of civilization where the elite patronized the arts and were served by foreign artisans and traders (United States Army Handbook, 1964:105).

The coming of Islam only superficially changed the basic social pattern. The well-born began to construct Moslem instead of Hindu genealogies and derived their sanction from Allah rather than Hindu gods. Although Islam introduced an expansion of commercial activity, it called forth no true middle class. The princes and nobles dominated as they had. The host of peddlers and small foreign traders ranked simply as part of the masses of commoners. While the Islamic ideal of human equality gave the ordinary man a sense of personal worth impossible to him on the basis of the Hindu hierarchy, Islam actually did little to raise his social status or alter the stratified structure of society in the principalities (United States Army Handbook, 1964:106).

Dutch activity indirectly introduced social change both among the nobility and at the village level. The Dutch set themselves over the Indonesians and made Indo-Europeans a more advantaged group who filled many clerical positions. Thus, social status based on race came into the picture (Wertheim, 1956:119-120). Secondly, the Dutch rule raised the status of the foreign orientals who were used by the Dutch as traders and artisans. They occupied a position between the Dutch and the Indonesians, taking on a position much like a middle class (United States Army Handbook, 1964: 106).

The Dutch policy of ruling and administering through the native aristocracy both stimulated and inhibited social change. The princes and chiefs came to be no more than the agents of the Dutch. In time this led to a weakening and discrediting of the position of the nobles. The village chiefs, formerly no more than informally elected chairmen of the councils of village elders, under the Dutch system gained extensive and often hereditary powers as agents of the colonial powers in enforcing levies on agricultural production and manpower. This development undermined local autonomy and prepared the ground for the consolidation that was to come with independence and the Indonesian state. The introduction of money economy weakened the self-sufficiency of the Javanese villages. The Dutch policy of dealing with village heads rather than individual land owners also weakened the concept of private ownership. Private ownership did not disappear but was modified by village communalism. Many Javanese migrated to wage work while others struggled to maintain their land ownership pattern (United States Army Handbook, 1964:196-198).

The Dutch period introduced extensive social change.
Modern Indonesian society has moved away from obeisance
based on race or the old family hierarchy. Dutch and
Indo-European elements have also lost influence in the society.
While in practice, some prestige is still associated with the
former family background of nobility, in recent years the
courts are no longer regarded as models for behavior, culture
and social values (United States Army Handbook, 1964:108-109).
In some areas, such as eastern Sumatra, the former nobility
was massacred because of the suspicion that these former nobles
had conspired with the Dutch. In other regions, such as
Jogjakarta, because the nobles were active in the republican
cause and have been recognized as able and dedicated leaders,
the nobility has suffered only slight loss of status (Wertheim,
1956:138). The Sultan of Jogjakarta is the Minister of Finance
and Economic Affairs in Soeharto's administration. In
Surakarta the former nobles were stripped of their governmental
powers but left in possession of their kraton and their spiritual functions (cf. Kahin, 1958:186).
With social status based on race and heredity dis-
credited, the path was prepared for a new social structure in
Indonesian life. Modern education became the identifying mark
of membership in the elite and the passport for admission into
it from below. Military personnel rapidly gained in status
and power. Leaders of the various political parties and organizations were accorded increasingly active and important
positions in the social structure. However, one authority
notes that the tendency toward a status system based on individual prosperity and ability is being outdistanced by a new
trend, represented by the collective organizations which are
playing an increasingly important role in social evolution
(Wertheim, 1956:144,145).
Indonesian social structure today is facing a new day.
It offers a new challenge for church growth. The new freedom
and responsibility may bring thousands more of the Indonesians
into a position where Christianity will become a vital and
possible option.

Social Stratification

In spite of the evolution traced above, Indonesian
society still has definite social stratification. Three
primary levels, only two of which are very important to everyday life, are discernable in Indonesia. The wong tjiliq
(little people) comprise the great mass of the farmers, peasants and the lower strata of urban populations. The prijaji
include the administrative bureauracy and the academically
trained intellectuals. The third level is a relatively small
but still prestigeous noble strate or ndara. Distinct from
this horizontal stratification there exists a vertical

classification of Javanese society based primarily on the
degree of participation in Islamic practices. In this classification, wong abangan do not regulate their lives according
to the basic principles of Islam, while the santri follow these
principles seriously. Some of the santri form such a culturally distinct group that they are assigned a level in the horizontal stratification somewhat below the prijaji
(Koentjaraningrat, 1960:89). Indonesian society might be
pictured as follows:

The wong tjiliq are for the most part farmers who live
in the villages but there are increasing numbers of them living
in the cities and engaging in various types of menial labor.
They are contrasted with the bureaucratic hierarchy. Children
of some of the wong tjiliq are gaining higher education and
moving into government jobs and other less menial vocations
(Koentjaraningrat, 1960:90-91).

The differentiation of abangan and santri is basic in
Indonesian society. The abangan emphasize the animistic
features of Indonesian religious life and centralize the
selamatan (ritual feast) and live in complex beliefs in spirits,
curing, sorcery and magic. The santri, more identified with
but not confined to the trading element, pays strict attention
to Islamic practices (C. Geertz, 1960:5-7). The santri often
localize in communities called kauman and lead an exclusive
social life (Koentjaraningrat, 1960:91-92).

Social stratification is important to the society of
Indonesia. Javanese are aware of the major social strata.
Although they may not understand the entire range of Javanese
stratification, every Javanese knows the levels above and
below his own and is able to adjust his behavior, speech and
gestures appropriately in all relationships with those of
higher, equivalent and lower status (Koentjaraningrat, 1960:
93).

Present Indonesia, while preserving the traditional
stratification, is moving into a more modern classification
as well. The strata are based on occupation and education.
There is the small ruling elite, consisting of those on the
highest levels of government, business, military, and religious
life. A second strata is the intermediate and much larger
group of middle and lower level civil servants, junior grade
army officers, small businessmen, semiskilled wage workers.
Below all these are the great masses of village cultivators,
peddlers, handicraft workers, plantation hands and unskilled
laborers whose ties are largely retained even in the cities
(United States Army Handbook, 1964:110). Church growth must
take account of these obvious differences in Indonesian social
stratification and seek to provide churches that can reach each
of the various groups that make up the mosaic. No one type
of church will reach every section of the population. Special
attention should be given to those segments that at any moment

might be showing response.

Village and Suburb (Kampung) Social Structure

Most of the people of Indonesia live either in the
villages (desa) or in the urban counterpart, the suburb
(kampung). About seventy percent of the people live in rural
settings where most are engaged in farming, fishing or fores-
try. Increasing numbers of the wong tjiliq are moving to the
cities and towns where they are most often restricted to the
simpler kinds of manual labor. They remain basically rural
people in an urban environment (United States Army Handbook,
1964:116-117).

The structure in the rural desa and the urban kampung
have much in common. Naturally the farming orientation of the
desa contrasts to the kampung where more of the people are
active in working for wages. The governmental unit of the two
are quite similar. The basic unit is the village or dukuhan,
which is headed by a kamitua, elected by the entire adult
citizenry. Several dukuhan are combined to form the desa under
the leadership of the lurah, elected roughly in the same way
as the kamitua. These officials have permanent tenure, except
they can be removed by either the government or their own
people. The lurah is commissioned to keep records, collect
taxes, transmit information from the government to the people
and settle minor disagreements. Above the desa is the sub-
district with the tjamat as the administrative official
(H. Geertz, 1963:45).

The Javanese desa is a purely territorial grouping of
unrelated individuals and families. In this community the
kinship factor has relatively small significance (Palmier,
1960:38). In addition to the nuclear families there are alien
elements such as prijaji peoples who may have moved into the
community. The members of the desa are grouped into several
subdivisions. The nuclear villagers own their own agricultural
lands and household compounds and assume the full burden of
citizenship. Others own either a household compound or agricultural land and bear some community responsibility. Those
who own a house situated in another person's household compound
and persons who provide for their own food or who work for the
master with whom they live, make up the third classification.
Members of family groups are not considered a separate class
(ter Harr, 1962:78-79).

The desa's territory includes the surrounding rice
fields as well as the house land. The irrigation system is
under the supervision of an official from the central government who employs village men to properly maintain the works
(H. Geertz, 1963:45). There are two types of land, the free-
hold that can be disposed of at the pleasure of the owner, subject only to the inheritance rules, and communal land which is

the property of the village and over which the users have limited disposal rights (United States Army Handbook, 1964:117).

Authority in the Javanese village has tended to remain subject to democratic controls by the villagers as a corporate group (United States Army Handbook, 1964:117). There is a well developed equalitarianism among villagers based on the feeling that all are equal and none has the right to hold himself above his fellows (H. Geertz, 1963:45). Social relationships in the village are based largely on the concept of mutual aid (gotong rojong). This mutual aid, while involving extended families, is not restricted to families but extends to all citizens of the village (Koentjaraningrat, 1960:94). The public work of the village is done cooperatively through the concept of gotong rojong.

From the church growth standpoint, it is clear that the villages and kampungs represent a fertile field for evangelism. Large churches in main road locations will draw various parts of the population to the Gospel. However, to reach the masses the Church must go to the desa and kampung where they live and where the Church can grow naturally in the environment of Indonesia.

Urban Development

Although most Indonesians live in rural areas and must receive more and more attention from the Churches, it is equally imperative that the urban millions must be discipled. During the twentieth century the town and city population has been growing even faster than the exploding rural populations. The steady migration to the cities has not been accompanied by a comparable development of industry with the result that many sections of the cities have a strongly rural appearance, except that there are no fields and gardens, and facilities are inadequate for the crowded urban situation (H. Geertz, 1963: 33).

Different from the masses herded into the kampungs and below the foreign diplomatic and business communities, the foreign trading merchant groups (mainly Chinese but also numerous Indian and Arab peoples) and the small urban elite, is a relatively large and as yet unstudied urban middle class, made up of middle level civil servants and white collar workers. This group includes school teachers, the middle rank of army and police as well as many office workers. Closely related to this white collar segment of the city population, the skilled workers such as craftsmen, tailors, bricklayers, blacksmiths and the more successful market peddlers form an important population block. Many among these urban dwellers are recent arrivals. They are urbanites from various islands where people were given preference by the Dutch in education and employment, as for instance the Ambonese, Menadonese and aristocratic Javanese and Moslem merchant families (H. Geertz, 1963:37).

The most numerous body of the urban proletariat--the laborers, servants, small street peddlers and unskilled workers--are even less understood than the previous group. Socially and culturally this population block is different from the skilled and white collar workers. They participate minimally, if at all, in the metropolitan superculture. Their social allegiances and cultural identities lie in the villages from which they for the most part are recent migrants (H. Geertz, 1963:37-38).

The Churches must make special studies of this lower strata of urban population. This group could well be the most fertile field for multi-individual evangelism in Indonesia's teeming cities. It is possible for the Gospel to travel back to the villages by means of those converted in the cities. However, among temporary urban residents who are merely attempting to earn a specified sum for a certain purpose, little response should be expected. Wold calls such people "target workers". They will likely show the same resistance, if there is any, as exists in their village to which they still claim allegiance (cf. Wold, 1968:42-43).

Among questions that must be answered are: Do the peoples from one ethnic group tend to segregate themselves in one area of the city and if so would an ethnic church in that area serve them best? Secondly, are these people sufficiently cut off from their former villages so as to be more responsive in their new environment? Thirdly, are the kampungs becoming new villages with social ties and influences that could function in people movements almost as effectively as they would in tribes. Wertheim notes that the kampungs are showing strong tendencies to act collectively in their own interests (1956:165). Lastly, could the kampungs in the urban areas be subject to web movements through the extended families that exist in the kampungs? Web movements, based on strong family and marriage ties that exist apart from tribal and caste lines, are but another type of multi-individual conversion patterns (see McGavran, 1970:320-325). One further question that must be met is to what degree specialized groups such as students, workers in the same profession, club members and other sub-groups, might be good soil in which people movements could grow?

Urban evangelism has tended to concentrate on churches on the main streets with a multi-ethnic membership. From what is known of kampung life, it is imperative that a church be established in each kampung because the people prefer to stay within the kampung. This is a possibility that should be well investigated in urban areas.

Javanese Family Structure

The diversity of Indonesian family life reflects the
ethnic complexity. Both patrilineal and matrilineal as well
as other arrangements are found in various regions. The
bilateral pattern of the Javanese is, however, at least in its
general outline, followed by around ninety percent of the
total population (<u>United States Army Handbook</u>, 1964:129). Many
marriage customs show the influence of either Islam or Christian
or at times both (ter Harr, 1962:180).

The Javanese kinship system is bilateral and nucleating
in that descent is considered through both the mother and the
father and inheritance is the same for daughters as for sons.
The nuclear family, parents and children, stands essentially
on its own, usually having its own house and only minimal obligations with kin groups (H. Geertz, 1963:47). Kin ties, so
powerfully developed among many Asian peoples are relatively
weak in the Javanese scheme. The only well integrated
kinship-based entity is the household, the core of which consists of a married pair and their offspring, the nuclear family
(<u>United States Army Handbook</u>, 1964:130).

The few contributions made by the nuclear family
are of utmost importance. They include the provision of an
enduring group within which personal, economic, social and
psychological needs of society are met and within which social
values are transmitted and enforced. The process of sociali-
zation which includes the maintenance of normative continuity
from generation to generation as well as the maintenance of
some of the deepest and most pervasive Javanese values are
carried on not only by the teaching of the parents but by the
very structure of the kinship system itself (H. Geertz, 1961:
2-3).

The absence of large corporate groups does not mean
that kin feeling is unimportant in the Javanese system. There
is a very developed kinship terminology. In fact the Javanese
language incorporates in its very structure certain obligatory
distinctions in regard to the social relationships between
addresser and addressee. The recognition of status between
persons has given rise to at least seven styles or levels
that relate to seven distinctive social-status relationships.
The three most important levels are <u>ngoko</u>, used for those of
lower status , <u>krama</u>, used for equal and <u>krama inggil</u>, used
for those of higher status. The kinship terminology reflects
the social importance of the nuclear family but also the place
of the extended family. A special term, <u>sedulur</u>, is used to
designate kinsmen outside the nuclear family. Beyond the
nuclear family the kinship terminology is distinctive and
strongly classificatory (Koentjaraningrat, 1960:106-108).

There is a great deal of latitude in regard to obligations to the extended family. While families do look to

other kinsmen for aid in weddings, funerals and other ceremonial occasions, the ties are not so close nor do they entail such obligations as in many Asian societies (United States Army Handbook, 1964:133-134). Kinship ties are only one of the factors that influence the behavior of the individual toward others. If there is an awkward differential between kinsmen or a personal conflict, they can ignore the kinship ties or accentuate them as they wish in keeping with the pressures of their particular situation (H. Geertz, 1961:4).

The importance of the nuclear family is most adequately captured by Hildred Geertz:

> *Nevertheless, for each Javanese, his family--his parents, his children, and usually, his spouse-- are the most important people in the world. They give him emotional security and provide a stable point of social orientation. They give him moral guidance, helping him from infancy through old age to learn, and relearn, the values of Javanese culture. The process of socialization is a continuous one throughout the life of the individual; and it is a man's closest relatives who, by their day to day comment, both verbal and non-verbal, keep him from deviating too far from the cultural norms. (H. Geertz, 1961:5)*

The particular type of family structure in Javanese society seems to indicate the possibility of people movements of the "web movement" variety. Since the nuclear family is so well-defined, people movements in the well known sense of entire tribes, villages or clans coming to Christ in multi-individual decisions, would be less likely to develop (see McGavran, 1955:1-16). The term "multi-individual" does not appear in Bridges of God but has been employed by McGavran in Understanding Church Growth to correct earlier misunderstandings of what people movements really are (see McGavran, 1970:302). Web movements move from family member to family member and from one nuclear family to the other across these relationships (McGavran, 1970:320-325). The Churches of Indonesia must seek to bring about such web movements and stimulate them to continue. At the same time, the Churches should remember that the rather close solidarity in the villages and the solidarity among various types of professional and working elements in the cities can well provide soil for people movements that would sweep villages and groups into the Church, again through multi-individual decision for Christ.

Practices involving marriage, child raising and divorce also have meaning for church growth in Java. Although some marriages, mostly in the rural regions, are still arranged by the parents without the consent of the participants, Javanese

youth in general make their own choice of a mate. Still,
marriages require parental consent (Koentjaraningrat, 1960:
100). Extensive social change now allows a man to arrange his
own marriage without his family having anything to do with
it (H. Geertz, 1961:64).

There are some prohibited marriages in Javanese society.
These prohibitions include union between siblings or other members of the same nuclear family. Such unions are considered
so absurd that nobody even thinks of the possibility
(Koentjaraningrat, 1960:100). Persons of different generations
should not marry in general but men often marry women of younger generations. There is general disapproval of marriage between children of brothers. On the other hand cousins in some
cases are felt to marry to advantage (United States Army
Handbook, 1964:136).

The tendency in Java is for girls to marry early. In
fact, if the optimum age has passed and a girl is still not
married, she might be married to a man with the agreement that
after a week the marriage would be dissolved by divorce. Once
the girl is divorced she can more easily contract a second
marriage as second marriages require less elaborate ceremonies
and men will be more inclined to ask her hand (H. Geertz, 1961:
70). The attitude toward divorce in general is somewhat lax.
The ease of divorce is seen in the fact that almost fifty percent of the marriages end in divorce (H. Geertz, 1963:47).
Even for women divorce proceedings are relatively easy (United
States Army Handbook, 1964:138). Both Christian and Islamic
teachings have had influence on the government regulations
concerning divorce (see ter Harr, 1962:197ff). Generally divorce is legally more difficult for Christians than for Moslems.

Marriage to several wives at the same time is permissable among most Indonesians. One group on Bali forms the
most notable exception. While permissable, however, polygamy
is not common (ter Harr, 1962:194). According to the census
of 1930 only two percent of the marriages in Java were polygamous. A 1956 report found some six percent of polygamous
marriages in Central Java. Koentjaraningrat found only
thirty-six out of 364 households involved in polygamy in a
Central Java village (Koentjaraningrat, 1960:103-104). The
tendency against polygamy is economic rather than religious,
moral or legal.

When a man has more than one wife, the wives from a
lower class than he, assume a secondary status. The head wife
is of the same class as the husband. Usually, only the children
of the first wife, or her adopted children, have full rights
to inheritance or succession (ter Harr, 1962:194). Most polygamous families are divided into two households to avoid conflict. First wives can at times force the husband to divorce
the second wife, especially if the second wife was taken se-
cretly (H. Geertz, 1961:132).

In such a society in which the marriage and divorce
situation is confused the testimony of the Christian home has
great influence. The evangelistic thrust of the Christian
home and Christian living related to marriage and family has
been noted by Bentley-Taylor as a highly efficient evangelistic
influence (Bentley-Taylor, 1967:144). Here again is a point to
be considered carefully by the Churches of Indonesia. Bringing
Christian attitudes to bear on Javanese marriage customs and
practices can have enormous power to commend the Gospel to un-
saved Javanese. ⌐

JAVANESE SOCIAL VALUES AND CHURCH GROWTH

There has been radical change in Indonesian social
values. The Javanese philosophy and outlook is basic to any
understanding of the Javanese. People will accept only those
innovations that are meaningful to them (cf. Barnett, 1953:
336). Basic Javanese ways of looking at life, death, work and
social relations are essential to a meaningful presentation
of the Gospel to them.

The Javanese attitude toward life and death is basically passive. Life is accepted as it comes and the inevitability
of death viewed as part of life. Death is seen as part of the
natural order and is thus accepted. Javanese highly value a
sense of detachment (iklas) in which true feelings are veiled
rather than exhibited (United States Army Handbook, 1964:152-
153). Detachment is especially valued at the time of death
of loved ones. Javanese view death as tied up with their view
of fate. The fear of death is lessened as they view it as a
desired state which frees them of emotion. When dead, one
has no further needs and therefore no desires (C. Geertz, 1960:
74-74).

There are three main views of death among the Javanese.
The remarkable feature is that all three can at times be held
concurrently by the same person. The Islamic version includes
the concept of eternal retribution, punishment and reward in
the afterworld for the sins and good deeds in this one. Second,
and more popular among the abangan population is the idea of
sampurna (perfect, complete) meaning that the individual personality completely disappears after death and nothing is left.
The third view, also widely held by the abangan but rejected
by the santri, is the notion of reincarnation. This view holds
that when a person dies his soul enters into an embryo on its
way to being born and is thereby itself reborn (C. Geertz, 1960:
75). These views of death run throughout Javanese life.

The Javanese believe in fate but they are not simply
passive. They smile a great deal and sometimes give the idea
of being carefree. Javanese do not seek to evade responsibility.
Although they are restrained and seek to avoid unpleasant clashes,
they can at times be subject to outbursts of murderous violence,

called <u>amok</u> (one of the few words Malay has given to Western
languages). Modern Indonesian youth is developing a fighting
spirit that is more and more respected and is in some regards
replacing the traditional value of detachment (<u>United States
Army Handbook</u>, 1964:152-153). While Javanese do not avoid
responsibility, they do avoid involvement. The expression
"<u>tjampur tangan</u>" (hand mixing or involvement) is a vital part
of Javanese life. Perhaps this like the habit of quiet speech
has arisen because of overcrowded conditions.

Work and Leisure

The unfailing monsoon season in most areas and the
almost seasonal-less nature has resulted in a society that
has not had to be seriously concerned with long-range planning.
Indonesian life moves on from day to day and the future viewed
as a matter beyond man's control. Traditional Indonesian
culture did not count time as the calibrated and moving back-
drop of action it has become in the West. For Indonesians it
is not the length but the content and quality of experience
that are important. The indirect and subtle approach to
problems is valued above the directness and speed of Western
society (<u>United States Army Handbook</u>, 1964:154).

Change is especially noticable at the point of time
consciousness. Urbanization, the program of the political
parties and the activity of the government are highlighting
the need for planning. While the <u>United States Army Handbook
of 1964</u> was correct in its assessment that government leaders,
at that time, were failing to recognize the necessity of solving
practical problems, this judgment would not hold true for recent times (see <u>United States Army Handbook</u>, 1964:154). The
government of General Soeharto both recognizes and is taking
steps toward the solving of Indonesia's pressing problems
(see Pauker, 1967b:15-]7).

In keeping with the traditional idea of time,
Indonesians have not attached moral or ethical values to either
work or leisure. Work is a common necessity to be taken for
granted. Leisure is a luxury to be ejoyed by those who can
afford it (<u>United States Army Handbook</u>, 1964:154). The <u>prijaji</u>
do not engage in manual labor and have given to Indonesian
society a certain lack of respect for manual labor
(Koentjaraningrat, 1960:89). In this respect also, changes
are beginning to be seen.

Private property and ownership are firmly established
in the Indonesian tradition. While there has been joint ownership among the Javanese, it has never been dominant. The
communal tendencies were heightened under the Dutch culture
system. In regard to private ownership, there has been a highly developed sense of the need to share among the Javanese.
The amassing of wealth has not been highly valued in traditional

society which looked on position as more important than income.
This is again a point of extensive change in the new Indonesia
where wealth and luxury are coming to be items to be sought
(United States Army Handbook, 1964:156).

Relations With Others

Javanese tend to divide all people into four groups,
Javanese, Indonesians other than Javanese, non-Malay Indonesians
and foreigners. Most close relationships will be along kinship lines. High value is placed on friendships, but the
Indonesian concept of friendship involves a rather more intimate
relationship--even to the sharing of property, than in some
other cultures (United States Army Handbook, 1964:157).
The tendency toward passiveness and emphasis on harmony and cooperation has given rise to a basic tolerance among
Javanese. They have a great propensity for dealing with dis-
putes and deviant behavior by compromise and "musjarawah"
(discussion until concensus is reached). However, the limits
of their toleration can be reached as was seen in the events
following the Communist coup attempt in 1965 (Koentjaraningrat,
1960:90=92).
Indonesian culture involves a highly developed sense
of politeness and proper conduct. One seeks not to show his
feelings and to preserve a calm demeanor. A few examples of
polite conduct will demonstrate the complexity of Javanese
feelings on the subject. One should never touch another's
head. In the presence of elders or superiors (such as a judge)
one should sit with his feet flat on the floor and never walk
in front of an older person without lowering ones head.
Actually, it is impolite to sit or stand with one's head higher
than that of an important person. Objects should never be
given or received with the left hand. Kindness and courtesy
should be acknowledged. One should never point with the index
finger nor cross his legs in the presence of others. When
served food or drink one should always consume some, but not
all, of what has been offered. A closer degree of friendship
and respect is entailed when one feels free to enter the back
door of a home than when he is invited in the front door.
Open disagreements are to be avoided as they are both dangerous
and bad manners. Westerners are sometimes surprised to see
men holding hands, even soldiers. The greater a gift given
the less acknowledgement is made. Criticism should be avoided
if possible and delivered indirectly if necessary. All the
above mentioned matters should be closely observed by church
planters.

Tradition

Indonesian society should most likely be considered in

terms of Nida's "tradition directed" culture. This fact is
borne out by the fear of supernatural forces (ancestors,
spirits, etc.) so evident. Most decisions would be based on
what the group, in Javanese society, what the family would
do (Nida, 1960:124-132).

Owing to their basic tradition-based orientation,
Javanese will respond readily to Christian teachings that present God as Father and Lawgiver. Jesus should be presented
as the better way for man (Nida, 1960:128). Javanese, with
their background not only of tradition directed life but
Islamic concepts of the austerity of God, will most readily
respond to the message of Christ who brings God to man and
man to God. The message that God is love should prove a key
to the tradition based society of Java.

It is imperative that those interested in church growth
in Indonesia understand the Indonesian way of looking at
things. Effective church growth will take place only when the
organization of the Church is understandable to the people,
congenial to their social structures and efficient in its
correlation of form and function (Nida, 1965 :108). To
achieve such church organization, missionaries must thoroughly
understand every facet of the life,philosophy and social
structure of the people.

THE RELIGIONS OF INDONESIA

The amazing diversity of Indonesian culture is clearly
manifested in the variation of religious affiliation. The
accompanying map indicates the relative domination in the
various regions of Indonesia (page 50). The map shows only
the dominant religion in a certain area. It does not indicate
that other religions are not found in that area.

The map shows northern Sumatra, the area of Atjeh, as
being intensely, even fanatically Islamic. Five regions, the
Minangkabau of western Sumatra, the Sundanese of West Java,
the Bandjarese of southern Borneo, the island of Madura and
Macassar of southern Celebes are strongly Islamic. The fact
that West Java was more sheltered from Indian influences and
had a long history of hostility toward the Javanese Majapahit
Empire helps explain the Sundanese Islamic stance. The south
Borneo people boast that no "Orang Bandjar" (Bandjar person)
has ever become Christian. Madura and Macassar both experienced
cruelty at the hands of the Dutch and Portuguese which might
partly explain their anti-Christian stand. For whatever reasons, these areas remain strongly Islamic and the Gospel has
made little progress among these peoples (see Fisher, 1964:
251).

Islam holds a more nominal sway over other regions of
Indonesia. The north coast and the southern regions of Sumatra,
especially along the coastal regions, are Islamic but not with

FIG. 9

RELIGIONS OF INDONESIA

Fanatical Islam
Strong Islam
Nominal Islam
Javanese Islam
Hindu - Bali
P.olestant
Catholic
Animism

the intensity of Atjeh or Minangkabau. Likewise the coastal
areas of many other islands and part of the northern tail of
the Celebes is held by a relatively strong Islam. The region
of Djakarta is a cosmopolitan mixture but could be seen as
only nominally in the power of Islam. In many of these regions,
especially Borneo and some of the eastern islands, the Islamic
influence is a thin veneer along the coast with animistic
peoples in the interior (see Fisher, 1964:251). To Christian
missions this means that mission stations located in the main
towns on the coast will meet relatively steady resistance but
missionaries who live and witness in the interior will likely
meet responsive peoples.

Central and East Java are dominated by a particular
form of Islam, often referred to as Javanese Islam (cf. Fisher,
1964:251). Due to stronger influence from the Indianization
process, the religion of Java shows a greater syncreticism and
a less intense attachment to Islam. There is a strong continuing belief in the old spirits and ancestral ghosts of
traditional Javanese religion (Kennedy, 1942:105). Hendrik
Kraemer once pointed to this fact as the main reason the
Church had gained a measure of success in Moslem Java
(Bentley-Taylor, 1967:138). The strength of Islam varies
greatly even in Central and East Java. The northern coastal
towns, east of Semarang and around Tjeribon are more strongly
Islamic. This is the area where Islam first entered Indonesia
and also has a great proportion of Arabic people. Interior
areas are more animistic.

The Hindu-Buddhist tradition still dominates the
island of Bali and the portion of Lombok inhabited by Balinese
immigrants. Over 15,000 temples on Bali are dedicated to
Hindu worship (Cooley, 1968:62). Bali shows a religion that
is a combination of Sivaism and Brahamanism with definite
Buddhist elements and a substrata of older, animistic rites
(Kern, 1940:496). "Bali, indeed is a kind of museum place,
a living survival of fourteenth-century Java" (Kennedy, 1943:
21).

Animistic peoples are located mainly in the interior
regions that have been cut off from trade routes and the
different waves of invading religions. These pockets of
animistic worship, denoted by the white areas on the map,
related to the people of interior Borneo, Sumatra, Halmahera,
Timor and various other islands in eastern Indonesia (cf.
Fisher, 1964:251). It must, however, not be forgotten that
animistic beliefs and practices are found in every region of
the archipelago, even among adherents of the great religions.

Roman Catholic power is dominant in only restricted
parts of Flores, Wetar and Timor. Although Catholics pre-
ceeded Protestants, they have been restricted or severely
limited by government regulations (Cooley, 1968:43). Again,
while Catholic power is dominant only in the small regions

noted, they promote strong church, educational and medical
work in almost every section of Indonesia.

Protestant Christianity has been planted in almost
every section of the islands. As previously noted, the Bataks
in northern Sumatra form one of the strongest Christian denominations in Asia. The island of Nias is likewise strongly
Protestant. In the Sanghir-Talaud Islands and the Minahasa
region of north Celebes are great concentrations of Christians.
In addition a strong Christian movement is present in the
Central Celebes among the Toradja peoples. The Ambon region
is about half Christian and half Moslem. Several areas have
seen people movements into the Christian religion, i. e.
Minahasa, Ambon, Batakland and Timor (Thomas, 1968:297).

It must be remembered that there are Christians in
Moslem areas and Moslems in Christian areas. Also, it should
not be forgotten that many of Indonesia's Churches exist
in large ethnic populations and are primarily ethnic Churches.
The church planter must form a concrete judgement concerning
the degree of responsiveness in each area.

The Animistic Base

The animistic substratum of Indonesian religion is
important since the masses are basically animistic in spite
of a more or less superficial affiliation with one of the
world religions (Kennedy, 1943 :106). The indigenous beliefs
of nearly all Indonesian peoples demonstrate a belief in a
supreme deity. However, in keeping with most animistic concepts, the supreme god or gods are felt to have resigned their
control of and connection with the world. These gods have
little relationship with daily life (Warneck, n. d.:25).

One observer reports a conversation with a Javanese
Moslem in which the observer asked the Javanese if he really
believed in Tuhan Allah (God), why it was necessary to "keep
in" with the field spirits? The Moslem answered that Allah
was a very great God with great affairs such as the pilgrimage
to Mecca and the life. He could not be expected at the same
time to keep an eye on the rice fields to see that rats did
not eat it and that it grew properly. Such things are the
business of Sri Dewi, the rice goddess, and the field spirits
(Ponder, n. d.:101). The concept of God in Christ with its
personal meaning must have unusual appeal among peoples who
hold such ideas.

Among Indonesians, like most animists, the high gods
are absentee gods. Their feelings of dependence are directed
more to the spirits, powers and ancestral ghosts who influence
their daily lives. The high gods are thought to be powerless
in the every day struggles of life (Warneck, n. d.:27). Jesus'
love and care for the individual finds responsiveness in
Indonesian hearts.

Indonesian animistic religion rests basically on the concepts of spirits of innumerable varieties and the ancestor cults (Kennedy, 1937:294). The belief that spirits cause a multitude of phenomena provides Javanese with a ready-made answer to many puzzling questions of life. In general, Javanese conceive of three types of spirits: memedi, the gendruwos, in addition to playing various tricks, sometimes kidnap children and even assume the form of a husband and sleep with the wife without her being the wiser. Children of such unions are monsters. In contrast, lelembuts can cause illness or insanity. These spirits possess the person and can only be driven out by the dukun, a multi-functional magic man who is a healer, diviner and sorcerer. Western doctors are powerless against the sickness cause by lelembuts. To frighten away the lelembuts people often put potions on the heads of babies and lime or orange peals (as well as other potions) on the heads of adults who feel indisposed. Some people make a pact with a lelembut, called a setan or djin, by which the possessed one gains certain powers as payment for being in the power of the spirit.

The third type of spirits, the tujul, are often conceived as children. They can aid one in business or work, even helping one become rich. Many seek the help of a tujul who will steal for his master (C. Geertz, 1960:17-22).

In addition some Indonesians conceive of numerous place spirits, earth spirits, water spirits, air spirits, spirits in waterfalls, beaches, volcanoes and almost every local place (Cady, 1964:13). A stone or any unusually shaped object may be the abode of a spirit. The Waringen (Banjan) tree is a frequent and typical abode of spirits. One group of Indonesians considered the water in a certain stream as so sacred that it could be only used after proper ceremony (Ponder, n. d.: 196-198).

The place spirits are called demit, and their habitations are called pundens. These are important to Javanese animists. The punden may be a banjan tree, an old Hindu ruin, an old grave or some topographical pecularity. Gifts are brought to the punden to placate the local spirit (C. Geertz, 1960:24-25). Javanese also conceive of a guardian spirit, the danjang, who watches over the village (Djajadiningrat, 1958: 391). The danjang desa (village spirit) abide in trees and other special places and respond to pleas for help given through a slametan (communal feast). When the village spirit is thought to be the ghost of some great man, the punden will most often be that man's grave, where gifts will be sacrificed seeking the village's welfare (C. Geertz, 1960:26-27).

Characteristic of Javanese animism is the belief in the presence in both man and rice and other inanimate objects of life force or "soul" or life energy, which while of the same nature for all, may be stronger in some than in others. Former practices of head-hunting and cannibalism were based on this

concept. Those practicing these activities hoped thereby to
gain the strength of their victims (Vlekke, 1943:10). Unusually
shaped rocks were often used as amulets because they were felt
to have power (Vlekke, 1945:7-8).

Every human has its own soul, called the soemangat that
attends the person while he lives. After death the soul is
called the njawa (Landon, 1947:15). The souls of the dead
continue to take interest in the communal life and are angered
if their descendents give up the traditions or fail to fulfill
their duties toward the spirits. The ancestor cults tend to
make difficult any innovation (Vlekke, 1945:8). This is another
example of the tradition based nature of Indonesian culture.

There is a well defined belief in ancestor cults throughout the islands. Since these ancestors have passed beyond the
realm of death, they can, if kept satisfied, be helpful to the
living (Kennedy, 1943:48). The Javanese visit the graves of
their ancestors and a sort of flower petal is placed on the
grave while asking forgiveness and promising continuing devotion. Many Javanese beg their ancestors to help them get
a bicycle, a promotion, riches, passing grades or some other
material benefit (Jay, 1963:86-87).

While all humans possess some spiritual powers, there
are those who are specially adept at communicating with the
supernatural who serve as magic men or dukun. Most of the
purposes of the dukun are commendable, healing the sick, determining propitious days for planting, marrying or traveling.
Dukuns predict future events, find lost objects and insure
good fortune. They employ magic and sorcery (United States
Army Handbook, 1964:227). The capacity to be a dukun is
partly inherited but is also partly learned through apprentice-
ship. Most dukuns make extensive use of amulets, spells, herbs
and the like. A dukun's reputation is usually greater away
from his home village. An Indonesian considering sorcery will
always seek an out-of-town dukun (C. Geertz, 1960:86-90).

Dukuns are usually men but sometimes women become
dukun tiban or possessed people. These people receive their
power, not by learning, but through divine stroke. While
under the influence of this power, which often departs as soon
as it comes, the dukun tiban can perform wondrous cures and
other miracles. In the process the person often becomes rich
(C. Geertz, 1960:101-103).

When employed for sorcery, dukuns can cause sickness,
bad luck or even death. The only defense against sorcery is
a better dukun. When one feels the object of sorcery, he
obtains a dukun to off-set the spell. If the afflicted one's
dukun is stronger, the magic will turn back on the one who
instigated it, but both dukuns will remain unharmed. There
is never any direct confrontation among those who are practicing
or being affected by sorcery (C. Geertz, 1960:107-110).

Dukuns perform much of their curative and predictive

functions through the practice of a system of numerology
known as petungan. This system determines lucky and unlucky
days. It indicates propitious times for activities such as
weddings, travels and business ventures. Petungan uses complicated Javanese calendars. The petungan system provides a
way of insuring that one is tjotjok (fits, as a key with a lock,
or compatable) with the world. The Sundanese use the alphabet
instead of the Javanese calendar but the principle of prediction is the same (Landon, 1947:19-20).

At the very heart of Javanese animism is the ceremony
of the selamatan. This ceremony consists of the distribution
of food to neighbors and other invited guests at special times
and occasions during the year (Koentjaraningrat, 1960:95).
Only a small amount of the food is consummed at the slametan.
The rest is taken home for the family of the recipient (United
States Army Handbook, 1964:226).

Selamatans fall into four main types centering around
the main events of life, birth, circumcision, marriage and
death. Other slametans are associated with Moslem ceremonies
such as the birth of the Prophet, the fast, the Day of Sacrifice
and others. Another selamatan concerns the social integration
of the village. This ceremony, called bersih desa (cleansing
of the village) is to rid the village of evil spirits. Other
selamatans are given on intermittent occasions such as departing
for a long trip, changing residence, taking a new name, beginning harvest, illness, sorcery and so forth. There can be
a selamatan for almost every incident of life (C. Geertz, 1960:
30).

The animistic base of Indonesian religion has great ✓
significance for church growth in the islands. The Lord Jesus
must be presented as The Power that can overcome the spirits
that bring such fear to the Javanese life. Indonesians must
be led to see that the indwelling Holy Spirit can and will
protect from all evil. They must see that it is the personal
God who will Himself meet their needs, not ancestors.
Indonesians need to understand that God knows and cares for
each person in a personal way. Psalm 139 should have great
meaning in Indonesia.

In addition, the Church in Java must find some functional substitute for the selamatan. Selamatans, since they are part
of animistic religious practices, must not be followed by
Christians. However, the function they perform in the Javanese
society must be continued. Some selamatan-like procedure must
be found that can be entirely Christian and at the same time
fulfill the basic need of the Javanese in his society. Such a
substitute could also have an evangelistic function.

Animism forms the base of religious life in Indonesia.
The religions that have come to the islands have never fully
replaced the original beliefs. However, animism is not the full
story. Beginning in the 700s there were influences from India,

Hinduism and Buddhism, that added their teachings to Indonesian
religion.   Indianization forms an additive to Indonesian religion.

The Hindu-Buddhist Additive

The ancient Indians, the Dravidian peoples, who were
overrun by the white skinned newcomers, the Aryans about 2000
B. C., brought their religious beliefs and tribal laws written
in the Rig-veda. Two centuries before Christ they composed
the two epics, the Mahbharta and the Ramayana. The former
relates of a tribal war and the latter of the exploits of Rama
who fought demons to rescue his wife, Sita. Rama represented
the ideal king and Sita the model wife (Vlekke, 1945:9).
Three gods eventually arose to prominence in the Hindu
religious matrix. Vishnu, a minor sun god, became an almost
monotheistic figure for many Indian religions. He was conceived
as a personal deity who could be trusted. Brahman became to
be associated with wisdom. However, when Vishnu and Brahman
were associated, there arose the belief that Vishnu had ten
incarnations that reached their climax in Rama and Krishna.
These avatars or manifestations were objects of worship or
bhakti (Braden, 1945:338).
The third god, Shiva or Siva is the resurgence of a
Dravidian god eclipsed at the coming of the Aryans. Siva is
symbolized by the bull, Nandi, and by the phallic male and
female powers of the supreme deity (Frazer, 1920:92). The
Siva cult proved adept at syncretism, adapting to itself
many local deities. The most venerated of these adaptations
was Ganapati or Ganesa, symbolized as an elephant who led a
troop of demons in the task of attending the gods (Crooke, 1920:
701).
To meet the challenge of Buddhism, Hinduism strove to
form a single anthropomorphic deity, attempting to combine the
monotheism of Siva and Vishnu with a vast polytheism. The
Siva-Vishnu combination, known as Harihara, was completed by
the addition of Brahma.   These gods in time absorbed a multitude of aboriginal gods and paved the way for an increasing
readiness for other peoples to accept Hindu concepts (Briggs,
1951:230-231).
It was the syncretized and tolerant variant of Sivaism
that reached Indonesia around 700 A. D. The belief in Karma,
especially in the realm of unremembered misdeeds which bring
present suffering, gave Hinduism a definite fatalistic turn
which fit in with Indonesian feelings (Pitt, 1955:3-15). The
tolerant and syncretistic nature of the Hinduism that reached
Indonesia aided its spread.
Buddhism appeared in India partly as a protest against
the claims of superiority on the part of the Brahman priestly
class and the degrading implications of caste. Buddhism had

a message for ordinary men. It offered an approach to life
not dependent on priestly magic. Life's sufferings stemmed
from desire which could be conquered by following the meritor-
ious eightfold path of right belief, aspiration, speech, action.
honest livelihood, sustained mental exertion, alertness and
serenity. Buddhism was missionary in spirit and broadly
humanitarian in its appeal which was intended for all nations
and races (Cady, 1964:38-39).

Buddhism divided into two major sects, the Hinayana
and the Mahayana (the lesser and the greater vehicle). The
seventh century Buddhists of Sumatra followed the Hinayana
path but within fifty years had been converted to the Mahayana
sect (Vlekke, 1943:20-21). The Mahayana included three innovations that strengthened its impact on Southeast Asia.
First, it presented Gautama as only the most recent of a line
of enlightened ones and contended that others would likely
follow him. Secondly, it affirmed the possibility of transferring merit from Buddhist saints about to enter Nirvana to
weaker brothers still struggling. Thirdly, and most important,
it granted to rulers an almost divine status (Bodhisattra)
that could qualify rulers as emergent Buddhas. Since such
ideas were perennially popular with the rulers of Southeast
Asia, they enhanced the appeal and spread of Buddhism (Cady,
1964:40).

Buddhism and Hinduism entered Indonesia in different
ways. As a religion that repudiated caste and race Buddhism
was transmitted by Indian missionary devotees and Asian converts. It was a religion of traders, while Hinduism could be
spread only by high-caste immigrants. Hinduism on the other
hand, buttressed royal authority through the support of divine
kingship. Brahman advisors presided at coronations, assisted
rulers as clerks, scribes and astrologers and were specialists
in numerology. Except for the use of the Bodhisattra principle, Buddhism was less able to fulfill such functions. But
Hinduism could not attract popular support. Hindu culture
came to have more influence than Hindu religion (Cady, 1964:
40-41).

As the Indian influences came most Southeast Asians
(particularly the Javanese) preserved the essentials of their
own culture. Hinduism is and was the religion of the upper
classes and never has completely reached the Indonesian masses.
The masses remained attached to their Indonesian animism and
ancestor cults. This fact explains how Islam so easily supplant-
ed Hinduism when it reached the islands in later years (Coedes,
1968:33).

There was a tendency in Indonesia for Buddhism and
Hinduism to grow together. Mahayanism showed a distinct tendency to amalgamate with native Hinduism, particularly with
Sivaism. Ultimately this led to a Siva-Buddha cult (Briggs,
1951:247). Javanese thought has characteristically demonstrated

a close association between Buddha and Siva, even identifying
Buddha and Siva as one. The result was a development of a
Brahmanical religion that recognized Siva as the chief deity
(Landon, 1947:78). The syncretism is further demonstrated in
that while most of the beautiful temples are Buddhist, the
literature shows profound Hindu influence (Kern, 1920:496).

Modern Hinduism (the Hindu-Buddhist combination) is
found almost exclusively on Bali. Here Hindu and Buddhist
elements are combined with animistic factors to form a religion often called Hindu-Bali. Balinese religion permeates
every aspect of life. There is worship of Siva (<u>kala</u>) and
his wife Uma (Durga) as well as of Surya, god of the sun who
is sometimes identified with Siva. Other important gods are
Indra, lord of heaven, Yama, lord of hell, Ganesa, the
elephant-trunked god of wisdom and others. While Brahma and
Vishnu are not regularly worshipped, altars are built for
them. Buddha is worshipped as a younger brother of Siva and
Siva's wife, Uma, is identified as Sri, the goddess of rice.
This goddess is represented as a Balinese maiden and venerated
in little chapels near or in the rice fields (Cole, 1945:214-
215).

The Indian religions intensified and refined many
older Indonesian religious ideas. The regions most influenced
by the Indian religions are today the least fanatically
Islamic. The mildness and tolerance of Islam is sometimes
attributed to the basic temperament of the Javanese people.
Actually, the Javanese are not basically different from other
Indonesian peoples who are not known for their gentle ways
(the Madurese, for instance). "So", says Coedes, "we may ask
ourselves if the particular aspect assumed by Islam in Java
was not due rather to the influence that Indian religions exercised over the character of the inhabitants of the island
for more than ten centuries" (1968:253).

Indian influence has been most crucial in cultural
areas. However, Indonesians have used great selectivity in
their acceptance of Indian cultural concepts (Cady, 1964:45).
While Java and to a greater extent Bali, show signs of a caste
system, the system is not well defined. On Java the only
remnant of the caste system is seen in the respect paid to
certain "high born" and in the language that requires different
levels for those of different rank (Koentjaraningrat, 1960:111-
112). Even on Bali where there is still a caste system with
three upper castes, the caste groups amount to only about seven
percent of the population and the common people continue their
lives in their normal way (Landon, 1947:75). Bosch concludes
that while Indonesians know of the four primary orders, there
is not the slightest indication of a real caste system (Bosch,
1951:9).

Indonesians also rejected female inferiority. Even
with the coming of Islamic influences women are still a status

above that generally given in Hindu or Moslem cultures. Women
on Bali can even under certain conditions choose their own hus-
bands (Landon, 1947:75). Thus, Indian cultural patterns were
accepted, modified and used in Indonesianized form.

Indian influence is clearly seen in the art and architecture of Indonesia. Similarities between Indian and
Indonesian art and architectural forms might be even more
apparent had history not wiped out the intermediate stages of
influence as Indian culture spread across Southeast Asia (Coedes,
1968:255). The artists who created the great architectural
wonders such as Borobudur were not Indian artists, but Javanese
and Balinese craftsmen, inspired and perhaps taught by Indians
(Bosch, 1951:9). Indian ideas and techniques were taken over
and thoroughly Indonesianized.

The languages of Indonesia, especially Javanese and
Balinese, were stabilized and enriched by their contact with
Sanskrit (Coedes, 1968:254-]55). This influence of Sanskrit
of necessity came from contact with the Brahman priests who
would have used this sacred and scientific language. The
traders most likely had little knowledge of Sanskrit but used
Prakrit or Tamil languages, which were highly Sanskritized.
It is noteworthy that a great number of Sanskrit words are
found in Javanese, Balinese and Malay languages, Drandian words
are almost completely lacking (Bosch, 1951:8-9).

The greatest abiding Indian influence on Indonesian life
and religion is the literary field with its natural consequences
in the philosophical. Throughout the Indian period, the
Ramayana and Mahabharta along with other Indian epics were the
only sources of inspiration for Javanese literature (Coedes,
1968:254). The ethical and moral ideals of the Javanese are
expressed in the shadow plays (wajang) which are strongly influenced by the Indian epics (United States Army Handbook, 1964:
228). In the wajang stories the Hindu stories were not simply
translated, but were rewritten with a Javanese setting. It
is so well done that Javanese think of the events as local.
The Hindu stories were captured by the Javanese and whenever
possible, the essential view on life of the Javanese toward
their ancestors and spirits was retained. The indigenous beliefs were dressed in the Hindu garb (Landon, 1947:79-80).

Indian influence has given to Indonesian religion much
of its philosophical base, such as tolerance and willingness
to accept all religions. It has profoundly influenced the
literature which has in turn influenced the basic feelings
of the people. It must be seen as an additive to the basic
animism. It did not greatly change the substratum, but added
to it and intensified certain elements within it. The Indian
religions prepared the way for the coming wave of Islam.

The Islamic Incrustation

Islam began with Mohammed's preaching in Mecca but was developed only after the Hijra to Medina in A. D. 622. The religion of the Prophet was based on the ancient Arabic religion with many Persian, Jewish and Christian additions. While the ancient Arabian religion included a large number of gods, coupled with a multitude of idols and images, including stone fetishes, it had as well a belief in one supreme god, Allah (Kraemer, 1952:153). The pilgrimage to the Ka'ab, erected in 550 A. D. on the site of an older temple, was a part of the ancient Arabic worship as were the wearing of the single garment, the Ihram, the march around the Holy Place and the throwing of stones, all found in some form in modern Islam (Zwemer, 1920:4). The temple at Ka'ab and the black stone were retained by Mohammed when he abolished the many idols and forbade the practice of walking around the temple unclad (Noledeke, 1920:665).

With a strong and skillful government driven by a faith that inspired both its followers and armies, Islam within a few years controlled all of western Arabia and was looking for new worlds to conquer (Gibb, 1953:2-3). By 661 A. D. the Caliphates, Abu Bakr, Umar and Uthman, had pushed the borders of Islamic influence into the Persian Empire, Syria and Egypt. Islam overran North Africa and most of Spain before being thrown back by Charles Martel in 732 A. D. India was occupied before 1000 A. D. and Islamic influence had reached Atjeh in north Sumatra by the tenth century (Verhoeven, 1962:29, 59, 81-82).

Islam has not been without its divisions, in fact, the number of divisions runs ahead of the seventy-eight predicted by Mohammed (Wilson, 1959:48). Two of these divisions have special meaning for Indonesia. The division between Sunnite and Shiite branches arose as a result of the controversy in 660 when the Caliph Uthman was murdered. The less orthodox Shiites, followers of Ali, the son-in-law of Mohammed, held that the Caliph should be a descendant of Mohammed (Kraemer, 1952:61-62). The more orthodox Sunnites won out and established the Umayyad Caliphate (661-750) which is often called the expansive Caliphate (Verhoeven, 1962:30-31). The Shiites later supported a revolt in the Persian region that aided the rise of the Abbasid Caliphate (750-1258) under whose power most of India was subjugated. Since Islam spread to Indonesia from India, it was this less orthodox brand that found its way to the islands.

Even more important to Indonesian Islam was the rise of the mystical Sufi movement within Islam. This movement was a reaction to the Moslem tendency to overemphasize the transcendent, unapproachable quality of God which led to a position near deism. Sufism tended in the opposite direction (Wilson, 1959:49). The early Sufis pursued the mystical experience through certain ascetic and moral disciplines. These ideas

were combined with gnostic and Platonian doctrines and in
time led to absorption tendencies (Gibb, 1953:147-148). A
book by Al Ghazali made the Sufi movement acceptable to many
of the world's Moslems (Kraemer, 1952:139-141).

Islam became strong in southern India and Ceylon
along the sea coasts and at the terminals of commercial and
maritime routes (Planhol, 1959:116-117). From these maritime
centers, especially Gujarat and Malabar, Islam travelled to
Indonesia on the ships of Moslem traders (United States Army
Handbook, 1964:229). The Islam that came to Indonesia had
been influenced by the religious climate of India and was
thereby more acceptable to Indonesians who were familiar with
Indian religious concepts (Berg, 1932:252-253). The mystical
elements that had entered Islam enhanced its spread in Indonesia
(Simon, 1912:143).

Islam first established itself in Perlak in north
Sumatra through Moslem traders. A daughter of the Mohammedan
ruler of Perlak married a ruler of Pasai (Samudera) with the
resultant Islamic advance. Then a Pasai princess married into
a family from the city of Malacca and carried her religion to
that city destined to become the focal point for Islamic advance in the fifteenth and sixteenth centuries (Landon, 1947:
137). Islam was following family lines in taking Indonesia.

Islam enhanced its own spread by making conversion easy.
The Mohammedan method was: first, exterior mission to make
the people Moslem, be it in name only, and then, if possible,
bring them under Mohammedan rule. The second consisted in the
penetration of Islam into all fields of life and the creation
of a feeling of solidarity with the rest of the Moslem world
(Berg, 1932:251). In the beginning, Islam meant little more
for the masses than a change in the name of the supreme being
from Shiva-Buddha to Allah. Slowly, the people were educated
by Moslem teachers to a stricter concept of the Mohammedan
belief. It was not necessary to give evidence of genuine
belief or knowledge of Moslem law. One had but to utter the
two parts of the confession of faith (Nieuwenhuihze, 1958:39).
"No religion ever made conversion easier than did Islam"
(Landon, 1947:135).

Islam also used practices in its teachings and made
the faith seem useful in procuring things Indonesians desired.
The wajang shows and gamelang (native orchestra) were left
alone, even though they contained many non-Islamic elements
(Landon, 1947:136). Islam tried to make it more attractive
to be Moslem by making it more difficult not to be (Simon,
1912:14-15). Islam entered the society without great dis-
ruption or arousing extreme resistance.

The Islamic advocates did attack boldly the manufacture
of images and art objects of religious nature. Idol making
was brought to a sudden and definite stop. Indonesian sculptors
and architects were forbidden to continue work and consequently,

Islam produced no art or architecture comparable to the Buddhist Borobudur (Landon, 1947:136-137). Otherwise, Islam entered the Indonesian society with a minimum of displacement.

To understand Indonesian Islam one should study the practice of the basic tenets of the religion. Since the practice of Islam varies from place to place, to generalize about this matter is as difficult as it is likely to be inaccurate. The study will still throw light on Islam in Indonesia.

The first pillar of Islam, confession of faith and of orthodox belief and practice, is but incompletely fulfilled in Indonesia. The confession was converted to Indonesian use and in some areas considered a new incantation of great efficacy. Indonesians generally follow the regular worship, or salat (solot) but not always with equal intensity (Kraemer, 1952:177). Many Indonesians neglect the five prayers each day which is the second pillar of Islamic practice (Landon, 1947:144-145). Indonesian Moslems (especially in Central and East Java) are not careful of all the dietary laws which are kept perfectly by only the most devout (United States Army Handbook, 1964:231). However, almost all Moslems obey the injunction against eating pork.

The month of fasting, called Bulan Puasa, is generally honored because of the belief that through it one can atone for his failures and sins (Landon, 1947:138). There is however, a great deal of variation in the way and intensity the fast is practiced. Kraemer says, "The orthodoxy in which the Moslems carry out the fast varies according to their region" (1952:193). He points out that the Atjehnese, Minangkabau and Sundanese (and he should have added the Bandjar people of Borneo) are very strict in their fast observance. In Central Java and in many large cities there is a laxity to the extent that many Moslems fast only on the first and last days of the month (Kraemer, 1952:193). The most popular point of the fast in Indonesian life is the last festival day, Labaran, which marks the time of the reaffirmation of family ties and the asking of forgiveness. This day is observed by most Indonesians, even if they are not practicing Moslems (United States Army Handbook, 1964:232).

Indonesians call the fourth pillar of Islam zakat, which is a tax or gift, donated by each Moslem according to his ability (Kraemer, 1952:187). The most important part of the gift is the rice gift given to the poor through the officials of the Mosque. At the end of the fast a special gift, the pitrah, is given for the poor and orphans and is most generally honored (United States Army Handbook, 1964:233).

Every Moslem who can is required to make the pilgrimage to Mecca, the Hadji, which is the fifth pillar of Islam. To make the pilgrimage one must not only put up money for his travel but also for the care of his family while he is gone.

The prohibition against borrowing money for the pilgrimage
is sometimes disobeyed. While both men and women make the
pilgrimage, women who "niak hadji" must be accompanied by a
male who either is or cannot become their husband (Kraemer,
1952:197-198).

During this century Indonesian pilgrims have outnumbered those from any other country. Between 1900 and
1938 over 500,000 Indonesians made the pilgrimage and in 1962
8,280 went to Mecca. The returning Hadji assumes a place of
leadership in Indonesian Islam (United States Army Handbook,
1964:233).

Until recently mosques in Indonesia were usually not
built in the Arabic architectural form. Few mosques had min-
arets. The call to prayer was given by means of a drum or
bedug. However, newer mosques are now being built in the more
traditional style (United States Army Handbook, 1964:231).
In most mosques a niche in the western wall, called the mihrab,
points the way to Mecca. To the right of the mihrab another
niche provides a place for the one who delivers the Friday
sermon (Landon, 1947:14).

Since Moslem law requires at least forty people for a
mosque, many villages and some city areas use a langgar (little
mosque) which serves as a place for worship, for teaching and
a sleeping place for strangers caught away from home by darkness.
Often connected with the langgar are Moslem schools known as
pesantren or pondok where women and children are taught. These
schools form the backbone of the Moslem educational system
(C. Geertz, 1960:178-181).

Circumcision, while not one of the five pillars of
Islam, is practiced with more intensity than some of the more
central tenets. The popularity of circumcision is perhaps
partly due to the fact that the incision of the foreskin was
practiced by pre-Islamic Indonesian animism (Landon, 1957:153).
The ceremony of circumcision, called sunatan, is usually done
with full ceremony between the ages of ten and fourteen. It
marks the boy's entrance into adulthood (C. Geertz, 1960:51-
52).

The practice of Islam in Indonesia is aptly summed up
by the noted Dutch Islamist, C. Snouck Hurgronje:

> *To follow up the image of the five pillars (of Islam),*
> *we might say that the pointed roof of the building of*
> *Islam is still mainly supported by the central pillar,*
> *the confession that there is no god but Allah and that*
> *Muhammad is the messenger of Allah, but that this*
> *pillar is surrounded with a medley of ornamental work*
> *quite unsuited to it which is a profanation of its*
> *lofty simplicity. And in regard to the other four,*
> *the corner pillars, it might be observed that some*
> *of these have suffered decay in the long lapse of*

time, while other new pillars, which according to
the orthodox teaching are unworthy to be supports of
the holy building have been planted beside the
original five and have to a considerable extent
robbed them of their functions (Hurgronje, 1906:313).

There are a number of modern trends evident in
Indonesian Islam. The names of Sarekat Islam, Masjumi and
Partai Sarekat Islam Indonesia (PSII) are important to a
complete understanding of Indonesian Islam. However, the
three movements that demonstrate the most clear-cut variation
among Indonesian Moslems are Darul Islam, the Muhammadiyah
Party and the Natul Ulama Party.
      As indicated earlier, the Darul Islam movement arose
in 1930 but alienated most of the nationalist and Moslem
movements (Kroef, 1962:51). The expressed purpose of Darul
Islam was the establishment of an Islamic state and the resort
to terrorism and violence have marked its history (Nieuwenhuijze,
1958:162-165). Located primarily in West Java, the movement
has been in revolt against the central government. While it
has been dormant and had little influence in the last few
years, the anti-colonial and anti-capitalistic tendency of
Darul Islam is still mirrored in some Islamic thought (Sundstrom,
1957:149).
      The Muhammadiyah Party was founded in 1912 with the
expressed purpose of modernizing Islam (Berg, 1932:286-287).
Muhammadiyah has sought to create a more modern and personal
interpretation of Islam with a greater appeal to reason than
to authority. Schools, clinics, hospitals and other philan-
thropic endeavors have been incorporated in the policy of the
movement (Wertheim, 1956:180-181). In 1961 Muhammadiyah
reported over 250,000 members (Kroef, 1962:54) and has more
or less overshadowed most other Moslem factions (Benda, 1958:47).
      The conservative reaction to the progressive Muhammadiyah
Party is centered largely in the Nahdatul Ulama (Moslem Scholars)
Party (NU) which was founded in 1926 (Kroef, 1962:55). The
NU Party was originally strictly a religious movement but during
the Japanese occupation and revolutionary period, came to have
a more political orientation (Sundstrom, 1957:159-161). Since
its break with the Masjumi Party in 1952, the NU has assumed a
major role in the life of Indonesian Islam.
      This discussion of the variants in Indonesian Islam
should not give any idea of strife or complete separation. The
progressive or conservative tendencies in Islam no more obviate
their being Moslem than denominational distinctions reveal an
absence of Christianity among followers of Christ. The presence
of differing opinions among Indonesian Moslems is in some ways
a testimony to the vitality of the movement just as denomination-
alism among Christians, rather than the tragedy sometimes depicted, is actually a testimony to the strength of the religion

and gives room to the depth of expression called forth by
Christian experience. However, the presence of divisions within
Islam defuses the argument of those who call for church union
on the basis of an assumed but inaccurate belief that other
religions are without divisions or denominations.

The Confrontation of Islam and Christianity in Indonesia

The basic Indonesian outlook allows a striking tolerance,
but there exists today a basic tension between the Moslems and
the Christians. This tension has been dramatized in the intense
persecution in the Central Celebes and the fanatical opposition
to Christianity in Atjeh, Madura and West Java. The Darul
Islam movement was but the extreme expression of the Moslem
drive to make Indonesia an Islamic state.

The same climate following September 30,1965 that gave
Christians unprecedented opportunities for evangelism, brought
to Indonesian Moslems a revival of interest and militant
strategy (Moody Monthly, 1968:6). Leslie Newbigin writes that
there has been an increasing anxiety among Indonesian Moslems,
caused by the relatively large numbers of converts from Islam
to Christianity (IRM, 1968:13). Many publications, directly
opposing Christian doctrines, are appearing in Indonesia. One
Islamic scholar, Saleh A. Nalidi, uses the Qumran texts to dis-
credit Christian scriptures. He identifies the "Teacher of
Righteousness" with Jesus whom he says did not die on the
cross but continued to live and finally reached Kashmir
(Bakker, 1968:48-49).

The tension in several areas led to threats and open
violence against Christians and churches. In Makassar in
October 1967 anti-Christian riots led to the sacking of at
least twenty-five churches. Similar, though smaller incidents
were recorded in North Sumatra, in Djakarta and near Tjeribon
and other areas of Java (Brayn, 1967:312). In Borneo the
tension was directed more toward Chinese nationals than just
Christians. Some fifteen thousand Dyaks allowed long standing
prejudices and hatreds to boil over against the eleven thousand
Chinese in one area of West Borneo served by Conservative
Baptists (Humble, 1968:11). The situation was serious as many
Chinese were Christians, the riots in West Borneo caused much
suffering for Christians in the area. Threats were recorded
over most of Indonesia. Where there has been a movement toward Christianity, a Moslem reaction was almost certain to
follow.

The Moslems have accused the Christians of using outside financing to attempt to bring Indonesia into the Christian
orbit. Also, they emphasize the foreign aspect of Christianity.
Recently they have sought to manufacture a link between
Christianity and the nation Israel, which has no political ties
with Indonesia (Brayn, 1967:313). The greatest danger to

Christianity is that the Moslems might succeed in obtaining
some kind of comity policy. The most damaging law that could
be enacted would be something like what exists in Malaya,
that makes it criminal to witness to a Malayan Moslem. Should
the religious affiliation of Indonesians be frozen, it would
mark a definite blow to the expansion of Christianity and also
a refutation of the basic constitution of Indonesia which
grants to all freedom of religion. Islam and Christianity
today stand in basic confrontation in Indonesia.

Conclusion

        According to recent estimates some eighty-five percent
of Indonesians are to some degree committed to Islam. At
present population figures this would amount to around 97,700,
000 persons who are followers of the religion of the Prophet
from Arabia. What shall be the Church's attitude toward these
millions?
        Certainly, the Christian mission must be directed to
and concentrated on "those who are winnable now" (McGavran,
1959:9). The millions of animists who even now are emerging
from their old fears into the light of the modern world must
claim the attention of those who are seeking to "make disciples
of all peoples". Also, other millions, primarily but certainly
not exclusively in Central and East Java, called even by Moslem
leaders, Islam statisik (nominal Moslem) must be won to a
genuine faith in Jesus. These peoples are winnable now.
        But what of those fiercely Islamic people of Atjeh and
Madura? What about the peoples of the Minangkabau area and
inhabitants of Macassar? What about the "Orang Bandjar" of
Borneo and the Moslems of Ternate in Halmahera? These are
resistant peoples. What of them?
        Speaking of resistant peoples, Donald A. McGavran has
said, "We believe that the Gospel must be preached to all men,
resistant as well as responsive..." (McGavran, 1963:20). No
people should be left without a witness. Missions will not
withdraw from resistant peoples but will seek ways to turn
resistance tc glad hearing.
        The truth that God desires witness even among the
resistant peoples has dangerous possibilities. It can lead
mission societies to invest all, most or much of their resources
among peoples who are set like cement against the Message. In
the quotation from McGavran, given above, the latter part of
the sentence was purposely saved until now for added stress.
McGavran continues, "...and that the number of the redeamed is
important." He goes on to state that those who search sincerely but return empty handed will merit their "well done".
This truth should not, however, be twisted into an assertion
that God cares nothing about how many are won. "We dare not,"
says McGavran, "...affirm that coming empty handed out of ripe

harvest fields pleases God" (McGavran, 1963:20).

In the approach to "resistant" peoples the Church must first ascertain if the people are really unresponsive or if the methods by which the Gospel has been presented have tended to make them resistant. If the people have actually turned stony hearts from the Gospel, they should still be served. But Churches and missions are unwise--even unfaithful--to employ a large or even sizable percentage of their resources among resistant peoples when ripe fields lie beckoning for harvest.

In serving resistant fields the Church or mission must keep in mind that it should be constantly seeking an entrance into the society. There will likely, almost certainly, be some segment of the population where the Gospel seed can grow. Ministry in resistant fields will involve constant probing to find entrance. In addition the Church must draw neither its strategy nor its basic attitude from the resistant fields, but should look to those regions where men are being won to produce its plans, methods and attitudes.

To missions in Indonesia this principle has an urgent message. The bulk of the resources will be employed discipling those peoples who are being won now. The mission will spend what is necessary to establish a continuing search for pockets of winnable peoples. A token force will be maintained among those whose ears are closed to the Message--so the Gospel will be preached to every creature, but more than that, so that when these stubborn hearts begin to soften, the Church will be there, ready to reap the harvest. Approach to the Moslem and Hindu mosaic of Indonesia should travel such a plan.

SYNCRETISM

The Indonesian religious mind has created a synthesis of the varied and conflicting religious traditions that have found their ways to the islands. The Indonesians have listened to and accepted from each of the invading systems of belief, but they have clung tenaciously to their ancient beliefs and practices as well (Kennedy, 1937:297). Each new religion has been Indonesianized. The current Indonesian religion is a combination in different proportions of Hindu-Buddhist teachings, Islamic doctrines and Christian dogma--all built on the animistic base and presently colored by an expanding nationalistic tendency. Syncretism might be called the story of Indonesian religions. Only as Christianity becomes effectively Bible-based at the hand of the local congregation is it likely to escape the calamity of syncretism.

CONCLUSION

This study of the peoples, social structures and

religions of Indonesia reveals how imperative such understanding
is for church planters. To fail to come to grips with cultural
realities in the society most often consigns the missionary
to a non-relevant ministry. As Nida has pointed out, missions
have all too often created a kind of Christian subculture by
the approach taken to non-Christian societies. In addition
missionaries have failed to communicate because of faulty
understanding of the social structure of the peoples served
(Nida, 1960:95).

Indonesian social structures and religions lead this
student to the following conclusions: first, Christian missions
must be thankful that ethnic, historical and religious factors
have given to many Indonesians a tolerance and willingness to
hear the Gospel. These responsive masses must be served.

Second, Christianity must be on guard lest essential
Christian elements be adulterated until they are no longer
Christianity. This principle is not to champion any form of
paternalism. It should not lead to forcing a "Westernized"
type of Christianity, church structure or procedure on the
churches in other lands. The history of religion in Indonesia
demonstrates the assimilative tendency of Indonesian society.
Christianity could, like Hinduism, be merely assimilated into
the Javanese pantheon. The goal of the Church should be to
possess the Indonesian cultural factors for the Gospel. Bavinck
says, "The Christian life does not accomodate or adapt itself
to heathen forms of life, but it takes the latter in possession
and thereby makes them new" (1960:178-179).

Third, Christianity must be presented in the language
and culture of the people. The Church must live and grow in
the Indonesian soil--in a word must become thoroughly Indonesian.
"The task of the church, therefore, is to make Africans into
African Christians, Indians into Indian Christians, Japanese
into Japanese Christians--not into American or European
Christians" (Luzbetak, 1970:344).

The pervasive temptation of the missionary is to
establish a Church patterned on his own customary denominational
structure. This use and insistence on American methods without
any real attempt to adapt to national psychology and methods
is one of the foremost reasons for failure to establish churches
that can live, grow, reproduce and share the life in their own
communities (Hodges, 1953:9). The tendency to reproduce cultural
factors in missionary churches is called by McGavran "cultural
overhang" and has, he says, "...a profound effect on church
growth" (1959:85). The Church in Indonesia must become
Indonesian in heart, soul, attitude and practice.

Fourth, Christianity must find Christian substitutes
for Indonesian religious practices that have such animistic
meaning as to demand replacement. These practices must be
achieved through accomodation which is defined as "...the re-
spectful, prudent, scientifically and theologically sound

adjustment of the church to the native culture in attitude, outward behavior and practical apostolic approach" (Luzbetak, 1970:341).

The missionaries must find those cultural parallels which will make the message meaningful in the culture (Nida, 1960:50). The mistake of early missionaries in Java of turning from indigenous practices because they were foreign to the missionaries' understanding and experience must be avoided. The eternal message of God must be transmitted in the voice and thought understood by those to be discipled.

The personal Saviour who has knowledge of and interest in each of his children will win wide acceptance when presented in the Indonesian's cultural pattern. The teaching of Jesus as the Power who can overcome the spirits and therefore bring peace, will meet universal response in Indonesia. But these truths must be presented in an Indonesian sarong and kain kebaja (traditional men's and women's dress).

The message and methods must be thoroughly Indonesian. Christianity must learn to use the cultural stepping stones over which the Gospel can bridge the chasm and enter fully into the main stream of Indonesian life. To so do, the Christian mission must take full note of the ethnic, cultural and religious mosaic of Indonesia.

3

Some of the Major
Churches of Indonesia

No Church can, nor indeed, should attempt to serve in
isolation from other Christian groups. Therefore, other Churches
in Indonesia and their growth (or lack of it) are important to
Baptists as they participate in discipling Indonesia's millions.
The purpose of this chapter is to give some understanding of
some of the Churches of Indonesia.

The historical setting of many of Indonesia's Churches
has been noted in Chapter I. This chapter will not attempt
to study all Indonesian Churches but only some of the most
representative ones. Discussion will center on the Churches
that show instructive glimpses into church growth. More detailed studies of the Churches of Indonesia are found in
Sedjarah Geredja di Indonesia (Church History in Indonesia)
by Muller-Krüger and in the less detailed but very helpful work
by Frank Cooley, Indonesia: Church and Society.

THE CHURCHES IN EASTERN INDONESIA

Eastern Indonesia represents those islands east of
Java, but not including New Guinea. The Churches to be dis-
cussed are: the Moluccan Protestant Church, the Churches in
Minahasa, Central Celebes, Timor and on the island of Bali.
The history of these Churches reveals significant accounts of
church growth.

The Moluccan Protestant Church (Geredja Protestan Maluku)

The Moluccan Protestant Church, founded around 1537,
is the oldest evangelical Church in Asia. At least seven congregations were functioning in 1546 when the Jesuit, St. Francis
Xavier, arrived in Ambon (Cooley, 1966:343). Of the 900,000
people in the Moluccas slightly less than one half are Christian,
a like number Moslem and the rest animists or some other religion (Cooley, 1968:52).

The Moluccan Church, while it is centered on Ambon,

serves many of the smaller and lesser known islands as well.
Ternate, Tidore and Batjan to the north as well as Ceram, Bubu
and Banda are served also (Muller-Kruger, 1959:79). The
Church is actually not an ethnic Church but serves a variety
of peoples. There are two major divisions of the Church. The
older, tracing its origin back three or four centuries, numbers
around one hundred and fifty congregations and holds to strong
traditions and deep-rooted feelings about Christian belief and
practice. The younger congregations have a history of only
around one hundred fifty years. Many started in this century.
Some have no pastor and remain isolated and weak (Cooley, 1962:
26).

Remarkable growth is seen in the first period of the
Moluccan Church's life. See the graph on page 72. Between
1537 and 1590 the Catholic Church in the Moluccas reached a
membership of 47,000, showing a definite response to the
Gospel in the region. Portuguese priests came to minister
to the people and often sided with the people against the
colonial authorities (Muller-Kruger, 1959:22,23). St. Francis
Xavier had unusual influence in these islands which he named
"the islands of divine hope". While Hall indicates that
Xavier was discouraged with the progress in Ambon (Hall, 1964:
222-223), there are other indications that he was highly ex-
cited about the possibilities. In 1546 he wrote, "And yet,
if only a dozen priest's helpers would come here from Europe
each year, it would not be long before the Moslem movement
ended and all in these islands would become Christian (McGratty,
1952:179).

There was a sharp decline in membership after 1560. In
this period the Moslem Sultan Baab led a revolt against the
Portuguese which purposed not only to expell the foreigners
but to Islamize the entire area. Thousands of Christians were
killed and the circle of Portuguese influence greatly reduced.
Xavier had left for China in 1552. It is not surprising that
the number of Christians declined to 16,000 by 1605
(Muller-Kruger, 1959:24-25).

The policies of the Dutch East India Company (VOC)
were not conducive to growth from 1605 to 1800. The Portuguese
priests were first granted permission to remain and then expelled. The VOC insisted just as strongly on a religious
monopoly as on a commercial one. Dutch pastors were both paid
and controlled by the Company. While some 254 pastors and
800 "visitors of the sick" were sent out, they were commissioned mainly to serve the Dutch nationals living in the islands.
The main motive for evangelizing the Indonesian population was
commercial--to keep them from becoming Moslem (Muller-Kruger,
1959:28,29).

The Church thus became a state church, patterned after
the Dutch style and using primarily the Dutch language. The
doctrines, hymns, practices and language all followed Dutch

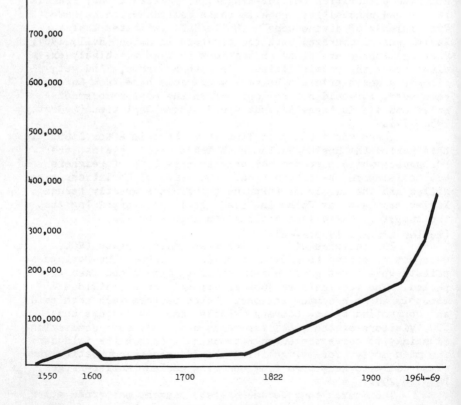

FIGURE 10

Graph of Growth,

MOLUCCAN PROTESTANT CHRISTIAN CHURCH

customs. Even the same hours of worship, the same kind of
clothing for deacons and elders and other features of the
Dutch Church were used. Indonesians had almost no voice in
the Church. There was no training program for indigenous leadership except during the period 1745-1755 and this program
resulted in only one national pastor. Little spiritual nurture
was given to Indonesians and Christianity was known as <u>Agama
Belanda</u> (Dutch religion). Some Indonesians were baptized but
because they had not been properly instructed were neither
allowed in the Communion service nor considered full members
(Cooley, 1966:351-354). In 1762, of 27,000 members, only 963
were considered full members. Muller-Kruger asks, "What kind
of spiritual life could be hoped for in a Church where only
about three percent of the people were allowed to partake of
the Lord's Supper" (1959:40).

The result was that the Church in Molucca developed a
Christianity greatly mixed with pre-Christian superstitions
and traditions. Since the Church was simply the Dutch Church
and the religion the Dutch religion, it failed to meet the
inner needs of the people. No functional substitutes were
sought for traditional practices. The Dutch by force denied
the Moluccans to practice their old traditions and superstitions.
However, the practices were continued in secret, even by devoted Christians. The Ambonese developed a mystical view of
the Eucharist which resulted in awe and salvation at the same
time. The religious needs of the Indonesians were not met.
Kraemer rightly notes, "Missions and Christianization mean
above all: digging channels for the expression of normal religious needs." He further states that the neglect of the
former religious life and the cruel repression of the former
practices actually resulted in the continuation of the animistic patterns (1958:21).

The coming of the British Baptist, Jabez Carey in 1813
brought a dedicated and productive ministry directed to the
Ambonese people. Carey was placed in charge of almost all
the educational facilities in the islands (Payne, 1945:19-21).
In contrast to the former Dutch workers Carey made extensive
and excellent use of the Malay language and formed close
associations with the Ambonese. He worked to alleviate many
of the serious social problems (Smith, n. d.:126-127). Of
Carey's ministry Muller-Kruger writes, "So close was Carey's
relationship with the Ambonese that it was with heavy hearts
and tearful eyes they parted with him when he was forced to
leave Ambon in 1817" (1959:75).

The growth of the Moluccan Church began in 1800 as the
fine work of Jabez Carey was succeeded by the Netherlands
Missionary Society and one of the finest missionaries of all
times, Joseph Kam, widely known as the <u>Rasul Maluku</u> (Apostle
of the Moluccas). Despite the work of Carey, the Church was
in decline when Kam arrived in 1816. He set about his work

with dedication and enthusiasm. Thousands were baptized. Kam
visited islands that never in the memory of any islander had
been visited by a missionary. Worship was improved, the understanding of the Christians deepened and churches planted. Kam
trained Indonesian leaders and secured help from the Netherlands
Missionary Society. Perhaps his most significant contribution
was the formation of a missionary society in Ambon. This
society recruited and supported Ambonese missionaries to take
the Gospel to congregations in isolated places. Concerning
this society, Cooley says, "This organization and, more significant still, this concern for missionary outreach, has continued in various forms until the present" (Cooley, 1966:358-
359).

    Regrettably, membership figures are not available for
all the history of the Moluccan Church. In 1762 the Church
numbered only 29,531 members (Muller-Kruger, 1959:26 and 40).
By 1933 the membership had reached 187,000 (de Bruine, 1935:
111). From 1933 there is a long gap in the records until 1953
when the membership stood at 276,000 (Cooley, 1968:6,7).
Muller-Kruger notes that in 1958 the membership was 277,000
which, if both figures are accurate, indicates a period of
very slow growth (1959:lampiran). Cooley notes a membership
of 280,000 which was most likely the report for 1960 or 1961
(1962:26). The next period reveals rapid and healthy growth
as the membership increased to 380,000 and the number of
congregations to 673 by 1967 (Cooley, 1968:53).

    From 1864 to 1935 the Moluccan Church was associated
with the Protestant Church in Djakarta and since 1935 has been
autonomous (Muller-Kruger, 1959:74). The Church experienced
severe trials during the Japanese occupation. Church buildings
were bombed, congregations scattered and in one period over
ninety pastors were killed. The 1950s brought great difficulty
as all support was withdrawn from the Church. Before, the
government had subsidized the Church but with the formation
of the Indonesian Government all subsidy stopped. Since the
Moluccan Church had not been trained in stewardship and most
giving was only symbolic, the Church experienced difficult
days (Cooley, 1966:366-369).

    The closeness of the Ambonese to the Dutch led to the
next problem. The Ambonese had long been favored by the Dutch,
receiving better education than other Indonesians and making
up a large segment of the Dutch civil service and army (Kraemer,
1958:13,14). Fearing their favored status might be threatened
by the Indonesian Republic, the Independent State of South
Moluccas (Republik Maluku Selatan) was established in 1950. The
bitter conflict that ensued as the central government put down
the revolt caused much suffering for the people and consequently
difficulty for the Church. This conflict could help explain
the slow growth between 1953 and 1958.

    In the 1960s the Moluccan Church began a serious attempt

at reform. A Department of Evangelism was set up. Local
congregations were revitalized and missions undertaken to
both animists and to Moslems (Cooley, 1962:28,29). The mission
to the Moslems was a new service for the Moluccan Church.
Hendrik Kraemer had taught that the Moluccan Christians needed
to feel some constraint to witness to their Moslem neighbors
(Kraemer, 1958:21-22).

The Moluccan Church almost insisted on being Christian.
Many methods and situations developed that could have stifled
the moving of the Spirit. Through it all, the Church has progressed. Should the reform of the 1960s continue, the Moluccan
Church could well be one of the outstanding Churches of the
world. Cooley says, "This little-known, oldest evangelical
church in Asia...is among the more active, creative,
self-reforming churches in Asia today" (1968:53).

The Church in Minahasa

Around 600,000 of the 700,000 people in Minahasa are
Christian. The Evangelical Christian Church (Geredja Masehi
Indjili Minahasa, GMIM) numbers some 500,000 members. The
graph on page 76 shows the growth pattern of the GMIM Church.
Other Churches such as the Roman Catholics and "sects" (as
viewed by the GMIM Church) claim another 100,000 members
(Cooley, 1968:56). A study of these Churches is inspiring
and instructive.

Christianity reached Minahasa around 1563 when the
Protuguese priest Magelhaes baptized a "king" and 1500
of his followers. Magelhaes reported that he refused to
baptize many other Minahasans. In 1588 a small group of
Christians still existed but the movement had almost vanished.
The first Dutch pastor arrived in 1675 and found a small
congregation (Muller-Kruger, 1959:92). Herein lies a church
growth tragedy. The people of Minahasa have from the first
been responsive. Without doubt many Minahasans died without Christ who would have been saved had resources been made
available to evangelize the area before 1800.

Dutch ministry in Minahasa was little if any better
than had been the Catholic effort. Part of the time Minahasa
was cared for by a pastor from Tidore. In 1707 a Dutch
missionary registered 5,000 Christians in Minahasa. From
1789-1817 shepherding in Minahasa was almost nil and this
among a people who had demonstrated their willingness and
desire to become Christian (Muller-Kruger, 1959:92,93).

The period 1822-1875 is known as the years of the
"Christianization of Minahasa" (Muller-Kruger, 1959:94). At
the urging of Joseph Kam, the Netherlands Missionary Society
(NZG) began serving the Church in Minahasa which numbered only
3,000 (Cooley, 1968:55). The decline could most likely be
attributed to the failure of shepherding. After 1822 the

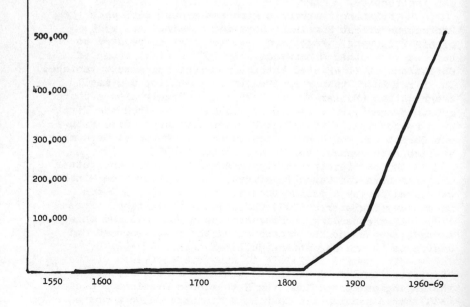

FIGURE 11

Graph of Growth,

MINAHASA EVANGELICAL CHRISTIAN CHURCH

evangelization of Minahasa proceeded remarkably. Cooley says,
"By 1870 as a result of well-conceived evangelistic efforts
by the Netherlands Missionary Society, the basic task of
Christianizing Minahasa was completed." By 1876 the membership
of the Minahasa Church had reached around 80,000 (Cooley, 1968:
55).

Muller-Kruger explains the rapid growth between 1822
and 1876 by being partly due to the work of two unusual missionaries, Riedel and Schwarz, who landed in Minahasa in 1831.
He further explains that the missionaries "...perhaps for the
first time in Indonesia gave major attention to the area
language." He applauds their efforts to learn the local tongue
rather than using the national or trade language (1959:95).

Other factors also rendered the Minahasans receptive
to the Gospel. Whatever these reasons were the Spirit of God
moved across Minahasa and the Church grew from 3,000 in 1833
to over 80,000 less than fifty years later. The student of
church growth, seeing growth like this in many countries,
believes that this sweeping tribe-wide growth within one
language unit is what normally should occur. This is the way
peoples become Christian. The slow, hesitant, one-by-one growth
exhibited by so many missions is actually contrary to what
is normal and healthy. Multi-individual movements to Christ
can happen, should happen, are happening and will happen again
(see McGavran, 1955:43-99).

A tragic event took place in 1876. The Netherlands
Missionary Society, partly due to financial reasons, decided
that since the "Christianization of Minahasa was complete",
they should move their activities to other areas. Other Dutch
societies were unable to assume the work and the Dutch government refused to allow missionaries from other countries, such
as the British Baptists, to enter. The Church in Minahasa
passed into the hands of the Dutch Protestant Church
(Muller-Kruger, 1959:98).

The change brought a great difference to the Minahasa
Church. The development of the Church indicated that rather
than leaving the "already Christianized" field, the NZG should
have reinforced the Minahasan Church. The Church was restricted and subjected to a religious neutralism, especially in the
schools (Muller-Kruger, 1959:99-100). In addition to the
religious neutralism of the civil servants and Dutch workers
there was a decided modernism and liberalism among the pastors
who did come from Holland. This narrow modernism had dis-
asterous effect on the young Minahasan Church (Kraemer, 1958:
38,39).

The Minahasan Church shows that when there is a great
sprritual movement almost nothing will stop it. It shows
also, however, that people movements must be adequately
shepherded--lest they develop along lines not conducive to the
greatest spiritual attainment. Cooley notes that secularism

has grown steadily in the region and admits that the formal and
traditional character of the Church has given room for this
development (1968:56). Kraemer goes further to state that there
is religious indifference and moral laxity among some leaders.
Still, Kraemer sees far more vitality in the Minahasan Church
than such statements might indicate and calls for more education
and leadership until the Minahasan Church truly appropriates
the Gospel to itself (1958:36-40).

The 500,000 members of the Evangelical Church (GMIM)
are gathered in 502 congregations served by 110 ordained
ministers and 500 assistant ministers. There are around 5,000
members per ordained minister. The secularism and traditional-
ism of the Church are pointed to by Muller-Kruger as reasons
for the Church being vunerable to erosion by other Churches,
of which there are many. Muller-Kruger counts twelve different
Christian denominations presently working in Minahasa (1959:
104).

The presence of competing Christian groups in Minahasa
points up the fact that anytime any Church allows its spiritual
life to cool other denominations will spring up to fan the
nominal Christians to a more vital faith. When this happens,
the established Church should welcome the incoming groups and
in no wise accuse them of breaking the body of Christ. The end
result will be a new spiritual life for all, including the
established Church.

Minahasa is a delightful area. Among its thousands
are many spiritual giants. Christians from Minahasa have fanned
out over most of Indonesia and in many places have assumed
spiritual leadership. With further training and spiritual renewal God will be greatly honored in Minahasa. The history of
this Church demonstrates the tremendous need for shepherding,
especially in people movements.

The Churches in the Central Celebes

The central region of the island of Celebes (Sulawesi)
is inhabited by the Toradja peoples who are roughly divided
into northern and southern Toradjas (Kennedy, 1943:19).
Christianity has made unusual progress among these peoples who
are now served by three different Churches with a combined
membership of over 350,000 members. The Makale-Rantepao
Christian Church (Geredja Kristen Toradja Makale-Rantepao)
and the Mamasa Toradja Christian Church (Geredja Kristen Toradja
Mamasa) have shown great fortitude under persecution (Cooley,
1968:80-83). While the history of all these Churches is instructive and inspiring, the press of space forces us to discuss the growth pattern of only the Central Celebes Christian
Church (Geredja Kristen Sulawesi Tengah).

The Central Celebes Church is located in the northern
region of the Toradja area and serves more different tribes than

the other Toradja Churches. It was born almost by accident.
The NZG had planned to open work in the Gorontalo region but
their first missionary, Dr. Albert C. Kruyt, decided that the
almost completely Islamized area did not offer sufficient
opportunities for evangelism. He turned from the closed field
to the more promising area of north central Celebes where he
arrived in the town of Poso in 1893 (Muller-Kruger, 1959:112).
In turning from the unresponsive region (and Gorontalo to this
day has proved unresponsive) to the more promising, Kruyt
complied with good, sound missionary strategy and his example
is worthy of serious consideration of all who seek to communicate
the Gosepl.

Kruyt and his fellow missionary, Dr. N. Adriani, shared
many basic missionary convictions that influenced their methods.
Kruyt's convictions may have been partially the result of his
having been born and reared in a missionary home on Java.
Central to the missionary strategy of Kruyt and Adriani was
the conviction that the Gospel can only take root in any people
if presented in their language and in forms compatible to their
culture. This conviction drove the two missionaries to begin
their ministry by studying in depth the language, customs and
culture of the Toradja peoples (Muller-Kruger, 1959:112-113).
So thorough was their study that their voluminous writings on
the ethnology of the region earned high praise from professional anthropologists (Cooley, 1968:81).

Their thorough knowledge of and appreciation for the
culture of the people allowed the missionaries to approach the
Toradjas without many of the mistakes often committed by
missionaries. Kruyt stated that to overlook superstitions
and attempt to exterminate unChristian acts by force would
drive people to continue the traditions and sometimes reject
Christianity. He said that new converts have to go through
a period of training in Christianity before they can fully
accept the glory of the Gospel (Kruyt, 1924:267-274).

The missionaries were convinced that the Gospel had
to be purged of foreign elements. Adriani wrote that if the
Gospel had been presented in the Malay language, the Toradja
people would have considered it "Dutch religion". Using the
regional language avoided this problem and helped rid the
Message of foreign overhand so the Church could be a Toradja
Church (Muller-Kruger, 1959:113).

Adriani contended that those who came into the Church
should have a genuine conversion experience. He rejected the
use of Ambonese teachers out of fear that such a policy would
draw many into the Church who simply desired to raise their
status. There would be the danger of producing a Christianity
in name only, while the old religion would continue unchanged
(Muller-Kruger, 1959:113).

Perhaps the most important conviction of these two
pioneers in missionary strategy was their insight that people

should come to salvation in clans, villages, families or other
groups, rather than as individuals. Kruyt and Adriani realized
that the Toradja society was collective rather than individualistic. Any Toradja who individually accepted the Gospel would
be automatically ostracized from his family and tribe. The
missionaries saw the necessity of people coming to Christianity
by families since only in this way could Christianity penetrate
to the roots of the culture (Muller-Kruger, 1959:113). This
same conviction concerning the multi-individual decisions forms
one of the principles of the modern church growth theory (see
Pickett, 1933:21-35; Tippett, 1967a:1-21; McGavran, 1970:296-
315).

So deep was the conviction of Kruyt and Adriani concerning the necessity of multi-individual decisions that they
refused to baptize individuals who requested it. Rather than
pull people out of their culture they waited seventeen years
for group conversions to develop. In 1909 a village head and
his people near the town of Poso decided for Christ. One
hundred eighty persons were baptized to begin one of history's
most inspiring examples of church growth (Muller-Kruger, 1959:
113).

The movement began to spread to other villages. By
1931 the first 180 had grown to 35,722 members (de Bruine, 1935:
112). Since 28,000 were baptized in the Luwuk area, the total
membership was 64,000 members. The Church was pressed to provide leadership during these periods of rapid growth. By
1953 the membership had increased to 80,000 (Cooley, 1968:6,7).
The problems of World War II and the removal of the missionaries
partially explain the slow down in growth. The membership of
the Church is reported as 85,000 in 1962 (World Christian
Handbook, 1962:156). Between 1962 and 1967 the Church registered a net gain in membership of 51,000 members, reaching a
total membership of 126,000, organized into 339 congregations
and served by fifty-six ordained ministers (Cooley, 1968:81).

The history of the Central Celebes Church could almost
be used as a text book on mission methods. While the wisdom
of delaying baptism for seventeen years might be questioned,
the results that followed demonstrate that in this particular
case it was the proper approach. The growth of the Church
is an inspiring account of the working of God's Spirit.

The Timor Evangelical Christian Church (Geredja Masehi
Indjili Timor)

The Timor Evangelical Church has received some of the
greatest blessing of the Spirit's work in recent times. It is
one of God's greatest miracles in Indonesia. The Portuguese
introduced the Catholic faith into Timor before the end of the
sixteenth century. The Dutch attempted to build on the
Catholic foundation but the lack of pastoral leadership made

real development difficult, if not impossible (Cooley, 1968:
54). There is a dearth of information about the Church's early
history. However, it is known that one important group in the
church in Kupang was known as the Mardijkers. This word is a
Dutch derivation of the Malay word merdeka, freedom. The
Mardijkers were composed of military personnel from other islands, freed slaves and Timorese who were serving in the Dutch
army. Since these people enjoyed a higher social status than
others, being a Christian came to be synomous with being of
higher status. The idea developed that Christianity was only
for chiefs (Middlekoop, 1960:36,37). This mistaken idea may
have had something to do with the meager growth before 1930.
See the graph of growth on page 82. In 1758, almost two centuries after the Catholics had first come to the island, the
Church numbered only 13,000 members (Muller-Kruger, 1959:119).

Around 1930 many began to enter the Church. Awakenings
in the interior regions of both Timor and Alor eventuated in
people movements. The Church was not able to keep up with the
care and instruction of those becoming Christian. The result
was some unfortunate syncretism and nominal Christianity according to Cooley (1968:54). The highly developed animistic religion of Timor naturally contributed to this condition
(Middlekoop, 1960:23-35).

By 1933 the Church boasted 154,500 members (de Bruine,
1935:112). These figures reveal a truly phenomenal rate of
growth. This growth continued as in 1953 the Church reported
a membership of 253,500 and in 1958 had reached 300,000
(Muller-Kruger, 1959:lampiran).

Around 1964 one of the truly miraculous movements of
the Spirit in modern times broke out in Timor. Much has been
written about this movement but much is still unclear. Among
factors that are both clear and substantiated are the following:
the movement began around 1964, before the Communist failure
(Bryan, 1968:48); it has been largely accomplished by lay
evangelistic teams (Bradshaw, 1967:83); it has been accompanied
by signs and miracles (Bryan, 1968:48); it has spread from the
coastal regions to the largely unevangelized interior tribes
(van Capelleveen, 1968:29); it has added over 200,000 members
to the Church in three years time (Bradshaw, 1967:83). The
awakening Timor is one of the Spirit's greatest works.

The authenticity of this awakening has been substantiated. Detmar Scheunemann, a missionary to Indonesia who recently visited Timor, reports continuing fruit from the movement. Christians are beginning to tithe, animistic practices
are vanishing and spiritual progress continuing in many areas.
One community, long a center of drunkenness and black magic,
has become law abiding since conversion. Emphasis in the
movement is changing from miraculous elements to the education
of the converts. While some problems did develop during the
movement, they were minor and have been overcome (Scheunemann,

FIGURE 12

Graph of Growth,

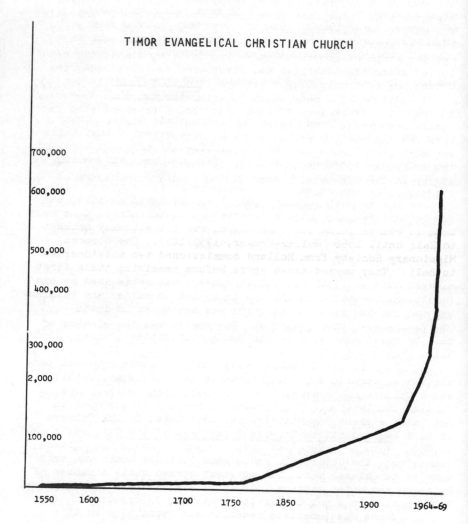

TIMOR EVANGELICAL CHRISTIAN CHURCH

700,000

600,000

500,000

400,000

300,000

2,000

100,000

1550   1600   1700   1750   1850   1900   1964-69

1969:3-8).

Obviously a genuine movement of the Spirit has been experienced on this little of island of Timor. Some have wisely determined not to write more about the movement for fear that wide publicity will in some way hinder the further working of God. Four factors stand out concerning the Timor awakening. It has been largely a lay movement. Secondly, it has moved from an awakening in the coastal churches to evangelization among the interior tribes. Thirdly, it has added greatly to the Church and is continuing to produce development in Christian graces. Fourthly, it has been a genuine movement of the Spirit. Future study will add to our present knowledge of this wonderful movement.

The Bali Protestant Christian Church (Geredja Kristen Protestan Bali)

Christianity has made little progress in the strongly Hinduized culture of Bali. There is some evidence that since the Communist failure of 1965 the Hindu-Bali religion has been strengthened (Bradshaw, 1969:19). Bali has been and remains basically resistant.

Christianity was late coming to Bali. Although permission for evangelistic work was given as early as 1630, the VOC authorities were more interested in buying slaves from Bali than in evangelizing it. The Gospel was not actually brought to Bali until 1866.(Muller-Kruger, 1959:124). The Utrecht Missionary Society from Holland commissioned two missionaries to Bali. They worked seven years before receiving their first convert (Cooley, 1968:64). This convert was ostracized by his family and society. In 1881 he conspired to murder the missionary and for his part in the crime was sentenced to death (Muller-Kruger, 1959 124-125). The result was the closing of Bali to missionary work by the Dutch authorities (Cooley, 1968: 64).

In 1929 the Christian Missionary Alliance obtained permission to serve among the Chinese on Bali (Kraemer, 1958:159) and a Chinese colporteur, Tian Kam Foek, began serving the Chinese (Muller-Kruger, 1959:125). From a rented chapel in Den Pasar a preaching ministry was undertaken to the Chinese of Bali (Report of the Foreign Department of the CMA, 1930: 44,45). Although there was little response among the Chinese themselves, the Gospel did reach some Balinese women who were married to Chinese men. The movement spread until a number of Balinese requested baptism. In 1932, 113 Balinese were baptized by immersion in a public service (Kraemer, 1958:160).

There was immediate reaction and opposition to this baptism. Artists, anthropologists and tourism promoters objected to the possibilities of any interference with Balinese religion. Balinese rulers were opposed. To placate these

groups the Dutch authorities withdrew permission for mission
work on Bali (Cooley, 1968:64). This halt in the spread of
the Gospel on Bali came in 1933 (Muller-Kruger, 1959:125).
        Dr. Hendrik Kraemer suggested that the East Java Church
supply evengelists to aid the Church on Bali. Due to the
Church's participation in the revolutionary struggle and the
attitudes of the evangelists, the Church achieved a new reputation among the Balinese. The Church began to grow, although
slowly. By 1958 the Church's membership had reached 2,800
(Muller-Kruger, 1959:lampiran) and had increased to 6,900 in
seventeen congregations by 1967 (Cooley, 1968:65).
        Cooley notes that the Church on Bali is now turning its
attention to the "larger mission on the island." Schools,
hostels and relief work as well as several development projects
are being supported by the Church (Cooley, 1968:64). It is
hoped that the Church will not become so engrossed in these
fine and important tasks that it overlooks or neglects the
primary task of evangelism. Church growth theory, while not
questioning the necessity and propriety of rendering helpful
service to men, contends that the first task of the Church is
discipling the peoples of the earth. The tension between evangelism and service must never be resolved by neglecting the
task of bringing men to Christ. Service must grow out of
evangelism, not be substituted for it (McGavran, 1970:31-48).

THE CHURCHES ON SUMATRA

        Sumatra has been the scene of some of God's greatest
victories. The Toba Batak Church developed from animistic
peoples to a thriving Church. The island of Nias witnessed
one of history's greatest revivals. Modern times have seen
the miracles among the Karo and Simalungan Bataks. The study
of church growth in Sumatra is a rewarding and instructive
venture.

The Batak Protestant Christian Church (Huria Kristen Batak Protestan)

        The Bataks of northern Sumatra are divided into five
groups. The Mandailing and Angkola in the southern Batak
region are solidly Islamic. The Simalungan Bataks are rapidly
becoming Christian while the Karo Bataks, the most northern
group, reflect a mixture of Islam, Christian and animistic beliefs. They have experienced a movement toward Christianity
in recent years. The great jewel of Christianity in Sumatra is
the Toba Batak Church which numbered some 819,000 members in
1967. Kraemer rightly observed, "It (the Batak Church) belongs
to the finest results of missionary activity in modern times"

(1958:43). The graph of growth of the Batak Church on page 86 shows how God has wrought a miracle among this people.

The first missionaries to the Bataks, the British Baptists, Nathaniel Ward and Richard Burton, penetrated into Batakland in 1824. These missionaries were warmly received. They brought back important information regarding Batak manners and customs, reporting that Batak religion was akin to Hinduism and their language related to Malay (Payne, 1945:47). The missionaries were venerated almost as gods and Burton was requested to take up abode with the Bataks (Nance, 1969:18). The good beginning came to nought as the British Baptists were forced to leave (Payne, 1945:47). Before leaving in 1825 Burton completed a translation of the Gospel of John in the Batak language (Nance, 1969:19). Ward stayed on in Sumatra until his death.

In 1834 the second missionary venture to the Bataks, this time by the Americans, Lyman and Munson, ended in tragedy. With Batak speaking guides the two entered Batak country in June 1834 and met their deaths at the hands of frightened Bataks. According to some accounts the two suffered the fate often faced among cannibalistic peoples. When informed of the tragedy, Lyman's mother is reported to have said, "My son is dead. He was my only son, but my sole regret is that I have no other to send to the Bataks in his place" (DeWaard, n. d.:16-18).

The same year, 1834, Ludwig Nommensen was born in the Netherlands. From a poor family, he was seriously injured at twelve and it was feared he would never walk again. He placed his trust in the verse that says, "Whatsoever ye shall ask in my name, that will I do." Through the help of a new doctor he regained his strength and at the age of twenty-seven went to Sumatra as a missionary to the Bataks (DeWaard, n. d.:20-23).

Nommensen led the Rhenish Missionary Society to the animistic peoples of the Toba region. Warneck writes, "After a time some responsive souls, then families, and later whole groups, became genuine Christians. The little communities had much to suffer in their early days from the hostility of the heathen" (Warneck,1912:21). Edward Nyhus adds that some of the early converts were slaves who were ransomed by the missionaries and that villages were founded to protect the first Christians who were ostracized because they had broken the communal unity and refused to take part in the public sacrifices (Nyhus, 1968:39).

From the meager beginnings in 1861 the Batak Church grew to 1,250 in 1871. The next decade saw the Church grow to 4,958. That was a critical year for the Batak Church (Nyhus, 1968:38). A mass movement began in 1883 (Cooley, 1968:67). The report for 1891 registered 21,779 members, representing a tremendous increase in ten years (Nyhus, 1968:38). The Church counted 47,784 in 1901 and 103,528 by 1911 (Nyhus, 1968:38). It was more than doubling every decade.

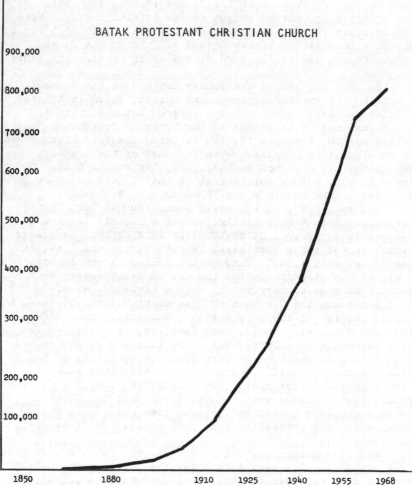

FIGURE 13

Graph of Growth,

BATAK PROTESTANT CHRISTIAN CHURCH

The Church reached a membership of 273,000 by 1930
(Kraemer, 1958:50) and three years later declared its membership at 342,000 (de Bruine, 1935:111). In 1936 the membership
was reported as 381,600 (Nyhus, 1968:38). The Batak Church
could count 400,000 members in 1938 (Davis, 1938:ii) and continued to almost double every ten years which is a remarkable
record of growth.

The Batak Church came through difficulties of the late
1930s and 1940s with a new sense of its own strength. After
gaining autonomy and suffering the rigors of the war years, the
Church demonstrated it could stand on its own feet. The period
was not without problems. Financial difficulties hampered some
educational ministries (IRM, 1938:28). Problems relating to
indigenous practices, such as using indigenous music, arose
and the Toba Batak independence incited other areas to seek
independence from the Toba Bataks (Gramberg, 1942:325). Some
Europeans were amazed to realize that despite difficulties
the Batak Church was able not only to function under its own
administration but to thrive. In 1938 it was written that the
results of the independence of the Church was "less drastic
than might have been expected" (IRM, 1938:28). In 1940 the
admission was heard that, "The success of the churches in
continuing their work under the new system set up in 1940 has
surpassed all expectations" (IRM, 1941:21).

The membership of the Batak Church was reported as
502,855 members in 1952 (World Christian Handbook, 1952:152).
The difficulties of the war years with the German missionaries
interned, the Japanese occupation and the general unsettled
conditions might have predicted a lesser rate of growth. By
1953 the report counted 650,000 members (Cooley, 1968:6,7).
Some question must be raised about these statistics. Still,
there was obviously a spirit of growth around the early 1950s.
The rapid growth continued, reaching a membership of 713,704
in 1957 and on to 740,000 by 1958 (Muller-Kruger, 1959:lampiran).
By 1967 the Batak Church numbered its membership at 819,000,
divided into more than 1,300 congregations and served by 220
ordained pastors (Cooley, 1968:69).

The history of the Batak Church is one of the most
inspirational accounts of the expansion of Christianity. However, the important matter is to ask what factors were operable
in allowing such a movement to begin and continue. A study of
these factors will show that preparation and policy greatly
contributed to the movement.

There were definite preparations for the coming of
Christianity to the Bataks. The isolated nature of the Batak
country and the fertility of the land gave the Bataks a shield
from the missionary waves of Hinduism and Mohammedanism. When
Christianity arrived, the people were still immersed in their
animistic beliefs and practices (Davis, 1938:1). Another preparation was the coming of the Dutch. The Toba Batak region

had been isolated but the Dutch opened roads, established peace
and prohibited many corrupting practices, thereby paving the
way for the missionaries (Warneck, 1912:21). J. Merle Davis
accurately noted, "The extraordinary growth of the Christian
Church in Batakland...cannot be understood apart from the
geographical, historical and cultural background of the race"
(1938:1).

Another preparation for the Gospel in Batakland was
the war led by Imam Bondjol which not only sought to expel
the Dutch but also purposed to capture slaves and Islamize
the tribes (Muller-Kruger, 1959:181). These Moslem raids just
preceded the coming of Christianity and had the dual effect
of helping to break down the isolation of the Bataks (Nyhus,
1968:37) and reinforcing the Batak resistance to Islam. Kraemer
says, "...the strong Batak sense of independence and the memory
of the atrocities perpetuated by the Padris or balak Bondjol
have always constituted a strong barrier against Islam" (1958:
56).

A second factor in the growth of the Batak Church was
the location of the missionaries among a receptive people.
Before 1850 the Dutch linguist, Neubronner van der Tuuk, had
studied the Batak language and in addition to his linguistic
work, had established a guide for Batak missions. He wrote
that the Angkola and Mandailing Bataks were already largely
Islamic and that there was little hope of evangelistic activity
among them. However, he pointed to the Toba Batak area as
open for the Gospel. The wisdom of his advice is seen in that
missionaries from Ermelo in Holland went to Angkola in 1850
and when in 1931, they combined their Church with the Toba
Batak Church, the Angkola group numbered less than 5,000 members (Muller-Kruger, 1959:132).

The Rhenish Missionary Society (RMG) was forced to
withdraw from South Borneo because of the rebellion of 1859.
The head of the Rhenish Missionary Society, traveling in Holland,
saw the book by van der Tuuk and took it as the leadership of
God. Thus, the RMG entered the Toba Batak area in 1861
(Muller-Kruger, 1959:180). Again, the history of the Batak
Church illustrates church growth principles that advocate con-
centrating on receptive populations. McGavran has asked "Why
Gospel-ready masses should be neglected". He insists that the
Church should see that good seed are planted in good soil.
Evangelism should be increased especially among receptive
peoples. McGavran says, "In the presence of receptivity the
one thing to do is to bring in the sheaves" (1966:770).

The quality of the missionaries of the Rhenish Missionary
Society was a factor in the growth of the Church. Dr. Ludwig
Nommensen spent a life-time and rightly became known as the
"Apostle to the Bataks" (Cooley, 1968:67). Not only was
Nommensen a spiritual power but a wise missionary strategist.
Taking Toba as his goal he allowed nothing to deter him. His

reward was the tremendous miracle among the Bataks (Kraemer, 1958:47). Another unusually gifted missionary, J. Warneck built on the foundation laid by Nommensen. Warneck drew up the constitution adopted by the Batak Protestant Church in 1930 (Granberg, 1942:322). Kraemer says it is impossible to mention the history of the Batak Church without reverently recalling the privations and sacrifices endured by the first missionaries and their wives, who endured all because of the burning desire to preach the Gospel to the Bataks (1958:43).

A vital factor in the growth of the Church was a historical event that took place in 1883. The Toba area was regarded as sacred, the home of Singamangaradja, the Priest King who was the highest representative of Batak animistic religion. A sacred mountain near Toba was considered a shrine of the Bataks. Singamangaradja had led raids that had forced missionaries from some areas. Many Bataks, as well as Europeans, were denied access to this sacred area, called Silindung (Kraemer, 1958:48-49).

In 1883 a Batak army led by Singamangaradja engaged the small Dutch contingent. Thousands of spectators watched as the Bataks were routed by the Dutch and Singamangaradja was wounded. This battle, known as the Battle of the Stone Steps, was the most decisive defeat in Batak history. It left many Bataks disillusioned with their religion and tradition. It is significant that the great movement to Christ in the Silindung area began in this same year (Kraemer, 1958:49).

Another factor in the Batak Church's growth was the freedom, responsibility and autonomy given the Church, sometimes against the will of the Rhenish Missionary Society. The Rhenish missionaries were no more free from paternalistic feelings than most other missionaries. But when the mass movement into the Church began, the missionaries were unable to keep complete control of the churches. They instituted a program of elders who were responsible for church-discipline, local church organ-ization and the administering of funds. In addition there were pastor-teachers who combined the function of teaching in the village schools with conducting worship services and pastoral care of the congregations (Beyerhaus and Lefever, 1964:76,77). Davis sees the value of the teacher-preacher as being that it fit in with Batak custom. In addition these men were re-quired to have practical as well as scholastic training (Davis, 1938:3,4). Most important, an indigenous leadership was pro-duced.

Independence, given somewhat grudgingly in 1930, pre-pared the Church for the difficulties during World War II. The establishment of the training school in 1868 furthered the possibilities of autonomy for the Church (Cooley, 1968:67). J. Warneck stated that the Holy Spirit could work through and guide the Church in its independence. He foresaw that mission-aries might sometime be forced to leave. His words were

prophetic. The missionaries did have to leave and the Church
was able to administer itself (Beyerhaus and Lefever, 1964:80).
    Self-support was from almost the beginning attained.
This attainment has proved a factor in the growth of the Batak
Church. The ability of the Church to support itself was stimulated by declining to give money to the developing churches.
The idea of self-support was early communicated to the Batak
churches. The little communities built their own buildings
and supported their own leaders. It has been accepted as
natural that every Christian has responsibility. In addition,
every church came to be required to give twenty-five percent
of its income to a central fund, established to aid poorer
churches and the unsubsidized schools (Davis, 1938:3 and 11).
Thus, the Church achieved self-support and was not hampered
by a financial dependence that often delays true adulthood.
    One of the foremost factors in the growth of the
Batak Church was the successful adjustment of Christianity and
the Batak adat or customary law. Batak adat covered every
area of life--birth, death, family life, social, economic and
political activities, business relations and many other facets
of life. It even controlled the treatment of the poor, widows,
orphans and strangers. This adjustment of Christianity and
custom was made easier because Batak custom involved a minimum
of idol worship and sacrifice to gods and enjoined fidelity
to marital relationships. When the Bataks first heard the
Ten Commandments they admitted them to be superior to their
own law, but contended they were similar to the Batak law. It
was said by some Bataks that Christian law was more exacting
but that Christ gave the power to live up to the Law, a factor
completely missing from their own laws (Davis, 1938:17,18).
While some of the adjustments made were not totally satisfactory
to the missionaries, the social framework of the Batak community
was preserved and this considerably facilitated mass conversion,
especially in the Toba district (Beyerhaus and Lefever, 1964:
75).
    Church growth theory teaches that Christianity, entering
a new society, must make efforts to plant itself solidly in
the matrix of that society while remaining entirely faithful
to the Lord. Nida teaches that for effective church growth,
the organization of the Church must be understandable to the
constituency, congenial to the social structure and efficient
in its correlation of form and function (1965:108). Such
adapting to the culture will often involve functional substitutes for pre-Christian forms. The value of finding substitutes is that the felt needs of the people are met in such
a way as to bring greater faith in God and at the same time
create no cultural void (Tippett, 1967b:269-272). One of the
foremost factors in the growth of the Batak Church has been
the dedicated mission work of the Bataks themselves. In
addition to a witness through changed life, the Bataks felt

strong responsibility to engage in active evangelism. Encouraged by Nommensen, bands of young Christians proved highly
effective in winning other Bataks to faith. In 1899 the Batak
Christians founded the missionary society, the <u>Kongsi Batak</u>,
for the work of spreading the Gospel into the animist and
Moslem areas (Beyerhaus and Lefever, 1964:76).

Besides direct witnessing, the Bataks used colonies
of Bataks who moved to new areas for evangelistic purposes.
These colonies moved into new areas where they cleared land
and settled among the original inhabitants. While it is
true that at times they failed to evangelize and even were
absorbed by the non-Christian population in other cases, most
often colonies evangelized the new areas. The Batak colonies
were a factor in Batak church growth (Davis, 1938:23-26).

An all important factor in the growth of the Batak
Church was the willingness of the Rhenish missionaries to
accept the multi-individual nature of the conversions of the
Bataks. The mission turned its back on the old pietistic aim
of converting individuals and accepted the idea of peoples
coming to Christ in groups. The Gospel was thus allowed to
evangelize the entire nation in a way that would have been
impossible had the concept of one-by-one conversion been
continued (Beyerhaus and Lefever, 1964:74,75).

Modern church growth theory teaches the possibility,
validity and desirability of multi-individual decisions for
Christ as a basic principle. The term "mass movement" has
been replaced by the term "multi-individual decision".
Multi-individual decision means that many people participate
in the act. Each individual makes up his mind. The decision
comes as a group of related individuals together decide for
Christ. The saved persons thus remain in contact with their
culture, their families and their friends (McGavran, 1970:
296-304). The desirability of multi-individual decision is
a central principle in church growth theory.

The growth of the Batak Church is one of God's most
gracious miracles. Besides the inspiration, the history of
the Church is instructive for missionary strategy. The Toba
Batak Church stands as a monument of the Holy Spirit's
power in this world. ⌣

The Simalungun Protestant Christian Church (<u>Geredja</u> Kristen
                              Protestan <u>Simalungun</u>)

The Rhenish Missionary Society began evangelization
efforts among the Simalungun Batak people in 1903. The first
twenty-five years saw only thirty-one congregations and 900
baptisms reported. The growth in the Simalungun area did
not begin until, under strong pressure from Simalungun leaders,
the local dialect was used rather than the Toba language.
Materials in the Simalungun language began to be used in 1930

and by 1940 the Church had grown to 5,700 members in sixty
congregations (Cooley, 1968:69). The experience of the Church
among the Simalungun Bataks illustrates the church growth
principle of using the heart language of a people rather than
relying merely on the trade or national language (see McGavran,
1970:204).

The development of the Church among the Simalungun Bataks
was aided by the efforts of the Dutch authorities in opening
the country after 1903. Also, many colonies from the Toba
Batak region came into the area of the Simalungun Bataks and
brought their religion (Muller-Kruger, 1959:285-286). There
was increasing pressure for autonomy and reaching the Simalungun
culture with the Gospel. During the Japanese occupation, the
missionaries were interned and the missionaries' resistance to
independence overcome. The wisdom and timeliness of granting
autonomy to the Simalungun Church is borne out by the remarkable
increase during the trying time of war and revolution. By
1952 the Church had increased to 21,600 members and the number
of congregations to ninety (Cooley, 1968:70).

Autonomy alone could not account for such an increase
in membership. A lay movement called "Witness for Christ"
carried the Gospel to increasing numbers of Simalungun Bataks
who were looking for firmer ground than their old beliefs
could provide. In 1963 the Toba Batak Church formally declared
the Simalungun Church independent. The Church continued to
show remarkable growth, reaching a membership of 85,257 by 1967
(Cooley, 1968:70).

The Simalungun region represents a wide open opportunity
for Christianity. Over 300,000 people make up the population
which means that thousands remain to be won. Cooley calls for
greater cooperation among Churches in aiding this Church to
reach the multitudes (1968:70).

The Karo Batak Protestant Church (Geredja Batak Karo Protestan)

Serving among some 450,000 people, the Karo Batak
Church has more than doubled since 1965 (IRM, 1968:17). Things
were not always so encouraging. The Netherlands Missionary
Society worked among the Karo Bataks for fifty years and reported only 5,000 members in 1946 (Muller-Kruger, 1959:199).

Of the Karo Batak Church Muller-Kruger said, "It can
be pictured as a plant which was planted in an arid region
and which received neither correct fertilizer nor proper
cultivation" (1959:199). The slow growth between 1890 and
1940 can be attributed to several factors. The Gospel was
planted for worldly reasons. The Dutch plantation owners
requested the Netherlands Missionary Society to undertake
evangelistic efforts in the hope that Christianization would
make the Karo Bataks better workers and overcome their tendency
to be destructive (Muller-Kruger, 1959:199).

A second reason for the slow start was timing (Cooley, 1968:71). While in the Toba area, Christianity had preceded the opening of plantations and the modernization of the land, in the Karo country secular forces preceded the Church. The inhabitants, still in a primitive stage, were corrupted by the secular forces and learned to sell and buy in a money economy. The result was not a happy one for church growth (Muller-Kruger, 1959:199-200).

A third reason for the slow growth relates to the method of planting the Gospel. The first missionary, a Dutch teacher, Dr. Kruyt, came from Minahasa and brought with him four national teachers. He apparently overlooked the fact that nearby the Toba Batak Church could have supplied Batak evangelists. Muller-Kruger concludes that the Netherlands Missionary Society failed to ask aid from the Toba Batak Church or the Rhenish Missionary Society because the ecumenical spirit had not yet developed (1959:200).

Institutions were promoted by the Netherlands Missionary Society from the beginning but all the schools were closed in 1909 because the missionaries were not satisfied with the results. This action, according to Muller-Kruger, lost what relationship the mission had with the Karo Bataks. In 1935 the schools were reopened with little result because World War II forced their closing once again. Two hospitals and a leper colony were well received (Muller-Kruger, 1959:200-201). One is forced to wonder if the schools and hospitals might have been a factor in the slow start as they surely occupied a great deal of the missionaries' time at this crucial period.

The Karo Batak Church began to grow around 1940. Cooley sees the attainment of national independence and church autonomy as factors in the new growth. He also points to the fact that the Church had been firmly planted among these people before 1940 which formed a foundation for the eventual growth (Cooley, 1968:71). The Bible was translated into the Karo Batak language only in 1940. There developed an intense desire for Christianity in the Karo Batak area in the 1950s. In 1953 one entire battalion of Karo Batak soliders embraced Christianity. The response began to spread throughout the Karo area, especially in the cities (Muller-Kruger, 1959:200-201).

By 1965 the Church had grown to 30,000 members. Reports indicate that after the Communist failure of 1965, response increased. Thirteen thousand five hundred thirty-seven infants and adults were baptized in 1966 with 2,379 more baptized during January and February of 1967. At that time over 6,000 were awaiting baptism. The Church's membership had doubled in a two year period (IRM, 1968:17). Most of the converts were animistic peoples but some were former Moslems (Cooley, 1968:71).

Muller-Kruger contends that the growth in the Karo Batak Church came at the prepared time. He says, "Is it not the Lord himself who sets the time of the harvest before his people?" (1959:201). Could it not also be possible that the harvest might have come sooner had the emphasis been placed earlier on the scriptures in the Karo language, the evangelization through Batak peoples and other more fruitful means of discipling? The Karo Batak Church stands on the brink of even greater victories.

The Nias Protestant Christian Church (Banua Niha Keriso Protestan)

With 225,000 members in 1967, the Nias Church was the second largest Church on Sumatra (Cooley, 1968:71). The Church was like those in the Batak area in that it was started by the Rhenish Missionary Society. The first missionary, Rev. Donniger, was unable to accompany the other German missionaries transferring from Borneo to the Batak area due to the illness of his wife. He settled in the city of Padang, West Sumatra and began evanglistic ministry among dock workers from Nias. Convinced that he could serve the Niasan people better on their own soil, Donniger moved to Gunung Sitoli, the only city on Nias under Dutch control in 1865 (Muller-Kruger, 1959:203).

Slow growth resulted in the first years. Note the graph of growth on page 95. In 1874 twenty-five persons were baptized on Easter Sunday (Kriele, 1927:91). The meager growth during this beginning period can be attributed to the geographic isolation which made communication difficult, the close kinship ties that made each village virtually a closed community, the lack of roads and security and the heavy weight of custom (adat) that was at that time unchallenged (Cooley, 1968:72). The missionaries were restricted to three cities along the coast and were prohibited from visiting the interior due to the savage tribes who often practiced headhunting (Kriele, 1927:91-92).

After the Dutch established security and opened roads in the last years of the nineteenth century, evangelism proceeded rapidly. By 1900 there were 5,000 Christians on Nias (Muller-Kruger, 1959:2-4). The Church reported over 20,000 members in 1915, a period covering fifty years (Kriele, 1927: 92).

The Nias Church almost tripled between 1915 and 1921, reaching a membership of 62,000 (Cooley, 1968:72). A large part of the reason for this renewal is attributed to the revival that broke out. This revival, known as the "fangesa dodo" (the great repentance) left an indelible mark on the Nias Church (Muller-Kruger, 1959:204). In 1915 the Nias Church celebrated the jubilee of the mission. A large meeting was planned at which the Nias Christians were asked to speak first about the blessing of the Christian religion on Nias and then about the unfinished task. The revival is traced

FIGURE 14

Graph of Growth,

NIAS PROTESTANT CHRISTIAN CHURCH

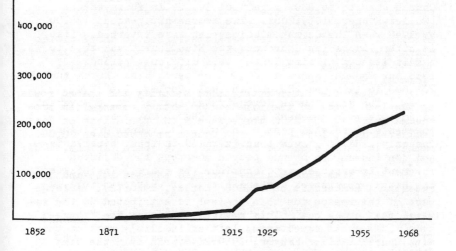

directly to the spiritual impact of this meeting and genuine
awakening came to church after church (Kriele, 1927:95-96).

This revival manifested a great conviction for and
confession of sin. Through confession, Niasans found freedom
and release from guilt. Some excesses occurred in the form
of extravagant and frienzied fanaticism but the movement was
in the main healthy and spiritual. Most of the excesses were
registered at stations where there was no missionary (Kriele,
1927:95,96). This fact shows the value of missionaries to
the Church during times of great spiritual outpourings.

The genuineness of the revival was testified by the
real repentance of sin including in many cases reparation,
a new desire for deeper spiritual knowledge, an enlarged
witness and the provision of spiritual leaders. The mission
was forced to begin a program of training for lay pastors
that resulted in an increase of lay pastors from six in 1916
to over one hundred in 1925. The Church was renewed and set
to the task of evangelism (Kriele, 1927:96-101).

Between 1921 and 1925 the Church grew at less than
1,000 per year which revealed a marked slowing of the growth
rate. This fact demands consideration because it would seem
that the one hundred new lay pastors should have stimulated
growth. A great part of the answer lies in the epidemic of
influenza that devastated the island in 1919 and 1920 (Kriele,
1927:104). It is likely that the deaths incurred in this
epidemic give the appearance of slow growth to the record
of the Church during these five years.

Rapid growth returned between 1925 and 1929 when the
Church grew to 84,000, a gain of 19,000 in four years
(Muller-Kruger, 1959:206). The membership reached 135,000
by 1940 when the German missionaries were interned. Like
in other Indonesian Churches, the Nias Church was able to
handle its own affairs during this difficult period. By
1958 the Church reported 180,000 members. The Church numbered
205,000 in 1965 and 220,000 in 1967 (Cooley, 1968:72).

The Nias Church demonstrated that a people movement
is not one mass movement into the Church but a series of
movements of related people in multi-individual decision.
The only kind of growth that is valid is that which lasts
and continues. In a true people movement the Christward
movement is often seen to continue for years. The Nias and
the Batak experiences are indicative of this principle.

THE CHURCHES ON JAVA

There are three main ethnic groups on Java. The
Javanese inhabit East and Central Java and number some 51,000,
000. The Sundanese, a people separate in language, religion
and outlook, occupy West Java and number about 24,000,000 people
The Chinese, some 2,000,000 strong, form the largest minority

group and are scattered in the towns and cities over Java. At least 260,000 Chinese or about 8.8 percent are Christian. Some 170,000 Javanese or about .35 percent are Christian. The strongly Islamic Sundanese people show only .074 percent of the population Christian, numbering but 15,000 (Cooley, 1968:96 and 99-100).

The church growth story on Java is important. The growth realized, though small in relation to total population, cannot be paralleled in the history of the Christian mission in any other land already drawn into the Moslem fold (Bentley-Taylor, 1967:138). Historical and ethnological factors have contributed to the growth in Java.

The Background of Church Growth in Java

The Javanese search for and desire of a mystic and secret way of life and wisdom forms a factor in church growth on Java. Javanese refer to this trait as <u>mentjari ngelmu</u> (seeking wisdom). The Javanese seeking of peace and fulfillment through some mystical experience provides a point of contact for the Gospel with Javanese society (Kraemer, 1958: 74-76).

Closely related to this search for wisdom is the type of Islam with its high tolerance, forming a factor in church growth. The religious background of animist, Hindu, Buddhist and more recently Islamic factors, has brought about a religious situation not found elsewhere among Moslem peoples. Each successive religion has been absorbed by the Javanese. The Javanese willingness to consider any religious message and tolerance constitutes a major factor in Central and East Java church growth (cf. Bentley-Taylor, 1967:138).

Church growth on Java was influence by the ministry of the British Baptists in the years following 1811. This ministry represented the first mission work directed toward the Javanese people (Muller-Kruger, 1959:135). One of the most regrettable failures in mission history was the 200 years during which the Dutch Church sought only to minister to Europeans with only the slightest effort to evangelize the indigenous population (Bentley-Taylor, 1967:16,17). Of this deplorable condition, Cooley says, "Developments during the first period of the East Java Church's history (1830-1848) suggest that quite a different situation might have evolved had the Dutch authorities permitted and encouraged missionary work among the Javanese" (1968:87).

When the British Baptist, William Robinson, was sent to Java in 1813 with instructions to consider himself primarily a missionary to the Javanese people, he was the first missionary to have ever been so instructed (Bentley-Taylor, 1967:22). The London Missionary Society also sent three missionaries to Indonesia, Joseph Kam, John Supper and Gottlob

Bruckner. The latter two served on Java. In Semarang Bruckner
became a Baptist. He did so partly because of disillusionment
with the spiritual condition of the Dutch Church he served and
partly because his study brought new conviction. After the
death of Thomas Trowt, the Baptist missionary in Semarang with
whom Bruckner had been close friends, Bruckner was adopted by
the Bristish Missionary Society and continued to serve in Java
until his death at the age of seventy-four (Payne, 1945:17).

Bruckner directed his energies toward publication and
translation work. He produced many tracts in Javanese and
finally with strenuous effort finished a translation of the
New Testament in Javanese (Muller-Kruger, 1959:161). Even
after Bruckner supervised the printing of the Javanese New
Testament (which was printed in India), he experienced difficulty in distributing the Bible because of the fear of the
Dutch authorities that any Christian work might cause trouble
with the Moslem population (Bentley-Taylor, 1967:46-49).

While the Baptist missionaries planted no lasting
churches on Java, their ministry was highly important. The
provision of the New Testament in Javanese and Gospel portions
and tracts was destined to have great influence on future
development. Also, the British Baptists, especially Bruckner,
stimulated the Netherlands Missionary Society to undertake
mission work among the Javanese (Payne, 1945:79-80). This
fact underscores a lesson that must not be lost by any who
in their intense compulsion toward unity fail to see the
stimulating effect of separate bodies working in cooperation
toward a common goal of discipling the nations.

A third factor in church growth on Java was the witness of two radically different lay Christians who began discipling the Javanese decades before the Dutch allowed formal
mission work. The coming of Johannes Emde to Indonesia was as
remarkable as was his subsequent ministry. When he heard that
there was no winter in Indonesia, Emde felt this contradictory
to Genesis 8:22, "Summer and winter and day and night shall
not cease." Resolving to see for himself, he gained passage
and arrived in Indonesia in 1800 (Bertley-Taylor, 1967:56).

Emde settled in Surabaja where he worked as a watch-
maker. He was profoundly influenced by Joseph Kam. After Kam
sailed to Ambon, Emde assumed leadership of the Surabaja congregation. He taught a "Westernized" Christianity which tended to separate the converts from their Javanese culture and
community. By 1845 the congregation in Surabaja, known as
"The Pious of Surabaja", included some 220 baptized Javanese
(Cooley, 1968:87).

The second European, C. L. Coolen, came from a Dutch
family. His father had immigrated to Russia and then to
Indonesia as a mercenary in the VOC army. Coolen's mother was
a descendant from the Mataram princess, a royal line among
the Javanese. From her Coolen inherited the mystic, symbolic

spirit of Javanese culture. He was the mingling of the
Western individualistic spirit with Javanese traits. He became expert in Javanese shadow plays and native orchestra
(wajang and gamelan) (Muller-Kruger, 1959:141).

In 1827 Coolen began clearing land and established
his own plantation near a town called Ngoro. Many Javanese
were attracted to Ngoro (Muller-Kruger, 1959:141-142). Coolen
began teaching the Javanese about Christianity, translating
extemporaneously from his Dutch Bible into their language.
Attempting to purge Christianity of its Western forms and make
it more Javanese, he used wajang plays to portray Bible truths.
The worship services resembled Javanese religious meetings,
even intoning hymns and prayers in the typical Javanese way,
the way also used by the Moslems. Converts were accepted on
their reciting the Lord's Prayer and the Apostle's Creed.
Baptism and the Lord's Supper were rejected by Coolen because
of the fear of the Javanese becoming too Dutch. He felt the
Javanese Christians should remain strictly Javanese
(Bentley-Taylor, 1967:59,60).

Both Emde and Coolen had part in the development of
a Christian community at Wiung near Surabaja. A faithful
Moslem teacher in Wiung, Pak Dasimah, had for years led a
religious meeting. Among those who attended was a Madurese
man, Kiai Midah, who made holders for ceremonial daggers,
kris. On a trip to Surabaja to sell his wares, Kiai Midah
was offered a Javanese tract by Emde's daughter. The tract,
produced by Bruckner, was a Javanese translation of the Gospel
of Mark. Kiai Midah contended that, since he could not read,
the tract would not help him. Miss Emde insisted he take it
in the hope someone could read it to him (Bentley-Taylor, 1967:
60).

The Gospel of Mark travelled back to Wiung in the hand
of Kiai Midah and thus passed on to Pak Dasimah. The idea of
a "Son of God" was too new for Pak Dasimah and he laid the
Gospel aside. However, he could not escape from the Message
and so came back to the book. The idea of a "Son of God" continued to attract the attention of the group and fill their
discussions (Muller-Kruger, 1959:140).

A providential incident moved the Wiung group closer
to Christianity. One of the Wiung group, Pak Sadimah, attended
a wedding at the home of one Kiai Kunti in Wonokali. In the
celebration, Kiai Kunti offered a prayer Pak Sadimah had never
heard. The prayer, acutally a Javanese translation of the
Apostle's Creed, had been taught by Coolen at Ngoro. When
Pak Sadimah told Pak Dasimah of the prayer, the similarity to
the Gospel of Mark was recognized and the leaders of the Wiung
congregation hastened to Wonokali seeking further information.
In this way they were led to Coolen. Ten members of the Wiung
congregation made the twenty-five hour journey to Ngoro to
seek instruction from Coolen (Muller-Kruger, 1959:140). These

ten leaders were instructed by Coolen and carried their knowledge of Christianity back to Wiung. They returned each year
for further instruction from Coolen (Bentley-Taylor, 1967:60).
    The Wiung Congregation used wajang plays to spread
their faith and soon several villages were interested in
Christianity. A member of the Wiung congregation, on a trip
to Surabaja, made known to Mrs. Emde that he was a Christian.
Mrs. Emde told her husband who extended an invitation to Pak
Dasimah and the next day Pak Dasimah stood at the door of
Emde's house in Surabaja. The Wiung congregation had thus
made contact with both Coolen and Emde's Church (Bentley-Taylor,
1967:60,61).
    These background factors are all important to the spread
of the Gospel in Java. The two hundred years of neglect must
be viewed as a period of missed opportunity. The conversion
of many Javanese to Christianity before 1850 indicates the
possibilities. Hendrik Kraemer has strongly stated this fact
(1958:76).
    Equally instructive to the church growth student is
the account of the highly "Javanized" Christianity taught by
Coolen. Kraemer states that Coolen Javanized Christianity
"beyound recognition." It is true that Coolen used Moslem-like
rituals involving the rapid repetition of Christian phrases
and using statements of the Ten Commandments, the Lord's Prayer
and the Apostle's Creed as magical formulae. By these and other
practices, Coolen, in the opinion of Hendrik Kraemer, kept
Christianity "utterly on the level of Javanese religious life"
(1958:77).
    Kraemer further contends that Coolen abandoned Christian
beliefs to the ethnic atmosphere. Admitting that Coolen was
correct in his idea that the Javanese could not comprehend the
Gospel in its European form, Kraemer disagrees with Coolen's
procedures of visualizing and interpreting the faith in Javanese
forms. The correct element in Coolen's approach according to
Kraemer, was the necessity to adapt the Message to Javanese
life and society. Kraemer notes that European missions stand
in daily need of reminder of this principle. Still, Coolen's
Javanized approach kept the Gospel too exclusively enclosed
within Javanese forms instead of making it stand out more clearly in its essential characteristics against the Javanese background (Kraemer, 1958:77).
    What Kraemer is saying is that Christianity must not
be accommodated to the extent that it gives up its essential
elements and allows a deadening syncretism to set in. In this
he is obviously correct. However, the church growth student
must look with less jaundiced eyes at the work of Coolen. If
Coolen went too far in adapting the Gospel to Javanese forms
(and his rejection of baptism, the Lord's Supper and the use
of magical forms indicated he did), at least his mistake was
not the usual one committed by Western missions. The fact

remains that in Ngoro and Wiung Christian movements began
which reached out to new peoples and grew naturally in their
own climate, being thoroughly adapted to the culture and time
in which they spoke. Kraemer also sees this value of Coolen's
work saying, "Yet we must never forget that evidently God used
Coolen as well as Pak Dasimah to start the course of the Gospel
in Java and to rouse in some profound minds the realization
that in Christ the deepest longings of the Javanese people are
fulfilled" (1958:77).

Missions have often overlooked the principle that
Christianity must be presented to people in the form most acceptable to their culture and philosophy. While the Gospel
must remain thoroughly Christian, it can be adapted so those
who become Christian need not leave their own culture. The
changes that come as a natural result of Christianity will be
effected by the Christian members of the society not by foreigners. Concerning the work of Coolen, the church growth student
must ask what would have been the result had the Church in East
Java tended more to his method than to the highly European
version of Christianity which developed around 1842?

Emde's congregation also is instructive as it became
enmeshed in exactly the opposite extreme from Coolen's. The
congregation led by Emde sought to impose on the Javanese their
pietistic interpretation of Christianity in its undiluted form.
Kraemer notes that missions still suffer from the tendency to
present the Gospel in an undiluted form and thus make difficult
its acceptance (1958, 78). The Surabaja congregation prohibited the wajang and gamelang and prescribed the wearing of trous-
ers and cutting of hair short in order to become "more human".
Kraemer contends that the Surabaja congregation was mistaken in
issuing these orders without entering more deeply into the
Javanese mind and without seeking equivalents for the practices
denied the converts. He correctly observes, "They simply want-
ed to mould them (the converts) in their own image" (1958,78).

The church growth student must agree with Kraemer's
assessment that the Surabaja congregation failed to understand
or respect the Javanese culture. They failed to provide for
the Javanese need for fixed ceremonies surrounding the tragedies
and joys of life. The greatest need of missions is to learn
to plant churches that can live a normal, healthy and repro-
ductive life in their own cultures. The Church that depends on
outside forces to produce for it a "hot house" existence will
never show the normalcy of extensive reproduction. The
Church must, while remaining faithful to the Lord and the Word,
be adapted to live naturally in the matrix of the culture in
which it is planted.

The East Java Christian Church (Geredja Kristen Djawi Wetan)

The East Java Church might be seen to have originated

in 1846 with the visit of L. J. van Rhijn of the Netherlands
Missionary Society who was investigating possibilities of
mission to the Javanese. Accompanied by Jellesma, van Rhijn
visited in the home of Gottlob Bruckner. Bruckner urged van
Rhijn to influence the Society to send missioaries. So impressed was Jellesma that he immediately began studying
Javanese. At the recommendation of van Rhijn the Netherlands
Missionary Society appointed Jellesma to Java and he arrived
to take up residence in 1849 (Bentley-Taylor, 1967:53-54 and
80).

          However, church growth had not stood still waiting
for missionaries. Thirty-five Javanese from Wiung were baptized in 1843 and these were followed by others until in 1845
around 220 Javanese names were on the membership book of the
Surabaja Protestant Church. Because of Emde's emphasis,
these Javanese Christians came to be known as "Kristen Londo"
(Dutch Christians). Emde's insistence that they cut their
hair and follow Dutch dress customs caused these Christians
to be known as "Dutchmen without hats or shoes" and Christianity
as "Agama Belanda" (Dutch religion) (Muller-Kruger, 1959:145).

          In the rural areas there was more opportunity for
Javanese Christians to remain Javanese. Several Christian
communities sprang up as the result of the work of Indonesian
evangelists such as Singotruno, Paulus Tosari and Matius Niep.
The Christian community, Modjowarno, actually became the
mother congregation for the Church in East Java (Muller-Kruger,
1959, 145).

          The work began to advance more rapidly after the
arrival of Jellesma who was "...a man of apostolic temper,
truly consummed by the desire to convert the Javanese"
(Kraemer, 1959:79). Before his death Jellesma baptized over
2,500 Javanese (Cooley, 1968:88). He was not willing to
evangelize one area alone but sought out wider horizons.
The seed was sown in an ever widening circle (Kraemer, 1959:79).

          Hendrik Kraemer is convinced that Jellesma's policy of
wide outreach would have achieved more had he concentrated on
fewer and more strategic centers (1958:79). This is a usual
criticism leveled at a rapidly expanding movement. Shepherding
is necessary. However, there is also the danger of stunting
a movement by excessive fear of over-expansion. The problem
could have been helped not only by more missionaries but by
the training of more national leaders and the transfer of
missionaries from other and perhaps sterile fields.

          Jellesma established a training program for Javanese
evangelists. He conflicted with the followers of Emde because
he was convinced the Javanese Christian should remain Javanese
but conflicted with Coolen's followers on the subject of baptism and the Lord's Supper (Muller-Kruger, 1959:148-149).
Eventually Jellesma succeeded in reconciling the two groups
and by 1853 had baptized almost 400 in Ngoro itself

(Bentley-Taylor, 1967:82).

The growth of the Church in East Java was effected largely by the Javanese evangelists. The missionaries gave instruction for the development of the new congregations (Muller-Kruger, 1959:148). By 1854 there were nine congregations with 1,100 members (Bentley-Taylor, 1967:86). The membership reached 29,000 by 1933 (de Bruine, 1935:110). The year 1937 revealed a membership of 32,665 (Kraemer, 1958:81-82). The churches usually started in the rural areas and moved into the towns along with the children of Christians who migrated to the cities (Muller-Kruger, 1959:145-150).

The policy of establishing Christian villages was suggested by the Mennonite missionary, Jansz, who felt that since Javanese life was wrapped up in the village, mission work could be best carried on by establishing such villages where converts could be gathered (Bentley-Taylor, 1967:87). These communities became the backbone of the Church (Cooley, 1968:88). They alleviated the problems of the Church in a Moslem land of persecution and economic discrimination and opened the possibility to many of being a Christian (Bentley-Taylor, 1967:141-142). The use of Christian communities may have been the only way to begin in Moslem East Java. Perhaps such methods would still be useful in highly resistant, antagonistic fields. However, the expected result of the Christian villages was a sense of isolation of the Christians from their neighbors. They became introverted to the needs and problems of their community. The attitude arose that responsibility for the spread of the faith rested with the foreigners. Bentley-Taylor says, "Spontaneous joy over the treasure found in the gospel, and consequently much of the spontaneous expansion, fell into the background" (Bentley-Taylor, 1967:88). The loss of the sense of outreach is an ever present danger in any approach that involves withdrawal and isolation.

An added problem of the isolation of the Christian communities was the increasing paternal influence of the missionaries. The masses of the Moslem community disappeared from the Christian's sights and the missionary involuntarily became the protector (Bentley-Taylor, 1967:90). Kraemer states that the evangelism of the period was "almost accidental" (Kraemer, 1958:83).

The growth of the Church on Java was stimulated by the fact that family conversion was considered the normal way into the Church. The importance of this pattern both in Java and in other fields is captured by Bentley-Taylor:

> *Just as at Philippi it was Lydia and her household,*
> *the gaoler and all his house, so it has generally*
> *been in Java. Western missionaries have too often*
> *underestimated the social cohesion of an oriental*
> *race, appealing to them individually to turn to*

Christ, as though their young people were free to
make personal decisions like the youth of London
or Washington. While it is undeniable that the
Javanese churches have frequently been in danger
or forgetting the absolute necessity for personal
faith in each individual and in each generation,
yet this pattern of group conversion has more to
commend it both in modern oriental society and
in the New Testament than we are apt to realize
(1967:142).

Bringing peoples, that is family groups, tribes, clans, and
villages to Christ must become a prominent element in all
missionary thinking and strategy.
     By 1953 the membership of the Church in East Java had
risen from the 1937 total of 32,600 to 55,000 members (Cooley,
1968:6,7). The Church overcame its former isolation and promoted strong missionary emphasis--in Java, Bali and Madura
and sincerely attempted to serve Indonesia (Bentley-Taylor,
1967:145-146). The Church's support of the independence
movement gained Indonesian favor for its program (Cooley, 1968:
89). In 1964 the membership was reported as 64,300 (IRM, 1968:
18).
     Growth came partly as a result of strong lay witnessing.
Laymen used family gatherings and festivals as opportunities
for evangelism. Since 1960 the Church has promoted Gospel
Weeks, seeking to reach every village in East Java. From these
efforts, at least 1,000 adults per year were baptized between
the years 1954 and 1965 (Cooley, 1968:90).
     The Church in East Java has shown amazing growth in
the new spiritual climate and responsiveness following the
events of September 1965. The membership of the Church rose
from 62,300 to over 85,000 in three years (Cooley, 1968:89).
In July and August 1966 the Church reported 10,000 baptisms.
By 1967 the Church could report 24,456 new members since the
Communist coup attempt (IRM, 1968:18).
     The Church did not grow between 1965-1968 without
effort. The churches responded to the opportunity that was
apparent after the destruction of the Communist Party with
witness and service (Cooley, 1968:112). Extensive evangelistic
efforts were undertaken in the prisons where thousands of
Communists were being held. Evangelism also was stepped up
among the disillusioned masses who were seeking assurance and
peace (Indonesian Bible Society Record, 1968:55
     Frank Cooley notes that some of those who have entered
the Church were "Nicodemuses", that is, those who had been
secret disciples before, became bold enough to make public
their belief in the new climate of post 1965 Indonesia (1968:
90). Another observer feels that some of the growth in Java
(Central as well as East) came as a result of those who had

left Islam for Communism and after the Communist failure found
new meaning for life in Christianity (ENS, 1970:2).

The story of the East Java Church is one of the inspiring stories of Christian missions. No where else have
such results attended missions in a Moslem country. While the
95,000 members is small in proportion to the total population,
it is a cause for praise in a country already brought under
the banner of Islam. We can but regret the lost opportunity
of the vital two hundred years between 1650 and 1850 when to
all appearances great harvest could have been reaped had the
Dutch been willing to put in the scythe.

The Churches of Central Java

Many of the same influences and pressures experienced
in East Java have been felt in Central Java. Communism had
been strong in Central Java as it had in East and it is therefore not surprising that the aftermath of the Communist failure
occasioned new opportunities for the churches in Central Java.
The churches responded with dedicated service and effective
evangelism. In some areas the churches became the positive
and stablizing factors in the society (Thomson, 1968:18,19).
Growth was the result of an unprecedented turning to Christ
and a continuing expansion of the local churches (Indonesian
Bible Society Record, 1968:55).

As in East Java, the first efforts at evangelism in
Central Java came as the fruit of dedicated lay people who
began Christian work before any missionaries were on the scene.
A Dutch official, Mr. Anthing, established relationship with
several Javanese who were seeking the truth and led them in
Christian studies. Among these Javanese were several who later
produced great fruit in the evangelization of Central Java
(Muller-Kruger, 1959:168).

After moving from Semarang to Djakarta around 1865,
Mr. Anthing used his own money to further the outreach of the
Gospel among the Javanese. He gave full time to evangelistic
efforts after his retirement in 1870. Over fifty Javanese
evangelists were trained by Mr. Anthing in his own home in
Djakarta. Muller-Kruger says, "He asked them to not become
or work as tools of the Dutch but as genuine Javanese evangelists." Unable to secure missionary help from Holland, Anthing
continued his service until his death in 1883 (Muller-Kruger,
1959:168).

Another influencial layman, A. M. N. Keuchenius, furthered Christianity in the region around Tegal in north
Central Java. With the aid of two evangelists from Anthing's
school, Keuchenius planted a congregation of forty or fifty
Javanese Christians before 1860. Around 1860 Mr. Keuchenius
succeeded in obtaining help from the Netherlands Reformed
Church (Nederlands Gereformeerde Aendingsvereenining, NGZV).

The missionary who came, Vermeer, began by serving the congregation but soon decided that an orphanage would bring greater
results as it could train children who would become the backbone
of the Church. The Church was moved outside of Tegal where
the orphanage was built (Muller-Kruger, 1959:153).

It is one of the common mistakes in missionary strategy
to turn from planting congregations in the mainstream of the
life of a people to begin a policy of good works and service
ministries. History has disproved the policy of growing a
Church through school and orphanage work. The experience of
the Lutheran Church in Liberia is a case in point of the difficulty of developing a strong Church by means of work with
children in orphanages and schools (cf. Wold, 1968:101-106).

Two women, Mrs. Osstrom-Phillips in Banumas and Mrs.
Phillips-Stevens in Purworedja, also did much for evangelism
in Central Java. Mrs. Phillips-Stevens carried the Gospel
into the villages. The two women worked with Javanese evangelists from Mr. Anthing's school.

These Javanese evangelists brought many Javanese to
Christ but were denied the privilege of baptizing or leading
the Communion service because they were not ordained
(Muller-Kruger, 1959:153). This regrettable situation is often
encountered. Western missions have all too often imposed upon
national leadership standards of educational and other ecclesiastical achievement before admitting them to ordination and
full service in the ministry. Far better if ordination is
based on spiritual and leadership abilities rather than educational or ecclesiastical achievement. Men such as these
Javanese evangelists should not only be allowed, but should
be encouraged in every avenue of Christian ministry. Only
in this way can churches be planted that will grow naturally
in their own culture.

Sadrach, one of the Javanese evangelists, proved to
be one of the most effective evangelists in Indonesia's history.
Born on the north coast of Java, he attended a Moslem school,
but met Jellesma around 1855. Profoundly influenced by the
Dutchman, Sadrach returned to Semarang where he was won to
Christ by Missionary Hoezoo. Traveling to Djakarta, he came
under the influence of Mr. Anthing and was baptized in 1867.
Beginning in 1869 Sadrach continued to work with Mrs.
Philips-Stevens in Purworedja (Muller-Kruger, 1959:154).

Like Coolen in East Java, Sadrach sought to develop
a form of Christianity that would not involve a radical break
with Javanese culture (Cooley, 1968:91). He was convinced
that Javanese Christians did not have to adapt themselves to
Dutch customs and ways. His views were based more on
pro-Javanese feelings than anti-Dutch ones (Muller-Kruger, 1959:
154-155).

The effectiveness of Sadrach's efforts is seen in the
report for 1889 at which time he worked over a wide area of

Central Java. Sadrach's movement numbered twenty-one congregations with 241 members in Bageleh, thirteen congregations
with 213 members in Banjumas, four congregations with 341 members in Tegal, six congregations with 515 members in
Pekalongan and nine congregations with over 1,000 members in
Jogjakarta. The total membership was over 3,000 in some
fifty-three congregations (Muller-Kruger, 1959:154).

There were some 9,000 Javanese gathered into scores of
congregations in Central Java when the missionaries began
arriving in force in the 1880s. The missionaries sought to
take over leadership and develop the Church along the line
of the Gereformeerd theology and polity. While Sadrach
welcomed and desired to work with the missionaries, he was
understandably unwilling to turn leadership completely over
to them (Cooley, 1968:91). The missionaries were unwilling
to accept the Javanese flavor in Sadrach's congregations.
They accused him of syncreticism (Muller-Kruger, 1959:156).

After much discord and misunderstanding, the missionary
society decided to separate from Sadrach's movement. Even the
missionary who had been working with Sadrach in a productive
way was forced to withdraw from the Javanese evangelist. Most
of the Christians remained with the congregations associated
with Sadrach (Muller-Kruger, 1959:156). Of this deplorable
situation, Cooley says, "...the opportunity of building on a
broad indigenous foundation was lost and the missionaries had
to start from the beginning" (1968:91).

Herein is a church growth tragedy. The productive
efforts of the Dutch laymen and the Javanese evangelists led
to churches among a relatively responsive people. The beginning was not utilized by the missionaries who turned first to
social and benevolent work and then because of their refusal
to build on the foundation of Sadrach, found themselves beginning all over. In addition the indigenous churches lost
the benefits the missionaries could have brought. Without
doubt had a more valid mission strategy been utilized, thousands
of Javanese Christians and hundreds of additional congregations
would have resulted.

Several Church groups have developed in the Central
Java area. The Java Christian Churches (Geredja-Geredja Kristen
Djawa) have a Gereformeerd (Reformed) background (Cooley, 1968:
90). The Church or denomination was central in this tradition.
In this matter the Reformed mission was different from the
pietistic tradition. In the Reformed mission all missionary
work was channeled through the Church. Local churches in
Holland had direct relationship with local churches in
Indonesia--Utrecht with Purweredjo, Amsterdam with Jogja,
Rotterdam with Purbolinggo and etc.(Muller-Kruger, 1959:157-158).

The Churches in Central Java began in the cities rather
than the rural areas. Educational, medical and social work
were emphasized as a tool of evangelism. By 1937 there were

159 elementary schools and fifty secondary schools. Nine hospitals and a literature ministry played important parts in the
work (Cooley, 1968:91).
        The Churches of Central Java have experienced growth
since 1891. By 1933 some 15,000 members were reported but
this figure most likely included both the South Central and
North Central Java Churches (de Bruine, 1935:110). The report
in 1945 is likely accurate in recording 17,875 members (World
Christian Handbook, 1953:152). The figure in Cooley's book
for 1953 is likely a combination of the two Churches which at
that time numbered around 24,841. Since 1965 the Church has
experienced rapid growth, reaching a membership of 76,500 in
1967 (Cooley, 1968:6,7).
        The North Central Java Christian Church (Parepatan
Agung) has been associated with the names of Gottlob Bruckner.
Hoezoo and a Dutch lady, Mrs. Le Jolle. Mrs. Le Jolle actually
started the work by inviting Javanese to her home for evangelistic services. In 1857 the congregation moved to a small
town near Salatiga, Ngemoh, where it was led by an evangelist
from Modjowarno. When she returned to Holland, Mrs. Le Jolle
encouraged the congregation at Ermelo to send a missionary to
Ngemoh. This missionary, De Boer, arrived in Ngemoh in 1868
and served until his death in 1891. The Church spread over
north Central Java and became known as the Salatiga Mission
(Pekabaran Indjil Salatiga) (Muller-Kruger, 1959:162).
        The Church of north Central Java formed a more con-
gregational type of Church government than other Churches in
Java. The name of their organization, Parepatan Agung,
denotes a loose type of organization rather than a central
authority. In 1949 an attempt was made to unite the two
Churches in Central Java but the effort was short lived. In
1953 a group broke off and reestablished the Parepatan Agung
(Muller-Kruger, 1959:163).
        This Church has continued to advance. In the period
following the Communist failure of 1965 effective evangelistic
efforts both among former Communists and others who had no
contact with the Communist movement have proved fruitful. The
families of former Communists have been won in large numbers
(Thomson, 1968:12-13). There has been truly amazing evangelistic results in the mountains near Salatiga where churches
are being planted, using indigenous music, buildings and methods.
Thousands have been baptized. The Parepatan Agung demonstrates
the vitality of a separate tradition in evangelizing a population.
        The Java Evangelical Christian Church, located in the
region around Mount Muria on Java's northern coast, has a
Mennonite background. The strength of Islam on the north coast
lessened the early growth of the Church (Cooley, 1968:92).
Of this Church Muller-Kruger says, "With its conviction concerning adult or believers baptism, this Church brought to Java

a new note not heard since the last of the British Baptists who served in the area between 1811-1815" (Muller-Kruger, 1959: 163).

The Mennonite Missionary Society was founded in Holland in 1847 (Muller-Kruger, 1959:163) and in 1851 sent P. Jansz to Djapara where he worked for twenty years. He was able to baptize only sixteen men and twenty-four women. Numbers of children were also attending but due to the Mennonite conviction concerning believer's baptism were not counted as members (Cooley, 1959:164).

Jansz was the author of the tract "Mission Work through Opening Land". In this tract he stated his conviction that the village pattern was so strong in Java that opening new villages was the only way the Javanese could be evangelized. P. A. Jansz, the son of the pioneer, carried out this plan. In 1881 the village of Margoredjo was opened, in 1901 Margokerto and in 1925 Pakis. Anyone could live in these villages if he promised to not work on Sunday and attended services. The missionary remained the head of the village (Muller-Kruger, 1959:165).

These villages did not prove as fruitful as Jansz had anticipated. Considerable influence resulted from the hospital, clinic and leprosy ministry. After 1928, more stress was placed on working in the cities such as Kudus and Pati. In the cities Christian nurses, teachers, civil servants and students were gathered into congregations. These local congregations were often led by school teachers who as lay pastors were authorized to administer the sacraments (Cooley, 1968:92,93).

The Church experienced a slow growth. It suffered greatly during the World War and the Japanese occupation. The suffering was caused more from the fanatical Moslems than by the Japanese. Christians were killed and church buildings were burned (Muller-Kruger, 1959:165,166). However, the Muria Church proved its loyalty to Indonesia during the struggle for independence and thereby has been recognized and accepted (Cooley, 1968:93).

The figures on the growth of the Muria Church are slightly clouded by the fact that Cooley evidently gives the figure for total community and the Mennonite background of the Church leads them to list only baptized believers as members. In a letter dated February 16,1970, Adolf Ens gives the following historical account of the Church's growth. I would think the figures are very near correct as he has gathered them from the Mennonite Encyclopedia, the Mennonite Yearbook and from an original writing by Ds. Sastroadi (Ens. 1970:1.2).

According to Mr. Ens, the Church reported thirty-nine members in 1877 and 2,134 in 1932 (1970:1). Muller-Kruger notes a membership of 3,712 in 1933 which must be a figure for the community rather than membership (1959:166). The membership reached 5,284 in 1938 and had fallen, according to Ens, to

2,410 by 1953 (1970:1). Cooley reported 5,565 in 1953 (1968:6, 7). Muller-Kruger gives the membership figure for 1958 as 7,200 (1959:lampiran). The Mennonite Yearbook noted the membership in 1960 as 4,443 from where it grew to 4,800 a year later. In Ds. Sastroadi's paper, the membership is given as 8,400 in 1961, but this again must be the figure for the community. The Mennonite Yearbook reports 10,500 in 1963, a figure which agrees closely with Dr. Sastroadi's report of 15,300. Again the Mennonite Yearbook reports 13,600 in 1965, a healthy increase over 1963. In 1967, when Cooley gives the figure of 27,000 (1968:93), the Mennonite Yearbook notes 16,400 (Ens, 1970:1). The figure for membership in 1969 is 18,500 (Ens, 1970:1).

The drop in membership during the 1940s can perhaps be explained partly by the war, the general instability and the persecution from the Moslems. However, the apparent drop in membership during the fifties are most likely only statistical errors (Ens, 1970:2).

There is a four-fold increase in membership between 1959 and 1969. According to leaders of the Church, the increase began shortly before the 1965 Communist coup. However, the really rapid growth has been realized since 1966. The growth must be tied up with the spiritual void left by the failure of the Communists which left a multitude of disillusioned sympathizers. The Church's effective evangelistic ministry is also seen as a factor. The decree of the government that all Indonesians should have a religion without doubt inclined some to faith in Christ. In addition, as previously noted, some ex-Moslems who had embraced Communism, were not inclined to return to Islam but found new meaning for life in Christianity (Ens, 1970:2).

The Muria Church demonstrates the principle of working among homogeneous units as they have both a Javanese and a Chinese Church. In our Western anti-racism feeling, we must not overlook the fact that Christ cannot break down the middle wall of partition between men until first they are saved. Men prefer to become Christian by families, clans and tribes and worship with those who look like, dress like, talk like and think like they do. The policy of having churches for different ethnic groups is not an evidence of racism but rather an acknowledgement of the practicality of approaching evangelism in this fashion. Later, brotherhood, so desperately needed, will be achieved (see McGavran, 1970:198ff).

The Churches in West Java

The Sundanese people in West Java have proved resistant to the Gospel. The closely knit family structure which has been permeated by Islam has made the Sundanese culture largely impervious to the Gospel. The attempt to use Christian villages

in West Java proved uneffective. Schools and benevolent work
have not brought many turning to the Church. The Church in
West Java (Geredja Kristen Pasundan) reached a membership of
only 15,000 in 1967 (Cooley, 1968:6,7 and Kraemer, 1958:99-100).

Java therefore reveals some rather responsive peoples
and some highly resistant peoples. The Javanese with their
tolerance and less fanatical Islam have responded to the Gospel
in numbers truly amazing for a Moslem country. The Sundanese
and the Madurese have remained solidly impervious to the
Message of Salvation. Java is therefore a church growth contrast.

CHURCH GROWTH ON NEW GUINEA

The western portion of New Guinea, the world's largest
island, came under Indonesian control in 1963 at the conclusion
of the conflict with the Dutch. Claiming only 1.8 persons
per square kilometer, West New Guinea (Irian Barat) numbers
only about 860,000 persons (Cooley, 1968:60). Many of the
peoples of New Guinea live in the sealed off highland regions,
in valleys often at elevations of 4,000 to 8,000 feet. The
interior peoples are roughly divided into the Kapauku, the
Moni, the Uhuduni and the East and West Dani tribes (Bunda,
1963:1-3). The map on page 112 indicates the location of these
tribes and the coastal peoples--the Melanesians and Papuans
(Sterling, 1943:12).

First efforts at missionary work in West New Guinea
began around 1860 but all but three of the eighteen missionaries
sent out by the Utrecht Missionary Society up to 1900 were
forced to withdraw. The first twenty-five years produced meager
results as only twenty were baptized by 1878. More converts
were reported during the next fifty years. By 1931 there were
some 25,000 baptized members and in 1940, 80,000. By 1967 the
Church reported 170,000 members (Cooley, 1958:61).

Some of the most inspiring stories of rapid church
growth and missionary dedication have been written in the
highland interior of West New Guinea. In 1936 a Dutch flier,
J. F. Wissel, discovered three lakes, later named after him,
and also observed a concentration of population. By 1939
missionaries from the Christian and Missionary Alliance visited
the area and soon thereafter established a station among the
Kapauku tribe. World War II brought difficulties and finally
forced the missionaries to evacuate. The missionaries began
to return in 1946 and by 1953 there were some twenty-three CMA
missionaries serving in West New Guinea's highlands (Sunda,
1963:1-4). The CMA supported fifty-six missionaries in 1968
(Report of the Foreign Department of CMA, 1968:51).

The Evangelical Alliance Mission (TEAM) entered West
New Guinea in 1952. The first two missionaries in the area
were martyred but in 1970 the mission reports thirty-one

FIGURE 15
PEOPLE MOVEMENT MAP
OF NEW GUINEA

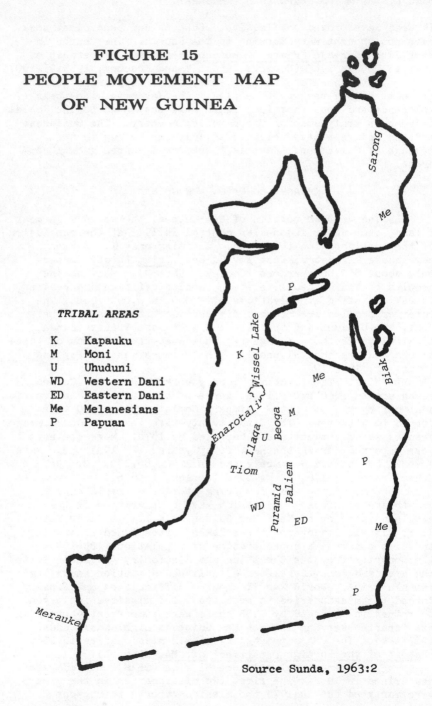

TRIBAL AREAS

K	Kapauku
M	Moni
U	Uhuduni
WD	Western Dani
ED	Eastern Dani
Me	Melanesians
P	Papuan

Source Sunda, 1963:2

missionaries, ninety churches, 3,415 members and 5,416 adherents who profess salvation but as yet are not baptized (Martin, 1970: 1-4).

Unevangelized Fields Mission, Inc. entered West New Guinea in 1952 also but it was 1957 before the first missionaries from North America arrived. Presently the mission counts thirty-six missionaries and forty churches. There is a total of 2,500 baptized members but may be as many as 30,000 believers in all. Most of the Unevangelized Fields Mission work is among the Dani tribe (Sarginson, 1970:1).

Regions Beyond Missionary Union entered New Guinea in 1957. They reported around twenty missionaries in 1967 (North American Protestant Ministries Overseas Directory, III-5). This mission also works largely among the Dani tribes (Sunda, 1963:6-7).

This study makes no effort to trace the history of all the unusual works of the Spirit in West New Guinea. Such material is available in other books. However, some illuminating chapters in the history of church growth--especially of the people movement type of growth have taken place in West New Guinea. To study the church growth lessons apparent in the history of the area is the purpose of this section.

The Christian and Missionary Alliance Mission in West New Guinea has experienced inspiring growth. When forced to leave the region in 1943, the CMA missionaries reported around 1,000 Kapuakus attending services and sixteen who had declared themselves Christian. When the missionaries returned in 1946, they found some still interested and others who had grown hostile. Baptisms totaled seventeen in 1947. The progress was very slow. Most of the converts came from the younger generation. It was 1957 before many adults were won.

There was an uprising among the Kapauku in 1956 which resulted in the destruction of houses, schools and the mission airplane and worse still the death of the Indonesian teacher and other Christians. Providentially, just before the uprising the missionaries and four of the Indonesian workers had left the village. The purpose of the uprising was the expulsion of the foreigners and their religion--both thought to be responsible for an epidemic among the pigs and the loss of influence on the part of the elders.

When the police put down the rebellion and restored order, it was a vindication for the younger men. Many felt that they could not return to the "old ways". A period of responsiveness and cooperation ensued. There is evidence that the Gospel began to flow through clans and villages. By 1957, 1,524 had been baptized and the figure reached 2,300 by 1961. The New Testament was translated into Kapauku and educational ministry had been undertaken (Sunda, 1963:9-13).

It was 1956 before a station was established among the Uhunduni peoples. This station was located in the Ilaga Valley inhabited by some 1,400 Uhunduni and 5,000 Dani tribesmen. The

showed little interest but there was receptiveness among the
Uhundunis (Sunda, 1963:15). The situation in the Ilaga Valley
underscores a basic principle in church growth theory--the
receptivity of homogeneous units. A homogeneous unit is some
section of society which has some common characteristics.
Missions must recognize and evangelize these units, be they
tribes, clans, language groups, or minority groups (McGavran,
1970:85). The importance of homogeneous units is clearly seen
by McGavran who writes:

> *Mankind is not one vast homogeneous mass; it is made*
> *up of many societies, classes, castes and tribes.*
> *Each receives or resists the Gospel in its own time*
> *and its own way. If we are to see humanity correctly*
> *we must see it as a great mosaic, each piece of which,*
> *though it is in contact with the others, has its own*
> *color and texture. That many pieces are today re-*
> *sponsive is of paramount importance to the Church as*
> *it engages in mission (1966:769).*

Witness was directed to these responsive peoples of
the Uhunduni tribes. On May 25,1957 after several weeks of
discussion among themselves, twenty leading men of one clan
came to the missionary to discuss "declaring their faith in
Christ and burning their charms." On May 26, one hundred
thirty men and boys and ninety women and girls declared their
faith in Christ. They together burned their charms and other
evidences of their former animistic religion. In August another clan of about sixty Uhundunis burned their charms. Subsequently the Gospel traveled to the Beoga Valley, some eight
to fifteen days journey from Ilaga Valley. In January 1958
four groups of about 1,000 people burned their charms and
declared for Christ (Sunda, 1963:16-17).
      Intensive instruction was given the converts in the
Ilaga Valley so that by April 1958, 130 had been baptized.
Other clans and villages continued to declare for Christ and
burn their charms until in 1963 most of the Unhundunis in the
Ilaga Valley--around 1,400 people--had become adherents of
Christianity. In the course of a few years most of the
Uhunduni population of Beoga Valley also followed Christianity.
Sunda calls the response of the Uhundunis in these two valleys
"good examples of 'clean sweeps' in people movements " (1963:
17-18).
      The movement among the Uhunduni in these two valleys
are almost classic examples of people movements. The movement
to Christ from among the Uhunduni was not a mass movement but
a series of decisions by small, homogeneous groups. One group
would decide this month and another several months later.
Numbers were achieved but only with the passage of several

months and years (McGavran, 1970:297).

The movement among the Uhunduni did not eventuate
in nominal Christianity as the Uhunduni have been extremely
active in evangelistic outreach--both among their own tribes
and also later carrying the Gospel over to the Dani tribes
(Sunda, 1963:18-19 and 23). McGavran has pointed out that the
assumption that Christians from people movements are nominal
Christians is usually based on prejudice rather than fact.
Nominalism is the problem of all Churches, not just people
movement Churches. "People Movements (sic) in themselves do
not encourage the production of nominal Christians" (McGavran,
1955:71).

The Uhunduni Christians came to faith through
multi-individual decisions as entire clans and families together expressed their determination to follow Christ. It
is both proper and desirable that peoples come to Christ in
groups as some social entity chooses together to follow
Christianity. Of multi-individual decision, Tippett says,

> *The period of decision for a communal group may be
> a long road. It may spread over years of village or
> family discussion, as individuals, one by one, come
> to the position where they can at last say that they
> are of one mind, and when they can burn their fetishes
> as a total group. This is a* multi-individual *decision
> (1967a:4).*

McGavran adds the idea of mutually interdependent conversion
to the discussion. Not only does he insist on the validity
of multi-individual conversion but declares that each one
making the decision intimately knows the others involved and
takes the step in view of what the others are going to do.
A people movement then becomes "...a series of multi-individual,
mutually interdependent conversions" (1970:302-303).

There was intensive instruction of the Uhunduni converts, a factor of extreme importance in any people movement.
The witness training school trained national workers to in-
struct those who would then train those coming to faith (Sunda,
1963:17). Training and other postbaptismal care is demanded
for people movements. To neglect postbaptismal care is to
invite failure of any people movement. "A people movement does
not involve careless accessions or hurried baptisms" (McGavran,
1970:297).

The miracle of the Uhunduni Church points to several
factors used by the Spirit of God to bring it about. The
missionaries seized the opportunity to disciple a prepared
and responsive people. The Uhunduni were prepared by their
own prophecies and expectations of some eternal truth that
would come. This eternal principle, called hai, was used as a
point of contact by the missionaries. Furthermore, the Uhunduni

were tired of war and searching for a way of peace. Very important was the decision of the missionaries to try to win the adults and their willingness to seek and accept group converions. The use of the local language and the stressing of the obligation of the Uhunduni to witness all played important parts in the movement (Sunda, 1963:19-22).

People movements are important to Christian missions. A quality is conveyed to the Christian Church through people movements which individual action seldom gives. Moreover, McGavran says, "At least two-thirds of all converts in Asia, Africa and Oceania have come to Christian faith through people movements" (1970:298). People movements are God-given and should be eagerly sought by Christian missions (McGavran, 1955: 68). McGavran defines people movements in the following words, each phrase of which is all important:

> *A people movement results from the joint decision*
> *of a number of individuals--whether five or five*
> *hundred--all from the same people, which enables*
> *them to become Christians without social dislocation,*
> *while remaining in full contact with their non-Christian*
> *relatives, thus enabling other groups of that people,*
> *across the years, after suitable instruction, to come*
> *to similar decisions and form Christian churches made*
> *up exclusively of members of that people (1970:297-298).*

The Gospel crossed a bridge from the Uhundunis in the Ilaga Valley to their neighbors from the Dani tribes. Some of the Danis burned their charms and declared for Christ. This started a chain reaction that led to over 2,000 Dani Christians in the Ilaga Valley. The news of these charm burnings spread to the Western Dani and to a lesser extent to the Eastern Dani. Numbers of Dani from the North Baliem area visited Ilaga and returned to their homes with glowing accounts of what they had seen and heard (Sunda, 1963:23-25).

The Danis continued to show interest. In December 1959 a Dani man from Ilaga preached to many of the Dani in the Baliem Valley, telling them they should make inter-clan war settlements and prepare to burn their charms. In 1960 missionaries and other Danis from Ilaga began a journey to preach in Baliem Valley. Large crowds welcomed them and the people desired to burn their charms. Some of the Australian Baptist missionaries felt the people did not understand enough to burn their charms and for this reason in the Baptist areas of North Baliem the tribesmen tied up their charms but others went ahead and burned them despite the protests of the Baptist missionaries (Sunda, 1963:26-27).

On February 13, 1960 over 8,000 Dani gathered in the North Baliem Valley. The Ilaga Dani preachers, themselves baptized only a few months before and still clad in their Dani dress (or undress) conducted the service. At the end of the service, some 5,000 Danis prepared a pyre and placed their charms upon it, often giving a shout of joy as they did. When all was prepared, the fire was lit. Around 3,000 of those assembled were afraid to burn their sacred ancestor charms. They were still of "two hearts". Before the night was over many of them had decided and on the following day around 3,000, having "found their hearts" participated in the outward dem-onstration of committment to the new "Jesus way". In two days time 8,000 had burned their charms and declared for Christ (Sunda, 1963:26-28).

The Dani miracle points to two principles, both enor-mously important to church growth. First, the Gospel crossed a bridge of relationships from the Uhunduni tribes to the Dani tribes and then from these Dani to their tribesmen in other areas. This is the natural course of people movements. The Gospel reaches to one people, overflows into a neighboring people across relational lines, floods this people and then overflows to still a third people. This conviction has been expressed by Donald McGavran in his important book, The Bridges of God. In another work McGavran has said, "Relationship, friendship and business bridge gulfs on every hand " (1959: 56).

The experience of the Uhunduni and Dani Churches also demonstrates the importance of a decisive encounter and commit-ment in conversion. For the animist to retain his animistic charms, fetishes or idols is to face the extreme danger of reversion. Tippett says, "With people who have just come out of animism there is a continuity of temptation when parapherna-lia are not destroyed" (1967b:109). The burning of the charms is the power encounter that gives a definite and public de-claration of intent to leave the old religion and follow the Jesus way. This declaration is made in the thought-forms and accepted ways of the culture. Such a power encounter is both a symbolic act and a step of faith for the convert (Ibid., 110). The power encounter is all important in the conversion process--especially for those of animistic background.

The Christian and Missionary Alliance has continued serving in the highlands of West New Guinea. Their report for 1968 counted 18,022 baptized members in 237 organized churches and ninety-eight unorganized congregations. Over 4,375 in-quirers were numbered. Significantly, there were 337 studying in full-time Bible School and 476 in short term Bible Schools. (Report of the Foreign Department, 1968:48-49). Surely, these movements have been and continue to be miracles of God.

The Australian Baptist Missionary Society, in coopera-tion with the CMA, UFM and RBMU, moved into West New Guinea in 1955 and settled in the region of Pyramid Mountain in North Baliem Valley. Their ministry was thus directed primarily to Dani peoples (Dube, n. d.:1). Stations were opened in four

different areas by 1961 and medical and educational ministries
were undertaken. One missionary wrote, "Early in the Missions
(sic) development here we realized the necessity of rapidly
bringing the people to a literate state" (Craig, 1963:1-2).
The medical work has attempted to meet the tremendous medical
needs of the area and has included training Danis in medical
skills (Dube, n. d.:2).

The Australian Baptists for a long time received very
little response from the Danis (Dube, n. d. 2). This is
surprising since the CMA missionaries were experiencing the
tremendous movement among the Danis in the Baliem Valley in
the early 1960s. When any Church is not growing in a certain
area, while other Churches in the same region are experiencing
growth, it is imperative for the non-growing Church to ask
why. Sunda mentioned that some of the Baptist missionaries
resisted the charm burnings by the Danis in 1960 (1963:26-27).
Perhaps the resistance to the moving of the Gospel at that
particular time slowed the Baptist advance. In addition, Dube
notes that the early period was concerned with the missionaries
learning the previously unwritten language, trying to understand the culture of the people and gradually sowing the seed
of the Gospel among them (Dube, n. d.: 2). The Baptists may
have been the victims of the policy of gradualism. For whatever reason, in 1962 the Baptists numbered only two churches
and eighty members (Dube, 1970:1).

The Baptist churches also, like the CMA churches, experienced the difficulty of an uprising against the new religion. The progressive freedom from the old superstitions
on the part of many Danis incited some of the chiefs, who
felt they were losing power, to instigate an uprising, resulting
in the death of several Christians and the burning of buildings. The uprising was put down by police action only after
much suffering and the destruction of many villages. The
final result of the uprising was a new sense of unity and
response on the part of many. Villages, contrary to accepted
Dani custom, were rebuilt and the work of the churches continued (Craig, 1963:4-5).

When response came to the churches aided by the
Australian Baptists, it came in fantastic numbers. The break
came after Good Friday services. The missionaries had discovered a new Dani word which meant "in my place". For the
first time they were able to explain to the Dani people that
Christ had died for them and in their place. Early on the
morning after the Good Friday service a red eyed Dani tribesman
came to the missionary's door and in picturesque Dani language
told him that during the night his "turned around heart had
come to him". Thousands of other Danis came to listen to the
"new talk". Bible Schools commenced, village services started,
baptismal classes were held and the first baptisms observed
and churches were planted in two villages by 1962 (Dube, n.d.:2).

Phenomenal growth was recorded after 1962 among these
tribesmen. By 1964 the Baptists were reporting 104 churches
and 1,100 members. While the number of churches remained the
same for 1965 and 1966 and declined to 81 in 1968 and 79 in
1969, this does not indicate a slowing of growth but only the
fact that some congregations were combining. The membership
figures show tremendous increases. In 1965 the membership had
grown to 1,500 and then doubled in the 1966 report, reaching
3,000. The report for 1967 noted 4,850 members, 5,450 in 1968
and 7,174 members for 1969 in seventy-nine congregations (Dube,
1970:1). God has seldom worked greater miracles than these
figures indicate.

The progress of the Gospel in the highlands of West
New Guinea demonstrate the power of people movements in discipling the multitudes of the earth. The accounts of God's
miracles in New Guinea must stand as some of the most inspiring of all missionary victories. God has richly blessed the
noble and sacrificial efforts of his people, both missionary
and national, who have labored in this fertile field and
brought from it the abundant harvest prepared by the Lord.

SOME INTERISLAND CHURCHES

While most of Indonesia's Churches are ethnic Churches,
serving in a certain region and primarily peoples of one
ethnic group, there are several that are serving on various
islands and among differing peoples. One such group is the
Seventh Day Adventists. The Adventists have their work divided
into East and West Indonesian Missions. The Eastern division,
with headquarters in Menado, includes Celebes, Sangir-Talaud
and the Moluccas. The Western division, with headquarters in
Djakarta, serves Java, Sumatra, Borneo and Southeast Indonesia.
A hospital in Bandung and a printing ministry as well as
clinics in several regions supplement the evangelistic and
educational work of the Adventists. In 1967 the Adventists
reported forty missionaries and 36,000 adult baptized members
(Cooley, 1968:48).

The Christian and Missionary Alliance (CMA) began work
in Indonesia in 1929 (Cooley, 1968:46). In 1930 the CMA had
nine missionaries in Indonesia and were projecting work (some
through national workers) in Makassar (where the headquarters
was located), Bali, Lombok, Sumbawa and Borneo. Translation
work was progressing in attempting to get tracts from Malay
to the different heart languages of the regions served (Report
of the Foreign Department of the CMA, 1930:43-46). By 1940
the missionary staff had grown to thirty-nine, the number of
national workers to 141 and total membership to 13,093. Total
baptisms in 1940 were 2,049. The CMA report noted seventy-one
churches, fifty outstations and 208 students in the Bible
School in Makassar (Report of the Foreign Department of the

CMA, 1940:50,51). Work had been opened in Buton, Moeni, South
Sumatra, Banka and Billition in addition to those areas already
served a decade before (Cooley, 1968:46).

The difficulties of war years are reflected in the
report of 1950 which counted a gain of only 2,000, reaching
15,205 total members. The same report claimed 132 churches
and 122 outstations. There were forty-nine missionaries and
1,320 baptisms included in the report (Report of the Foreign
Department of the CMA, 1950:48-49).

The CMA churches continued to grow and by 1960 reported
24,035 members in 202 organized churches and seventy-eight
unorganized groups. The churches reported only 682 baptisms
for 1960. The churches were assisted by 223 national workers
and fifty-one missionaries. Publication work was continued
as well as Bible Schools and other training ministries (Report
of the Foreign Department of the CMA, 1961:44-45 and 80-82).

The statistics are somewhat confusing as we study 1964
and 1965. The 1964 report claimed 27,308 members in 220
churches and forty-two unorganized congregations (Report of the
Foreign Department of the CMA, 1965:48,49). The next report
noted 3,504 baptisms, 343 churches, forty-seven unorganized
congregations and a total membership of 47,746. There were
fifty-four missionaries and 377 national workers (Report of the
Foreign Department of the CMA, 1966:48-49). No explanation
of the 20,000 jump is given but the answer could well be that
the 1964 report was incomplete, although it is not marked so
in the report.

The CMA churches evidently reaped the same harvest
as other Churches in Indonesia after 1965 as the report for
1967 notes 50,380 members in 410 churches and thirty-six unorganized congregations (but the figures of churches and congregations are noted as incomplete). Two thousand one hundred
seventy-eight baptisms were reported in 1967. Five hundred
fifteen national workers were aided by fifty-three missionaries
(Report of the Foreign Department of the CMA, 1968:48-50)

The CMA in Indonesia now has one national organization
which is known as the Gospel Tabernacle Christian Church (Kemah
Indjil Geredja Masehi Indonesia). Both the publication ministry and the Jaffray School of Theology located in Makassar
are under the authority of the national organization (Cooley,
1968:47). The CMA has a widespread ministry grounded solidly
in church planting, national leadership and adequate missionary
support.

Only with difficulty can accurate statistics be gathered concerning the Chinese Churches in Indonesia. There are
several Churches made up almost entirely of Indonesians of
Chinese descent. Many churches, especially in West Java, are
predominately Chinese in membership and other churches have a
mixture of Chinese and Malay members. Of the total Chinese
community in Indonesia, at least 263,000 or 8.8 percent are

Christian. Even more significant is the fact that Christians constitute 17.5 percent of the Peranakan (Indonesian born) Chinese (Cooley, 1968:99-100).

Chinese evangelization has been aided greatly in former years by Christian evangelists from Asia. Foremost among these was Dr. John Sung who in 1937 and 1939 attracted thousands of Chinese to his meetings and proved to be a strong stimulus to the growth of Chinese Churches in Indonesia.

In addition, many converts were able to win their families, which meant that the Chinese Churches were composed largely of family units. The financial condition of the Chinese people in general and therefore the churches also, has strengthened the growth of the Chinese Churches in Indonesia (Cooley, 1968:100-101). The Chinese Churches in general have better equipment and more paid leadership than other national groups.

Some representative Chinese Churches are the East Java Indonesia Christian Church (Geredja Kristen Indonesia, Djawa Timur) with a membership in 1967 of 15,000. The Central Java Indonesia Christian Church (Geredja Kristen Indonesia, Djawa Tengah) has a membership of 16,000 in twenty-six congregations. The West Java Indonesia Christian Church (Geredja Kristen Indonesia, Djawa Barat) has a membership of around 2,000 in thirty congregations. The Church of Christ (Geredja Kristus) has a membership of 4,000 in eight congregations while the United Muria Christian Church of Indonesia (Persatuan Geredja-Geredja Kristen Indonesia di Muria) has a membership of 5,000 in twelve congregations (Cooley, 1968:102-103).

A very vital and rapidly growing expression of Christianity in Indonesia is found among the Pentecostal Churches. Pentecostals appeared in Indonesia in the 1920s. The movement had a special appeal to the Eurasians who were nominal members of the Protestant Churches and felt neglected. Many Chinese, especially Indonesian born, were also attracted to Pentecostal Churches. Cooley mentions that recent estimates of Pentecostals show a membership for those Pentecostals outside the Indonesian Council of Churches 900,000 and for those associated with the Council around 438,000. Cooley states that both these figures are probably considerably inflated (1968:105).

Among the Pentecostal Churches in Indonesia, first to join the Council of Churches was the Church of Jesus the Messiah (Geredja Isa Almasih), an autonomous Church from the beginning (Cooley, 1968:106). This Church was founded in Semarang on December 18, 1945 under the leadership of Pastor Tan Hok Tjoan. The first baptism was observed in April 1946 when thirty souls were baptized by immersion. The Church now has twelve congregations, some as far from Semarang as Makassar, and 13,910 members. A Bible institute was founded in 1967 to train pastors and evangelists. This Church continues strong

evangelistic ministry to a primarily Chinese membership
(Tanutama, 1970:1-3).

Another Pentecostal Church, the Bethel Full Gospel
Church (<u>Geredja</u> <u>Bethel</u> <u>Indjil</u> <u>Sepenuh</u>) in 1964 reported 100,000
members. This is a national Church which had over 500 congre-
gations on Java, Sumatra and New Guinea. The churches have a
sense of local autonomy. The Pentecostal Churches are growing
rapidly, with members coming largely, but not exclusively,
from the Chinese community (Cooley, 1968:107).

CONCLUSION

This survey is by no means exhaustive. Many Churches
have not been mentioned and the stories of those discussed
have not been completely told. The graph on page 123 shows
the relative memberships of some of these major Churches
of Indonesia. The material given should, however, demonstrate
the miracles God has wrought in Indonesia and relate the
Christian situation of the country. It is with these and
other evangelistic Churches that Baptists will join hands to
evangelize the other millions among the islands of Indonesia.

FIGURE 16

GRAPH OF COMPARATIVE MEMBERSHIP

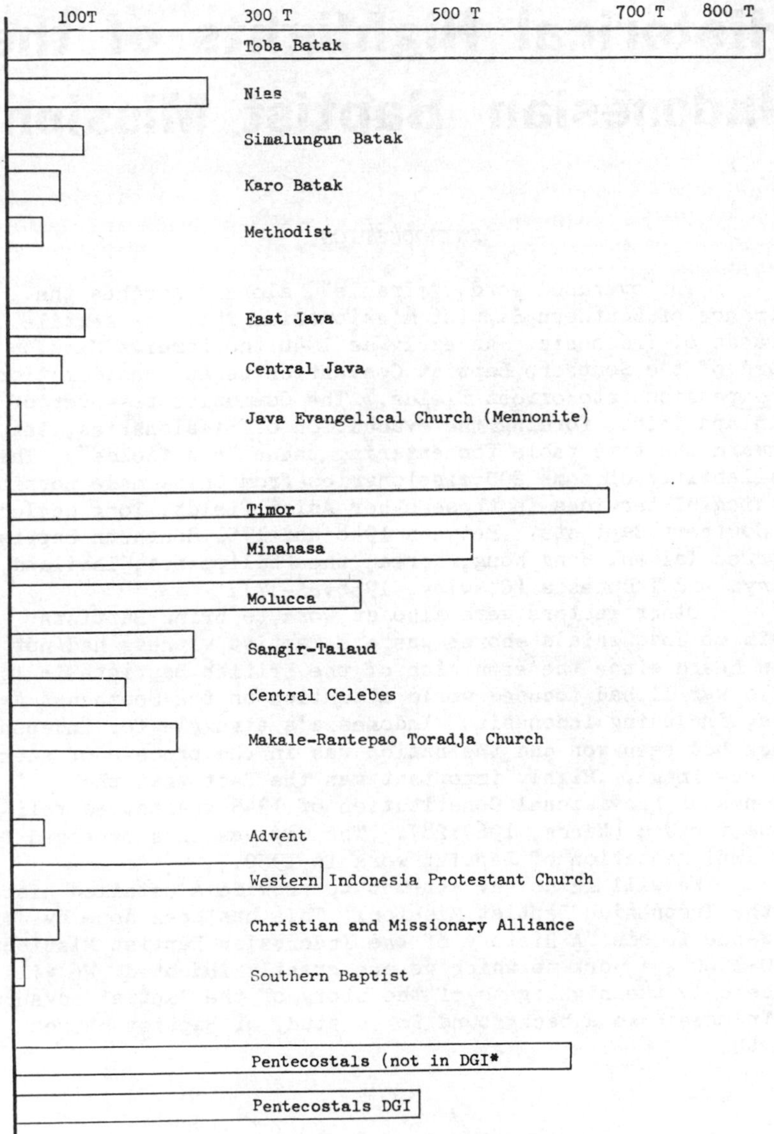

* Indonesian Council of Churches

4

Historical Highlights of the Indonesian Baptist Mission

INTRODUCTION

The overused word, "miracle", alone describes the entrance of Southern Baptist missionaries into the fertile islands of Indonesia. As early as 1948 the Foreign Mission Board of the Southern Baptist Convention began consideration of expansion into orient fields. The Communist takeover of mainland China, forcing the evacuation of missionaries, set forward the time table for entering these "new fields". The availability of some 200 missionaries from China made possible meaningful services in these other Asian fields, long neglected by Southern Baptists. Between 1948 and 1951 Southern Baptists entered Taiwan, Hong Kong, Korea, the Philippines, Thailand, Malaya and Indonesia (Crawley, 1958:25-]7).

Other factors were also at work to bring Baptists again to Indonesia's shores where a Baptist witness had not been heard since the expulsion of the British Baptists in 1815. World War II had focused world attention on the Southeast Asia area, including Indonesia. Indonesia's struggle for independence had been won and the nation was in the process of seeking its new image. Highly important was the fact that the Indonesian Provisional Constitution of 1945 guaranteed religious freedom (Nance, 1969:28). The way was thus prepared for the implementation of Baptist work in 1950.

We will in no way attempt to provide a detailed history of the Indonesian Baptist Mission. This has been done by John I. Nance in his "A History of the Indonesian Baptist Mission; 1950-1960", a work to which we are greatly indebted. We will trace only the highlights of the story of the Baptist advance in Indonesia as a background for a study of Baptist church growth.

GAINING ENTRANCE 1950-1953

In 1950 Dr. Baker James Cauthen, then Secretary for
the Orient for the Southern Baptist Foreign Mission Board,
surveyed Indonesia, Malaya and India. After conferring with
missionaries, pastors and government officials, Cauthen concluded that since no more than 150 missionaries from all
Christian missionary societies combined were serving among
the 70,000,000 Indonesians, additional ministry was needed.
Cauthen stressed that over 2,000,000 Chinese lived in Indonesia
and only some 20,000 (this was likely a mistaken figure) were
gathered into sixty-nine churches. Cauthen felt these Chinese
offered a great potential field for China missionaries. He
indicated that Baptists should enter Indonesia with members
of the China staff who could witness among these Chinese (Nance,
1969:23-29).

Seemingly the first plan upon entering Indonesia was
witness among the overseas Chinese living in the islands. In
the outworking of the Mission's expansion a different direction
was taken so that in time the majority of the members of the
Baptist churches came from non-Chinese peoples. The decision
not to concentrate exclusively on Chinese Indonesians was a
significant and far reaching one. There was merit in the fact
that the Chinese were seen as a separate ethnic group.

During the Foreign Mission Conference in 1951, ten
missionaries conferred with Cauthen concerning work on Java
and the group selected Buren Johnson, Stockwell B. Sears and
Charles Cowherd to be the pioneers to Java (Nance, 1969:30).
These three landed in Djakarta on Christmas Day, 1951, commissioned to investigate possibilities of Baptist mission work in
Indonesia (Crawley, 1958:67). Sweeping changes in the government structure of Indonesia had taken place between Cauthen's
1950 visit and the arrival of the pioneers in 1951.

Efforts to obtain permission to enter Indonesia were
aided both by the gracious and helpful attitude of Indonesian
officials and by the assistance of friends both within and
without Indonesia. The efforts were slightly hindered by a
lack of enthusiasm on the part of both the Dutch controlled
Mission Consultant and the National Council of Churches of
Indonesia. However, Mr. Abednego, head of the Protestant
section of the Ministry of Religion, requested more information
about the Baptists. After being informed of Baptist principles
and methods, he called the three Baptist missionaries for
conference, to which Dr. Cauthen was likewise invited. Letters
from M. Theron Rankin, Executive Secretary of the Foreign
Mission Board and Mr. J. W. Decker, secretary of the
International Missionary Council, were presented to further
introduce Baptists. At this conference there was a careful
presentation of Baptist principles and plans and an explanation

of why Baptists found it impossible to work organizationally
in the framework of the National Council of Churches. The
distinction between religious tolerance and religious freedom
was accepted by the Indonesian officials (Nance, 1969:42).

In the midst of a difficult time due partly to the
failure of the Indonesian cabinet, on the twenty-fifth of
February 1952, just two months after the three pioneer
Baptist missionaries had begun their quest for permission,
the Ministry of Religion and its head, Mr. Abednego, gave
official approval to the Indonesian Baptist Mission. In nine
months the picture had totally changed from a tentative seeking
to an official opportunity. The Mission had formal government
approval, the first missionaries were in the country with
permanent visas, other missionaries were preparing to sail and
the work of a new mission had been born (Crawley, 1958:68-69).

Gaining admission to the country was but the first
step. The Baptists immediately sought ways to proclaim the
Gospel and disciple the Indonesian people. The next years
saw the opening of churches in most of the major cities of
Java, with medical, publication and training ministries following as time and personnel made them possible.

THE FIRST CHURCHES AND CENTERS 1952-1955

Bandung, West Java

The Baptist missionaries held their first worship
service in the mountain city of Bandung on May 11, 1952.
Twenty-three persons attended the English language worship
service led by Charles Cowherd in the Masonic Lodge (Nichols,
1958:38). American, British and Dutch citizens were in attendance (Nance, 1969:54-55). Among the worshippers was the
Yo Tjin Thay family, who later became members. This family
helped in the organization of each of the five churches and
missions in Bandung. Their son, Billy Mathias (Yo), now serves
as the editor of the Indonesian Baptist paper, (Suara Baptis
(Willis, 1968:12).

The First Baptist Church of Bandung was organized on
November 23, 1952, just eleven months after the first missionaries had arrived. Under the leadership of Charles Cowherd
the church augmented the English worship services with Sunday
School programs in English, Dutch, Chinese and Indonesian.
Seven members were baptized in the borrowed baptistry of the
Seventh-day Adventist Church and took their places among the
twenty charter members (Nance, 1969:51-58). By June 1953 the
membership had reached thirty-six, including people of five
nationalities--Indonesian, Dutch, Chinese, British and American
(Minutes, 1953:17).

The church continued to worship in the Masonic Lodge
for about three years until an old residence was purchased and

remodeled for a church building. By the end of its fourth
year the church in Bandung had a membership of one hundred
thirty-five, with a Sunday School that averaged about three
hundred (Nichols, 1958:38-39). In later years the First Baptist
Church was joined by six other churches and chapels in the city
of Bandung (Minutes, 1968:151). Bandung also became the location of the Baptist publication ministry.

In Bandung, on November 28, 1952, eight missionaries
formally banded themselves together to form the Indonesian
Mission of the Southern Baptist Convention. W. B. Johnson was
chosen Chairman and Darlyne Sears, secretary. In January 1953
the executive committee, composed of the four male members of
the mission, approved Bandung, Djakarta, Surabaja and Semarang
as the cities for new mission stations (Minutes, 1953:26-27).

Djakarta, West Java

The mission office was of necessity located in the
capital city, Djakarta. Buren Johnson and his wife took up
residence there in January 1953. By October a large factory
building had been purchased and was in the process of being
remodeled for a church and Mission office space (Minutes, 1953:
18). Significantly, the first residence in Djakarta was located near the former residence of William Robinson, the
English Baptist who had proclaimed the Gospel there 140 years
previously (Nichols, 1958:41).

By April 1953 a small group of Indonesian believers,
under the leadership of Pastor Ais Pormes, were meeting in
the home of the Johnsons. Pastor Pormes had been converted
under unusual circumstances on his home island near Banda.
Attempting to enter a Dutch church for a Christmas program,
Pormes was refused admittance by the Dutch door keeper. Crush-
ed with disappointment the young man cried out in his heart,
"Oh God, they have closed the doors of the church against me,
but I know you have not closed the doors of heaven against
me!" He traces his salvation to that experience (Nichols,
1958:20-21).

The crash of an American bomber in January 1944 start
a chain of events of far reaching significance in the life ⌐
Ais Pormes. Helping to rescue the injured Americans, Porm
then hitched a ride on the plane that came to evacuate th
airmen to Australia. After studying several years in A'
Pormes journeyed to America where he was ordained by a
church. He returned to Indonesia in 1952 and began t
a group of his fellow islanders in Djakarta. Conta'
with the Baptist Mission and this small group beca'
leus of the Calvary Baptist Church which was late
(Nichols, 1958:21).

The little group meeting in the home c
varied from twenty-five to fifty. They cont⁴

the missionaries' home until the building was remodeled. Sixteen converts were received in the first three months (Minutes,
1953:18). The Calvary Baptist Church of Djakarta was organized
on May 1,1955 with forty-two charter members. Ais Pormes was
called as pastor. During the year of organization, some
thirty-four persons had been baptized (Minutes, 1955:46).
By 1968 Baptists in Djakarta counted four churches, all
self-supporting, two chapels and a membership of 865 (Minutes,
1968:151).

Surabaja, East Java

The third center of Baptist ministry, Surabaja, the
second largest city in Indonesia, was opened when the Stockwell
Sears family moved there in January 1953 (Nichols, 1958:73).
Through contact with a friend who had attended the same high
school with Stockwell Sears in China, the missionaries obtained
the opportunity of teaching English in a Chinese high school.
Five of the first six converts came from students in this
high school and invaluable contacts with the Chinese community
were realized (Minutes, 1953:19).
The Surabaja missionaries received permission to use
the chapel of Christ Church, which served the British community
and on March 1, 1953 held the first Baptist worship service,
using the English language. Of the nineteen persons attending,
nine later became charter members of the Immanuel Baptist
Church (Nance, 1969:63). The report of the Surabaja station
in 1953 noted twenty-three professions of faith, sixteen
baptisms and four additions by transfer. On November 22, 1953
the Immanuel Baptist Church was organized with sixteen charter
members. On June 7, 1954 ground was broken for the first
building for this congregation (Minutes, 1954:30-31).
An important event is recorded in the history of the
Baptist Church in Surabaja. Sears had written that there were
no Baptists in Surabaja. Later he found that there were congregations, who without knowing anything about Baptists, as
such, were preaching and practicing Baptist principles. These
congregations were independent, self-supporting groups that
practiced believer's baptism by immersion. Several leaders
of these congregations approached Sears about the possibilities
of becoming Baptists. The Baptist missionaries discouraged
this procedure. Friendly relations were maintained but out-
right merger was not effected. This wise decision avoided
any misunderstanding of Baptist intentions in Indonesia (Nance,
1969:64-65). The Mission has wisely steered away from any
attempts at proselyting other Christian groups. By-law number
eighteen in the constitution of the Mission makes clear the
Mission's rule against encouraging any non-Baptist group becoming Baptist or even changing their name to Baptist (Minutes,
1968:21).

Surabaja has proved a fertile field for Baptist ministry. In 1968 there were two organized churches, six chapels
and a total membership of 932 (Minutes, 1968:1515). Several
outstanding leaders have come from the churches in Surabaja.
Thus far, almost all the work is done within the city and little
outreach into the surrounding rural areas has been realized.
An attempted opening of the island of Madura proved unsuccessful but a probe into Djember in deep East Java, has planted a
church.

Semarang, Central Java

In July 1954 Baptists occupied their fourth Mission
station, the Central Java city of Semarang. The first Sunday
in Semarang the three missionaries, Buford and Mary Frances
Nichols and Catherine Walker, gathered with Samuel Sarendauta,
who had come to attend the projected seminary, for the first
worship service. Although several had promised to attend, the
four waited for over an hour but no one joined them. Visitation
and newspaper announcements resulted in twenty-nine attending
the worship service on August 1, 1954 (Nance, 1969:70).
By April 1955 seventeen baptisms testified to the
evangelistic fruit of the Semarang church. Services were held
in both Indonesian and English. The Seteran Baptist Church
(later named Sion) was organized in 1955 with twenty-four
charter members. A second church, planted near the site of
the seminary, reported twenty-five who were awaiting baptism
in 1955 (Minutes, 1955:48).
The missionaries in Semarang have been occupied with
the seminary from the beginning. However, evangelistic work
has not gone unattended. This fact is attested to by the
statistics of 1968 that show Semarang to have the largest
membership of any station in which Baptists are working. In
1968 Semarang reported three organized churches, eighteen
chapels and a membership of 1,720 (Minutes, 1968:161).

Kediri, East Java

After months of planning, negotiating and frustration,
the Baptists settled on Kediri as the location for their first
medical mission work in Indonesia. The first three missionaries
to Kediri were all medical personnel and all women. Ruth Ford
and Everley Hayes, nurses who had previous experience in China,
and Dr. Kathleen Jones arrived in Kediri in late 1954 and early
1955 (Nichols, 1958:118). Because the three ladies were
flooded with the medical work in the clinic, evangelistic
ministry was limited to what could be done on Sundays and what
could be done during clinic hours (Minutes, 1955:47).
A seminary student came in February of 1955 and greatly
increased the evangelistic ministry of the clinic. A Sunday

School attendance of over 100 and a worship service attendance
of thirty to forty was reported (Minutes, 1955:47). An
evangelistic missionary joined the medical missionaries in
early 1956. The first service at the location later to house
the hospital was held in December 1955, exactly four years
after the arrival of the first missionaries (Nance, 1969:92).
Sunday Schools were being held in two centers, at Bangsal and
at the Semampir site on the riverside. In July 1956 the total
Sunday School attendance for both centers was 584. Worship
services were attended by 137 adults and young people. While
Kediri was the latest of the five major centers entered by
Baptists, Sunday School attendance has increased faster in
Kediri than in other places (Nichols, 1958:130-131).

        Children's work has been important to the growth of
the churches in Kediri. The fruit of the evangelistic efforts
are attested by the fact that Kediri in 1968 reported 1,592
members in three organized churches and twenty-two chapels
(Minutes, 1968:161). Many leaders for the Indonesian churches
have come from the work in Kediri.

        Thus, by 1956, five years after their arrival, Baptists
had opened stations for evangelistic, medical and seminary
work. Five cities were occupied by missionaries and churches
had been planted in each city. A church was planted in
Surakarta as an outreach of Semarang but no other centers made
an appearance on the mission records until the Minutes of 1962.

EXPANSION AND DEVELOPMENT 1955-1969

        The period 1955-1969 provided the Baptist churches in
Indonesia opportunity to expand and develop in every area of
their ministry. New stations were opened, new churches planted,
special campaigns promoted and new ministries begun. Nation-
wide activities were promoted with advantageous results.
Churches and institutions continued to expand.

New Stations and Cities

        The opening of stations in Bandung, Surabaja, Djakarta,
Semarang and Kediri had been accomplished by 1955 but it was
1959 before the next station was officially opened in Solo
(Surakarta). Evangelistic outreach to the Solo area began
from Semarang. In 1956 a student from the seminary preached
Tjangkiring, a village near Solo. A high school student,
forced to leave his home because of his Moslem family's opposition to his conversion, moved to Solo and requested Bible study
leadership. The Bible study group grew into a small congregation of believers. The small number in the congregation did
not blind the Semarang missionaries to the possibilities in
Solo. They called for reinforcements to take advantage of
the open door (Minutes, 1956:36).

In 1958 the Semarang Station report noted that
twenty-nine converts had been baptized in Solo and continued
to point out the need for missionary personnel for the city.
Thanksgiving was expressed that the first missionaries for
Solo were "standing by" ready to enter the city after their
furlough (Minutes, 1958:37). The 1959 Minutes for the first
time included the station report of Solo, noting that the
work had been directed for the most part by missionaries from
Semarang (Minutes, 1959:46).

The Solo Station has proved a fertile field. Strong
outreach into the rural regions has been combined with a
progressive church planting mission within the city. The
churches have been active in outreach (Pennell, 1969:1). By
1968 the Solo station reported three organized churches,
seventeen chapels and a total membership of 874 (Minutes, 1968:
151).

The Baptists opened evangelistic work in Sumatra in
December 1961 when the Ancil Sculls moved to Palembang. Illness
in the family forced their return to the United States. The
church was not actually started until the Sculls returned in
September 1963 (Minutes, 1964:74). The church in Palembang
was organized June 13, 1965 after baptizing twenty-four members
and accepting seven by transfer. The church sponsored a
reading room, English classes and a children's school or
kindergarten (Minutes, 1965:88). The school promoted by the
Palembang church was the first instituted by a Baptist Church
in Indonesia. The opening of the school was against the
policy of the Mission in regard to schools. In 1968 the
Palembang Church reported ninety-three members (Minutes, 1968:
151). The present status of the church is somewhat uncertain
due to various problems.

In May 1961 the Personnel and Planning Committee of
the Indonesian Baptist Mission departed from the principle
of not sending missionaries directly from language school to
open new work when the Ed Sanders were assigned to evangelistic
ministry in Djogjakarta (Minutes, 1961:39). With Jogja
(shortened form of Djogjakarta) occupied, Baptists had extended
their witness to the three largest cities in Central Java. In
July 1962, after five months, the Jogja station reported sixteen conversions (Minutes, 1962:49).

Jogja has proved to be one of the more productive
stations due largely to aggressive church planting and the
student evangelism program that has utilized students in direct
evangelistic efforts. By 1968 there were three organized
churches, eight chapels and 907 total members (Minutes, 1968:
151). A significant fruit of the evangelistic outreach from
Jogja has been the planting of churches in several nearby
towns, Magelang, Klaten, Sleman and other villages (Minutes,
1968:119). Evangelistic services also were started in Purwokerto
by the Jogja Station in 1966. The city of Purwokerto later

was organized as a separate station with missionary personnel
to work with the existing church (Minutes, 1966:70).

    Bukittinggi in West Sumatra was authorized as a mission
station in December 1961. Plans for the station were laid
in 1961 and early 1962 with the station being actually opened
the latter year (Minutes, 1963:75). Since the city of
Bukittinggi is in the center of the Minangkabau people, who
have proved their strong attachment to Islam, the church has
experienced meager growth. A large percentage of the forty
church members are the missionary families and their household
workers. A church was planted in the port city of Padang
whose membership is included in the above report (Minutes, 1968:
151 and 97-99). The church promotes a student program and
continues witness in this difficult region.

    In 1965 the Mission planned to open another station,
this one in Bogor, West Java (Minutes, 1965:65). The evangelist, Avery Willis, moved to Bogor in 1965 and began an evangelistic ministry marked by its enthusiasm. Several large
public meetings were attended to overflowing and hundreds of
decisions were registered. The church numbered ninety-five
in 1968 (Minutes, 1968:151). The Church there worships in
two congregations. One is reported to have around seventy
percent Chinese members and the other ninety-six percent
Chinese (Trotter, 1959:1). As in Bandung most converts are
from the Chinese population substantiating the basic difficulty
of evangelizing the Sundanese. No breakthrough to the Sundanese
has been registered.

    The Mission next moved to North Sumatra where on July
6, 1967 the Bob Stuckey family opened Baptist work in the city
of Medan, a city of almost one million people (Minutes, 1967:
86). Several firsts were experienced by Baptists in North
Sumatra during 1967. July 6th marked the entrance of the
first Baptist missionaries since the British Baptists in 1815.
August 20th marked the first Baptist worship service and one
week later the first Baptist convert was reached. February
4th saw the first Baptist baptism and later in the month the
first Baptist revival (Minutes, 1968:151).

    Baptist missionaries arrived to build on the existing
foundations in Purwokerto, Central Java in 1967. The
twenty-five members were attending services when the Von
Wortens arrived. In addition to continuing the development
of the church in Purwokerto, churches have been planted in
Purbolinggo, Kroja and Tjilatjap, nearby cities, and in
Tjikidang, a village some ten miles from Purwokerto (Minutes,
1968:110-111). The development in this station has demonstrated the possibilities of rapid expansion in a responsive
region. It is to be regretted that staffing this station was
delayed by the deployment of missionaries to other less responsive areas.

    The last three stations opened by the Mission have been

in 1969 and 1970. In 1969 the Wendell Smiths moved to
the South Sumatra area of Lampung. This area, a resettlement
area in the government transmigration program, promises great
possibilities for evangelism. History has proved that the
Gospel is particularly effective among unsettled and resettled
peoples. Also in 1969 the East Java city of Madiun, where a
church had already been planted by churches from Solo, was
opened as a station when the Charles Buckners established
residence. Madiun had long attracted the eyes of the
Mission and rapid growth can be expected in this center. The
last station for the Mission is in deep East Java, at Djember
where evangelism was begun under the direction of the Avery
Willis family.

Within each of these stations, churches were constantly
being planted and more and more being led by national pastors.
In 1968 the Mission reported twenty-five organized churches
and eighty chapels led by national pastors (Minutes, 1968:151).
By 1969 the Mission counted a total of 159 churches and
chapels with only four churches being served by a missionary
pastor. These were years of expansion and development.

Programs Relating to Church Growth

The Indonesian Baptist Mission has ardently planted
churches. In addition to church planting by individual
missionaries, churches and stations, several productive programs have proved useful in church extension. These special
programs have done much to extend Baptist witness into rural
regions.

In 1962 the seminary instituted the Seminary Evangelistic
Extension Program that came to be termed popularly the Seminary
"Dropping". The major purpose of the program was training
of the students in personal soul-winning activities each week.
However, it soon became evident that in engaging in soul-winning
activities the students were at the same time planting new
churches. The main procedure consisted of house-to-house
soul-winning visitation. Five new congregations came into
being through the efforts during the first year and three more
during the second (Minutes, 1964:76-77). At present some
twenty-one congregations have resulted from the program
(Minutes, 1968:151).

In 1966 a program of village evangelism (called the
Desa Program) began as an outreach of the churches and hospital
in Kediri. The program was designed to take advantage of those
who made professions in the Baptist Hospital and returned to
their villages where there were no churches. Pastor Mulus
Budianto served as the evangelist and Mel Gentry was the
missionary. During the first year this program planted congregations in eighteen villages and registered 375 professions
of faith. Over 630 attended worship services and some 216 were

in new Christians classes (Gentry, 1967:1-2).

The program involves an initial visit to the home of
a person requesting religious services. The evangelistic
workers at the hospital seek those willing to issue an invitation to their village. The services are cleared with the
village authorities before starting services. Usually services
are held twice a month. On the night of the service a group
of trained Christians arrive at the village about one hour
early. These Christians are called Christ's Witness Corp
(Pasukan Penjaksi Kristus). They visit throughout the village,
giving tracts in the Javanese language and inviting the people
to the services. Most of the services, conducted in the
Javanese language, are held in homes. Usually no invitation
is given for four to five weeks. The converts are gathered
into new Christian classes led by the evangelist. The churches
are not subsidized and usually in time are served by lay
pastors (Gentry, 1967:1-2).

Services in several villages had to be discontinued
because of Moslem pressure. Hundreds have been baptized in
the program. There has been a determined effort at education
in recent days. The report for 1968 indicates that the congregations now associated with the "desa" program count 542
members (Rogers, 1969:1).

Church growth has come from the direct outreach of a
number of churches. While many churches have been active in
this type of ministry, the Bethlehem Church in Bandung, the
Sion, Tjandi and Iman Churches in Semarang, the churches in
Djogjakarta, the Penumping and Tjolomadu Churches in Solo and
the churches in Kediri have been most active in direct outreach. The future of Baptist expansion will depend largely
on outreach of local churches in Indonesia.

Lay training has been a part of the Baptist approach
in several centers and has contributed significantly to outreach. In 1960 the Kediri Station instituted a Preacher's
School that offered a two year program of study (Nance, 1969:
139). This school no longer is functioning but a short term
(four day) course was held in 1969. Several cities have held
extended courses for laymen, teaching biblical and historical
subjects. Another approach has been short term courses offer-
ing courses over a period of only a few days. In 1968 the
Mission asked the Ebbie Smiths to undertake a Bible School
project for lay pastors, located in East Java (Minutes, 1968:
77).

Mission-wide Emphases Related to Church Growth

In addition to evangelistic efforts on local levels
there have been two very special nation-wide efforts that have
significantly contributed to Baptist Church growth in Indonesia.
Both the Asian Sunday School Campaign and the GEHIBA Revival

aided the churches in reaching men for the Master. The fact
that these programs came at strategic times has enhanced their
results.

The Asian-wide Sunday School Campaign was held in 1966
after months of preparation. With teachers from outside the
country, study courses were held in every station. A total of
1,326 people enrolled in the courses and the average attendance
was 1,020. The report of the campaign listed ninety-nine professions of faith and seventy new teachers enlisted in the
Sunday Schools (Minutes, 1966:106-109). The campaign, coming
as it did at the very beginning of the more responsive periods,
laid a foundation for the rapid growth of the years between
1966 and 1969.

The Mission promoted a nation-wide evangelistic campaign in 1967 under the leadership of Ed Sanders. Through
preparation, including soul-winning clinics, conferences
and programs preceded the meetings in the churches. The campaign, named GEHIBA (Gerakan Hidup Baru or New Life Movement)
brought great blessings. The report of professions of faith
numbered 5,682 (Minutes, 1967:28). A second nation-wide campaign is planned for 1970, this time known as KABARIA.

To aid churches in providing needed equipment the
Mission established a Building and Loan Board in 1960. The
purpose was to help the Baptist Churches in Indonesia acquire
and improve church property, including equipment, transportation for the pastor, pastor's home as well as buildings and
building sites (Minutes, 1960:75). The Board, by making loans
to churches, has greatly aided churches to provide needed
equipment and has provided a step toward independence for
several congregations.

TOWARDS A CONVENTION

There was always a spirit of cooperation among the
Baptist Churches of Indonesia. This spirit has led to a
movement toward organized cooperation. This movement resulted
in the formation of regional associations, a Mission-wide
"Jajasan" (foundation) and toward a Committee of Cooperation
(Badan Kerdja-sama). The eventual goal is a national convention.

Associations

The purpose of associations among Baptist Churches consists of providing means of working together on projects too
large or extensive for any one local church and providing for
fellowship. The association has no control over the local
churches but exists only to serve and enlarge the possibilities
of service. It has been within this principle that the Baptist
Churches of Indonesia have formed regional organizations.

The first association was established in West Java among

the churches in Bandung and Djakarta and later Bogor and
Sukabumi. The churches in Kediri formed an association in
1964 and assumed responsibility for the laymen's school. The
association has provided for closer fellowship and communication
as well as closer cooperation in various ministries (Minutes,
1965:87). Cooperative efforts in lay training, evangelism and
other ministries have moved in the direction of forming associations in Semarang, Djogjakarta, Solo and Surabaja. These
experiences in associational cooperation have formed the basis
for the future formation of a convention.

Jajasan (Foundation)

        In September 1961 the Mission formed the Jajasan
(foundation) which was known as the "Jajasan Missi Baptis
Indonesia. The members of the executive committee were to be
the members of the Jajasan and Mr. Prawoto from Kediri was
the advisor. Stockwell Sears and Leon Mitchell were also to
be included on the Board (Mission Treasurer and Business
Manager) (Minutes, 1962:29).
        The stated purpose of the Jajasan was to act as a
legal holding body for all properties purchased with funds
from the Foreign Mission Board. The executive committee set
in motion at this September meeting the machinery to follow
all legal process for establishing this foundation with government officials (Minutes, 1962:29,30). Political conditions
in the country at the time had indicated that such a foundation
was imperative.
        In 1966 the Jajasan was changed in composition. The
Mission voted that the Jajasan Missi Baptis be recognized as a
legal property holding, property operating and money receiving
body--a legitimate vehicle for carrying out the program of
the Southern Baptist Mission in Indonesia. The membership of
the foundation was changed to include the executive committee,
Mission Treasurer, Mission Business Manager and four nationals
elected by the Mission (Minutes, 1966:30,31). Thus the Mission
had moved into a position of legality and more representation
for nationals in the administration of Baptist affairs in
Indonesia.
        Further progress in regard to the foundation was
achieved in 1968-1969. The name was changed from Jajasan Missi
Baptis Indonesia to Jajasan Baptis Indonesia. While the executive committee, the Treasurer and Business Manager continued
as members, the national membership was to be selected not by
the Mission, but by the Badan Kerdja-sama Kaum Baptis Indonesia
(Committee on Baptist Cooperative Work in Indonesia) (Minutes,
1968:22,23). This Jajasan is fulfilling the legal need of the
Baptist Churches and Mission for a legal holding body in the
nation.

Badan <u>Kerdja-sama</u> *Kaum* <u>Baptis</u> *Indonesia (Committee on*
    Baptist Cooperative Work in Indonesia)

    In 1968 the Mission and the churches of Indonesia moved
to the formation of a joint committee for cooperative work,
the <u>Badan</u> <u>Kerdja-sama</u> <u>Kaum</u> <u>Baptis</u> <u>Indonesia</u>. This committee
made up of four missionaries elected by the Mission and four
nationals elected by the churches is designed to work together
on all matters relating to Baptist work. The committee suggests
names for the national members of all boards and committees.
It is consulted on budget and personnel needs and assignments
(Minutes, 1968:22, 36-37).
    The work of this joint committee is the most far reach-
ing yet taken by the Baptists of Indonesia. Through this
committee the Baptists hope to move toward the formation of a
genuine, functioning convention, without experiencing the
problems that are often faced in the formation of such organizations. Time will prove the wisdom of this gradual approach
toward the formation of the convention of Indonesian Baptist
Churches.

INSTITUTIONAL BEGINNINGS

    Baptists early planned for institutional work to
undergird the evangelistic thrust. The seminary was planned
for Semarang, the hospital for Kediri and publication ministry
was placed in Bandung. Later the mission planted student
center ministries in four different cities, Djogjakarta,
Semarang, Bandung and Djakarta. The Mission instituted plans
in 1968 for an East Java Bible School to implement the training
of lay pastors. The story of the beginnings of these institutional ministries is an interesting and instructive one.

The Baptist Theological Seminary of Indonesia

    Semarang was at first envisioned as a center strickly
for evangelistic endeavor. However, after several surveys,
there developed the feeling that Semarang was the logical place
for the preacher training school. Buren Johnson encouraged
Buford Nichols to plan for the seminary in Semarang but suggested that it would be wise to locate the campus separate from
the "missionary residence compound" (Nance, 1969:69). Months
of searching brought Buford Nichols to the eventual home of
the school, twelve thousand square meters on the western edge
of the city. In a letter dated May 5, 1954, Nichols reported
to Dr. Cauthen that the land had been purchased two days previously and that the projected date for opening the school
was set for October 11 of that year (Nichols, 1958:89).
    The seminary actually had its beginning in the education-
al committee of the Mission. This committee recommended that

a seminary advisory board be established to consider building
plans, course of study and student aid (Minutes, 1954:19).
Later this board was called the Seminary Board (Dewan Seminari)
and gave welcome aid in systematic planning of the principles
and program of the school (Nichols, 1969:2).

     With only six months to lay the plans and provide the
physical facilities for the opening of the seminary, the
Nichols and Catherine Walker found themselves under heavy
pressure. Three semi-permanent buildings were constructed on
the hill to provide a girls' dormitory, boys' dormitory and a
kitchen. Despite inconveniences to the three faculty members
and the twelve students the seminary opened on schedule,
October 11, 1954. Since the kitchen was incomplete, food and
drinking water were brought from the city. The students were
forced to study by candle light and kerosene lamps as the
electricity had not been installed (Nance, 1969:70-71).
Nichols reported that the seminary at its opening had no fence
to prevent thieves from entering, the grass was tall, unkept
and filled with snakes and bathing water secured from the
river. In spite of all, the school was opened (Nichols, 1969:
3).

     At the time of its opening the seminary served but
two organized churches with a combined membership of less than
one hundred. The central location at Semarang allowed students
to commute to all parts of Java where Baptists were working.
Students from the seminary have rendered meaningful service
in the churches during their student days. It has been an
established principle at the seminary that students were not
only free to serve churches but were expected to be active
in church related service during their study. This principle
has aided not only the work of the churches but has placed
the seminary in the center of Baptist evangelistic outreach.
Most of the students are serving churches before they graduate.

     Just forty days after the seminary opened its doors
to students, it enlarged its ministry to welcome the first
Indonesian-wide Baptist Youth Conference (Nance, 1969:72).
This conference, held from November 29 to December 3, was
labeled the "first annual conference" and was led by Miss
Faye Taylor and Pastor Ais Pormes. Students from all five
stations in the Mission attended (Minutes, 1955:29). These
conferences have become annual affairs, in recent years being
divided into different age groups due to limited space at the
seminary. Hosting conferences of various types has been another contribution of the seminary to the churches in Indonesia.

     The seminary began with a four year course of study for
those with at least a high school education. The report of the
seminary board for 1961 noted a student body of nineteen. The
same report decried the inability to begin a second level of
study, for those with only junior high school education. The
hope was expressed that such a program would expand the student

body to as many as fifty (<u>Minutes</u>, 1961:75). The next seminary
board report announced that a two year program for those with
junior high background would be inaugurated in the fall session
of 1962. The same report noted that nineteen new students had
already been accepted, eleven for the new program. Added to
the eight students who were to return, this number guaranteed
the largest student body in the school's history (<u>Minutes</u>,
1962:71). This two year program was later expanded to a three
year program and has provided some of the most able and influential leaders in the Indonesian churches and ministries.

During the school year of 1962-1963, the seminary began
a program of Evangelistic Extension led by Keith Parks. This
program (named the "Droping") sought to help the students to
gain experience in soul-winning and at the same time extend
the evangelistic outreach (<u>Minutes</u>, 1963:113). During the
six years this program has been in operation, it has resulted
in planting congregations in over twenty-one areas in and around
Semarang (<u>Minutes</u>, 1968:110). These congregations are in the
most part served by student pastors and serve both their
communities and the education of the young ministers.

Beginning in 1968 the seminary further enlarged its
ministry. The course of study was further divided into
seminary and Bible school sections. The seminary division
(named the <u>Tingkat Baccalaureus</u>) accepts students with high
school or college background and offers a Bachelor of Divinity
Degree to those with a college degree. The Bible school division (named the <u>Tingkat Diploma</u>) accepts any student, irre-
gardless of his educational background. The two divisions
are taught in separate classes but both the period of study
and the curriculum is basically the same. The main difference
is the absence of the Biblical languages in the Bible school
division (cf. Nichols, 1969:4).

The seminary has continued to expand its physical
facilities and faculty. In January 1966 Pastor Ernest Sukirman
became the first national teacher in the theological subjects
(other nationals had taught music, languages, etc.). Two
other Indonesian pastors began part-time teaching in 1969. The
three temporary buildings have been replaced with the main
classroom and administration building which also houses the
twelve hundred volume library, four permanent dormitory buildings, a home for the president, a recreation area and an audi-
torium large enough for seven hundred people, complete the
campus. The land has been increased to 29,929 square meters
(Nichols, 1969:3).

A total of seventy-nine students have graduated from
the seminary. With two exceptions, every full-time pastor
among Baptist Churches is either a graduate or a student of the
seminary. Present enrollment is around 150 students (Nichols,
1969:3-4). The seminary stands at the center of Baptist work

in Indonesia, seeking to lend its influence to the ministry
of the Word.

Baptist Hospital of Indonesia

From the beginning the Baptists planned a medical
ministry in Indonesia. Finding that Indonesia had but one
doctor for every eighty-seven thousand people, Dr. Cauthen
rightly perceived the tremendous contribution a Christian hospital could make. Thus, medical work became a definite part
of the plan of the mission (Nance, 1969:74-75).

The Mission, through Buren Johnson, began conferring
with the Indonesian Ministry of Health as early as 1953 concerning the possibilities of medical work. These conferences
indicated that one of Indonesia's greatest medical needs was
a school for nurses. To operate such a school the proposed
hospital would be required to have a minimum of one hundred
beds. The Baptist plan for such a hospital met a welcome
response at the Ministry of Health (Nance, 1969:75).

The first doctor appointed for Indonesia, Dr. Kathleen
Jones, arrived in December 1953 (Nichols, 1958:121). Dr.
Jones along with nurses Ruth Ford and Everley Hayes, constituted the vanguard of Baptist medical work on Java. Soon
their numbers were swelled by new appointees of doctors,
nurses and medical technologists.

Settling on a location for the Baptist Hospital proved
a problem of no small dimension. At one time it was suggested
that the hospital be located in a little known village in
Borneo, served only twice monthly by mail. Other cities
strongly considered were Padang on Sumatra, the island of
Madura and the cities of Surabaja and Madiun. Eventually
Madiun was considered the most likely place for the first
medical venture (Nance, 1969:79-80).

However, Madiun for various reasons was not acceptable
to the East Java Medical authorities. These officials urged
Baptists to consider the city of Kediri. The missionaries
were not overly impressed with Kediri as the hospital site
but felt they should cooperate with the authorities. The
Mission Minutes of 1954 indicate that Kediri had been selected
as the site (Minutes, 1954:22-23).

Two houses, located on the banks of the Brantas River,
were purchased in 1954 and on September 7th of that year
nurse Ruth Ford arrived in Kediri to oversee remodeling. One
house was planned to serve as living quarters and the other as
a clinic. Everley Hayes arrived in less than two months and
Dr. Jones on February 3, 1955. Just twenty-five days later
the clinic began seeing patients (Nichols, 1958:118).

The three pioneer medical missionaries had been warned
to expect little response because they were "women, white, and
Christian" (Nance, 1969:85). The first day only ten patients

entered the clinic. By the end of the second week almost
one hundred patients per day were being treated. The first
year the clinic registered 17,200 visits involving over 10,000
different people. By the end of the second year over 20,000
different people had been treated at the clinic (Nichols, 1958:
119).

Baptists had opened a medical ministry in Indonesia.
Buren Johnson observed that the negotiation of permission to
open medical work was the "toughest problem" since the struggle
to obtain entrance into Indonesia (Nance, 1969:86). The
missionaries gave the credit to the Lord. Ruth Ford wrote,
"We believe the Lord opened Kediri to us and we want to go
forward with Him as we develop the full scale program in our
area" (Minutes, 1955:47).

Land for the permanent site of the hospital was cleared
in November 1955. During the last two weeks of 1955 Baptists
held clinic at the hospital site, two days each week in temporary quarters (Nance, 1969:87). The first permanent unit
of the hospital, formally dedicated on February 28, 1957,
housed forty-five beds and twenty cribs (Nichols, 1958:128).

Plans for a school of nursing were realized in 1961.
This school conforms in every way to the requirements of the
Indonesian Ministry of Health. Graduates of the school pass
a government test before being recognized as nurses. This
school, under the leadership of nurse Virginia Miles, continues
to help meet the increasing demand for trained nurses in
Indonesia (E. Smith, n. d.:130).

Plans were made for a second medical work in Indonesia.
After much consideration, the Mission decided to locate the
work on Sumatra. The Mission adopted as a policy for medical
ministry, that it should be located so as to open doors to
evangelistic work in an area which would be difficult to open
otherwise. A further suggestion called for evangelistic
workers to precede or accompany the new medical project
(Minutes, 1961:43).

In December 1961 the Mission executive committee accepted the recommendation of the personnel and planning
committee that the new medical project be opened in Bukittinggi,
West Sumatra (Minutes, 1962:31). Bukittinggi is the center
of the Minangkabau society which has proved itself so strongly
Moslem that it has been historically almost, if not, impervious
to the Gospel. For this reason it was felt that the Minangkabau
people would fulfill the requirement of a resistant people.
As to whether this principle is valid or not we must wait to
a later section to discuss. Due to various types of opposition
from both political and religious groups, the building of the
hospital in Bukittinggi has been delayed. A clinic has function-
ed for several years (Minutes, 1968:126-128). Permission was
obtained in 1969-1970 and the hospital will in time, it is
hoped, become a reality.

Publication Ministry

The production of Sunday School materials for the
Baptist Churches started in the home of the Stockwell Sears
who were assigned to evangelistic work and was done in addition
to their evangelistic ministry. The Baptist Press in Hong
Kong sent blank art outlays and the lessons, translated into
Indonesian, were memeographed onto the lesson leaflets. At
first this program was local only but as time passed other
stations requested the material. This involved a great deal
of time and the Sears' garage was turned into a publication
plant for translating, memeographing and sending out the
literature (Nance, 1969:96).

The suggestion that a publication committee for the
Mission be established led to the formation of a committee to
supervise and sponsor publications in 1953 (Minutes, 1953:13).
By 1954 the Mission had requested Grace Wells to "assume the
responsibility of production of literature on a temporary basis" and selected Bandung to be the temporary location for
publication work (Minutes, 1954:19-21) The "temporary" assign-
ment lasted until Grace Wells' retirement in 1962 (Nance, 1969:
97).

Increasing quantities and types of Christian literature
have flowed from the publication house. A hymn book, Njanjian
Pengharapan (Hymns of Hope) was published and an extensive
revision and expansion is in the process of being completed.
Tracts, books, plays, music materials, Vacation Bible School,
women's work and other literature have been added to the
Sunday School and Training Union materials produced. The
fourth annual Mission meeting permanently located the publication operation in Bandung and authorized the erection of a
Publication Building (Nance, 1969:98). The publication ministry has also been responsible for the promotional work of the
Mission. This responsibility has included the planning and
overseeing of the conferences and leadership clinics (E. Smith,
n. d.:130).

The lesson material has for some years been lessons
from America which were translated into Indonesian and revised
to fit the culture. This material has of necessity often been
less than appropriate for Indonesian society but has to some
extent met the needs of the expanding churches. Recently progress has been made toward a simple series that could be used
for starting new work. This material is being eagerly awaited.

Student Work

Thousands of students in many cities attracted the
evangelistically oriented eyes of the Baptists. However, the
Mission wisely postponed opening work among students until such
time as there was a strong church base in the city where the

student ministry would be undertaken. Thus, student work was delayed, awaiting the development of churches near the major universities (Minutes, 1958:53).

Baptists early settled on the city of Djogjakarta, the site of the leading university of Indonesia, as the location for their first student evangelistic ministry. The 1958 Minutes requested a student couple or single women for service in Djogjakarta (Minutes, 1958:66). A building was purchased for a student center and Frank Wells was sent as the first student evangelist. During 1963 the student center building was remodeled and began its services (Minutes, 1963: 80). Other student centers have been opened in Semarang in 1967 (Minutes, 1967:91), in Bandung in 1968 and in Djakarta in 1969.

Student work has been conceived as student evangelism and has been consciously tied to the ministry of local churches. In some cases productive results have been realized by using students in evangelistic outreach. Student evangelism promises great opportunities.

Radio and Television Ministry

While small beginnings in radio ministry had been undertaken earlier, the first genuine breakthrough in radio and television came in May 1965 when Pastor Hari Budaja and missionary Bill O'Brien presented a thirty minute program on the Indonesian National Television network. The program was so well received that Baptists were invited to prepare a quarterly program for television (Minutes, 1964:94). Due to conditions beyond anyone's control, it was impossible for O'Brien to continue on the programs, but Baptist Churches continued to receive opportunities for television programs (Minutes, 1965:108).

The Mission elected a Radio-Television Committee in 1967. A recording studio was built at the Student Center in Semarang and high quality program materials produced for radio stations across Indonesia (Minutes, 1968:118). Various opportunities on television are also being received and used to advantage.

CONCLUSION

In brief, this is the story of the Baptist ministry in Indonesia since its beginnings in 1951. It is the story of advance. The important question is, "Has the advance been as great as it might have been had other strategies been employed?" "Has the growth been what God desired?" The next section will analize the growth and ministry of the churches in Indonesia, the influences of the institutions and other factors. This analysis will provide valuable data for planning.

5

Growth Analysis of the Baptist Churches in Indonesia

INTRODUCTION

Analysis of church growth is imperative. Every church
(denomination, mission, association of churches, etc.) must
take a long look at both the methods it has been employing and
their effectiveness. One way, but not the only way, of
measuring the effectiveness of any program (indeed the most
logical and consistent method) is to notice the numerical increase of members, congregations, ministers and such factors
as stewardship and outreach. Such measuring is a spiritual
undertaking. The study is useful chiefly as it leads to an
accurate evaluation of the program and suggests ways of increasing effectiveness. Tippett says, "The motive of numbering
is not pride at our accomplishment but the seriousness of the
commission to us lesser shepherds to 'care for the flock of
God' until the Chief Shepherd comes (I Peter 5:2-4). Good
numbering is part of good shepherding" (1965:1-2).

Any successful analysis and evaluation demands that
certain attitudes be operative both with the entity to be surveyed and the surveyor. The surveyor must provide exact data
on the facets of growth. Vague approximations are of little,
if any help (McGavran, 1970:81).

Indonesia has proved a fertile field for Baptists. Beginning with 1951 the Baptist Churches have increased to
9,779 members in 153 congregations. This is a record of good
growth. However, the question must be asked, "Could it have
been more?" God's people must never be satisfied with the
thousands if the Lord has prepared and intended ten thousands.

In analysizing the growth of the Baptist Churches we
will note the overall growth, the growth in each area, the
very important matter of growth station-by-station and the use
of personnel and funds. The developmental growth of churches
will be studied also. In this way we hope to set forth the
growth and development of the Baptist Churches in Indonesia.

THE OVERALL PICTURE OF GROWTH

The Graph of Growth

The easiest way to perceive the growth picture of any Church is to construct a graph of growth. On this graph the ascending line represents the growth of total membership based on field total figures. One square represents one hundred members. Thus the graph rises from thirty-nine members in 1953 to a 1969 high of 9,779. The graph of growth of the Baptist Churches is found on page 146. The following table indicates the year-by-year statistics concerning total membership, total baptisms, total congregations, number of missionaries and number of national pastors.

Figure 17   *TABLE OF MEMBERSHIP, BAPTISMS, CONGREGATIONS, MISSIONARIES AND NATIONAL PASTORS*

Year	1953	1954	1955	1956	1957	1958	1959	1960	1961
Membership	39	61	126	282	538	793	967	1317	1580
Baptisms	7	30	82	135	153	308	201	371	339
Congregations	1	2	2	4	8	14	23	27	22
Missionaries	15	16	22	33	31	42	50	55	64
National Pastors	1	1	1	1	3	5	7	12	22

Year	1962	1963	1964	1965	1966	1967	1968	1969	1970
Membership	1979	2843	3169	3391	3965	5834	8186	9779	
Baptisms	463	581	821	521	798	1726	2381	2204	
Congregations	32	43	51	54	70	90	105	149	
Missionaries	64	71	79	89	82	95	103	105	
National Pastors	25	28	33	39	43	51	64		

Without at this time seeking reasons for the growth, we draw several conclusions from the graphs. First, the Indonesian Baptist Mission began with the plan of planting churches. The first years produced only a few congregations.

FIGURE 18

Graph of Growth,

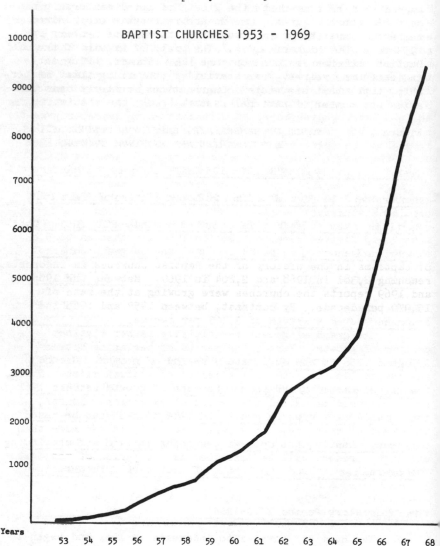

BAPTIST CHURCHES 1953 - 1969

After several years of earnest effort, the churches began to
increase more rapidly. After 1957, a consistent increase with
only slowing in 1958 is seen until 1962. The graph for 1962
to 1963 indicates a sudden increase. The figures for 1962,
1969 members, climbed to 2,843 in 1963, an increase of 864.
One is led to suspect these figures, since the total baptisms
reported for 1963 reached only 581. The increased baptisms
would not account for the growth in total membership. However,
an opposite problem is encountered in the period between 1963
and 1964 as the increase from 2,843 to 3,169 is less than would
have been effected by the reported 821 baptisms. If the
two years are combined, there would be a total baptisms of
1,402 which added to the 1962 figure would be fairly near the
3,169 figure reported for 1964. Most likely the statistics for
the two years became confused with some being improperly reported in one year or the other. The growth should in all
likelihood be seen as a rather sharper increase between 1962
and 1964, rather than just the one very rapid year of 1963.
This is the way with statistics. While any year or number
of years may be inaccurate for a variety of reasons, the
general trend is firm as a rock. Later entries correct
earlier mistakes.

An even steeper rise is noted beginning in 1965. The
membership figures rose to 3,965 in 1966 and then on to 5,834
in 1967. The next two years produced the largest numbers
of baptisms in the history of the Baptist Churches in Indonesia,
reaching 2,381 in 1968 and 2,204 in 1969. Between the 1965
and 1969 reports the churches were growing at the rate of
15,970 per decade. By contrast, between 1955 and 1965 the
churches showed a growth of 3,165 per decade.

The graph of growth reveals five rather distinct
periods of growth. First, the period of beginning between
1953 and 1956 is the exploratory period of growth. Second,
the period 1957 to 1962 is the period of gradual climb. Third,
the rather marked increase in the rate of growth between 1962
and 1964 could be called the period of expansion. Fourth,
the notable slow down in growth in 1964 to 1965 can be named
the years of pressure. This period actually lasted more than
one year. Lastly, the upsurge beginning in 1966 and continuing
until the present will be described as the period of response.
The overall growth of the Baptist Churches will be described
in each period.

The Exploratory Period 1953-1956

The Baptists moved into Indonesia in 1951 and began to
seek avenues of service. Most of the work revolved around
the missionaries and getting settled. It was a time of exploration and is therefore called the exploratory period. It
lasted until 1956.

Every mission begins with an exploratory period when there is no Church, the missionaries are learning the language and culture, making their first mistakes and winning their first converts (McGavran, 1965c:155). Keith Hamilton has called this stage of mission work "hot house growth" when so much depends on the missionary from outside rather than the people themselves. The leaders during the exploratory period are mostly missionaries and mission paid workers. There is only a handful of converts. Hamilton goes on to say, "This is the way churches begin in most areas. Indeed it is the only way possible under certain conditions" (1962:138-139).

This was the way Baptist Churches began in Indonesia. Missionaries and subsidized nationals did most of the work in mission provided facilities. This approach was and is not wrong in itself. However, care should be taken that this period not be needlessly prolonged. Hamilton says, "It (the exploratory period) should be recognized as only the first phase to be passed through as rapidly as possible" (1962:139).

During these years of exploration the Mission opened churches in five stations. The number of missionaries had grown to thirty-three, the total membership to 282 and the churches had reported a total of 254 baptisms. The beach-head had been established and secured; the future beckoned to the little band of Baptists.

Several factors must be noted concerning this first period of growth. First, the Mission from the beginning projected a program of church planting. Their purpose for establishing institutions was stated as being to serve the churches and aid in opening doors for beginning other churches (Nance, 1969:32). Even those stations heavily involved in institutional work were quick to plant churches. Semarang had church work before the seminary opened (Nichols, 1958:90-91). Church and Sunday School ministry were started in Kediri by the medical staff with the help of a seminary student as early as 1954. This church work was in addition to the clinic ministry (Minutes, 1955:46-47).

One of the Mission's most significant decisions during those formative years extended their witness to all the people of Indonesia. From the report of Dr. Cauthen to the Foreign Mission Board in 1950 it might have been expected that the Baptists in Indonesia planned to center their ministry among the Chinese minority. Four couples, who could speak the Chinese language while learning the national language to broaden their usefulness, were the first arrivals. In fact, fourteen of the first fifteen missionaries were transfers from China (Nance, 1969:67).

In spite of their understandable and commendable love for and attraction to the Chinese people, the missionaries early recognized the vast opportunity among the Javanese. Stockwell Sears, a China transfer, wrote in 1953, "We still

need workers proficient in the Indonesian language before
an effective work can be opened among the people in whose land
we live" (Minutes, 1953:19). The same year the chairman of the
Mission language committee, Buford Nichols, who had completed
over twenty years of service in China, wrote, "Though we in
Indonesia shall be able to continue some needed Christian witnessing in English and Chinese, most of our missionary work
must be done in the Indonesian tongue." Nichols contended
that only through this method could the masses be reached
(Minutes, 1953:15).

While the first preaching was of necessity done in
English and some Chinese language teaching was employed, the
Mission and churches early centered on using the national
language. Had the missionaries isolated themselves to one
minority language group they would have missed the opportunity
of serving the great masses of the Javanese. By projecting
a ministry to the entire population, the Baptists have been
able to win both Chinese and Javanese as well as Indonesians
from other islands who were living on Java. The decision to
major on the Indonesian language and all the people of
Indonesia greatly augmented the subsequent growth of the
churches.

Had the Baptists had more preachers in those early
years the growth could without doubt have been increased. In
1953 the Mission boasted only four men and two of these were
to be heavily involved either in seminary or Mission office
work. Although the workers did superhuman work, there was
still the lack of preachers. Only two men were engaged in
church development. In 1954 the ladies outnumbered the men
three to one since there were four men, their wives and eight
single women (Nance, 1969:67-73). This all points up the lack
of sufficient preachers in the early years.

The Mission also set the pattern for a subsidized
program with expensive buildings, during these beginning days.
Church buildings were purchased in Bandung, Djakarta and
Surabaja by 1954 (the Surabaja building had been started but
not completed by the 1954 Mission Meeting) (Minutes, 1954:26-
31). The seminary and hospital buildings had been provided
during the first period. While subsidy may have been necessary
in this period of beginnings, it set a standard that has yet
to be overcome and may in the future limit the possible outreach.

Southern Baptist Missions, not just in Indonesia, must
come to grips with the matter of subsidization. This is not
to say that all subsidization is wrong. When funds from outside can aid the planting of churches and discipling of men,
then by all means, funds should be used. Far better a growing,
but subsidized church than a stagnant though self-supporting
church. Still, it is imperative that recognition be given
to the fact that while subsidy can stimulate the start of a

church, it also has built-in limitations as to its outreach.
The resources of the sending body will stretch only so far.
Outreach will be limited to the number of buildings that can
be built, equipped and financially aided. This plan can reach
the thousands but will close itself off from the ten thousands.
On the other hand, a method involving the planting of hundreds
of village and neighborhood congregations with largely unpaid
ministers and indigenous buildings, suffers no such limitation.

        The first period was characterized by the beginnings
of church planting in the major cities and the establishment
of institutions. While there was active emphasis on churches,
the establishment of institutions diverted energy from the
planting of churches that might have been more productive during the first years. It must, however, be noted that the
seminary produced many workers for the churches who were
serving the churches while they studied. The exploratory
period provided a basis for the spiritual experiences of what
we are calling the period of gradual growth.

The Period of Gradual Climb 1957-1961

        By 1957 the Mission had planted firm roots in Indonesian
soil. Missionaries were proficient in the Indonesian language.
Stations in Bandung, Djakarta, Surabaja, Semarang and Kediri
were functioning. Seminary and hospital were making their
presence felt. The foundation was laid.

        This period saw a gradual climb in every area. The
membership of 538 in 1957 swelled to 1,580 by 1961. The growth
per decade was 2,600. The churches reported 1,219 baptisms
during the four years. The number of organized churches rose
from seven in 1958 to nine in 1961 and the number of chapels
had grown to thirteen.

        Most significantly, and the primary characteristic
that divides this period from that of the previous exploratory
period, were the twenty-two national pastors reported by 1961,
three having been reported in 1957 (Minutes, 1961:54). By
1960 most of the churches were being led by national pastors.
The report of 1960 showed five missionary pastors and twelve
national pastors (three other nationals were employed vocation-
ally). Since the Mission reported twenty-seven congregations
(nine organized and eighteen chapels), the majority were being
led by nationals (Minutes, 1960:22). The increase in national
pastors is indicative of increasing progress of the Baptist
Churches.

        The number of congregations also increased during the
period of gradual climb. In 1956 the Mission reported but
four congregations. In 1957 this number had increased to
eight. During these years the number of congregations gradually grew to twenty-seven in 1960.

        In some ways this period of gradual climb corresponds

to what Keith Hamilton refers to as the second stage of growth. However, Hamilton's concept of many churchlets of some dozen or so members with unpaid leaders was not the program followed by the Baptists during this period (Hamilton, 1962:139). Most of the Baptist Churches were located on main streets in the cities. They had memberships made up of peoples from various ethnic groups and either paid national leadership (largely subsidized) or were led by missionary pastors. One is forced to wonder what would have been the result had the plan of hundreds of churchlets been followed during this period.

The most distinct regret concerning this period is the word "gradual". For a new mission still getting started it was a fairly good record of growth. However, missions must always ask, could it have been more? Only in this way can continual progress be assured.

The Period of Expansion 1962-1964

Mention has been made of the increased growth between 1962 and 1964. In addition to the membership growth from 1,979 to 3,169 there was an increase in congregations from thirty-two to fifty-one. The churches reported twenty-five national pastors in 1962 and thirty-three by 1964. The missionary staff, sixty-four strong in 1962, numbered seventy-nine by 1964. The growth from 1,979 in 1962 to 3,169 in 1964 marked a growth at the rate of 5,950 per decade. It will be remembered that the rate of growth per decade for the entire period of 1955 through 1965 was 3,165 and from 1965 through 1969 was 15,970. The 1962-1964 period was characterized by expansion in every phase of Baptist witness. We must find those factors that were used of the Holy Spirit in achieving this increase.

History was written with a swift hand during these years in Indonesia. The period marked the emergence of "guided democracy" and the establishment of President Sukarno's concept of NASAKOM. NASAKOM was the attempt to combine in one philosophy of government the divergent elements of nationalism, religion and communism. The very existence of such a concept indicates the increasing power of the ever increasing Communist Party of Indonesia. "Guided democracy" was in effect from July 1959 to March 1966 and was therefore a factor during the period (Cooley, 1968:127).

In addition, 1962 brought the culmination of the confrontation with the Dutch over the control of West New Guinea. The end of this confrontation to some degree relaxed tensions within Indonesia and lessened the anti-foreign feelings that had been pronounced during the struggle. Beginning in 1963 the confrontation with Malasia brought increased tension. The fact that Russia did not fully support the Malasian confrontation as it had the New Guinea dispute may have fulfilled

the prediction that Societ policy in the matter could well
enhance Chinese Communist power in Indonesia (Derkach, 1965:11).
The ensuing tensions and anti-Western feelings were felt over
most of the archipelago.

From this brief survey of historical events one might
draw the conclusion that church growth would be hindered. The
facts, however, show marked increase. In all probability, had
the political conditions been more conducive to growth, even
more rapid advance might have been realized. Conversely, had
less aggressive evangelistic methods been employed, the churches
would certainly have realized meager advance.

The influx of new missionaries and the return of experienced missionaries was a factor in the increase during
this period. Difficulties in obtaining visa permits in 1959-
1960 had slowed the rate of missionary reinforcement. However,
new missionaries were admitted in late 1960 and early 1961.
These new missionaries were through language school and in the
work by 1962 and played a part in the expansion. Moreover,
several missionary families were returning from furloughs
and adding their experienced influence. Missionary influx
was one factor in the growth.

Associated with the increase in missionaries was the
opening of new stations. Solo was staffed with missionaries
during the 1959-1960 mission year and began to show marked
increase during the 1962-1964 period. Jogja was occupied
by missionaries in 1961 and began to report notable membership
gains in 1963 and 1964 (Minutes, 1962, 1963,1964). Palembang
had been established as a station but sickness in the missionary family delayed the development of the church.

Beginning in 1961 aggressive evangelistic efforts were
promoted in several stations. Kediri in 1961 promoted a
city-wide evangelistic campaign that resulted in 150 professions of faith. Postal cards were distributed that provided
blanks requesting information about Christianity. Over 400
cards were returned and evangelistic tracts and other materials
were sent. Evangelistic activities continued in the hospital
(Minutes, 1961:52=53). Outdoor evangelistic campaigns were
held in both Semarang and Jogja (Minutes, 1962:54 and 59).
These campaigns made use of Bible films and public address
equipment as well as extensive visitation. In addition the
Seminary Evangelistic Extension Program was instituted in 1962
and while providing evangelistic training for students, added
thirty-one baptisms to Semarang's total of 127 (Minutes, 1963:
87).

There was a base of established churches without which
the growth in 1962-1964 would have been impossible. Nine
churches had achieved self-support and the majority had national pastors. Of the twenty-nine congregations only nine were
directly led by missionaries. The churches reported thirty-five
Sunday Schools in 1962 with 4,384 enrolled (Minutes, 1962:82a-

82b). It should be noted that in accordance with general
Baptist practice the Sunday Schools provided for adults as
well as youth. It is apparent that the Baptist Churches were
progressing not only in numbers but in the growth in grace
(qualitative growth) and in the ability to work as churches
(organic growth). The growth of these two factors in the
churches, equally important with quantitative growth, must
never be overlooked or neglected (cf. Tippett, 1969:127-128).
     The more rapid growth of these two years was not
destined to continue. The years of 1964-1965 revealed a notable slowing of the growth pattern. This period, called the
years of pressure, constitute the subject of the following
section.

The Years of Pressure 1964-1965

     Almost every phase of the churches' work show a de-
crease in 1964-1965. Overall membership increased only from
3,169 to 3,391. The 821 baptisms of 1964 declined to 521 in
1965. Perhaps most instructive is the fact that <u>only three
new congregations</u> were planted in the period. In 1961-1962
ten new congregations had been opened. Between 1962 and 1963
eleven and between 1963-1964, eight. These comparisons make
the lesser number of congregations planted in 1964 the more
startling. The number of missionaries increased to eighty-nine
by 1965.
     The tension, confusion and general unsettled conditions
of 1964-1965 in Indonesia were an important factor in the report. The confrontation with Malaysia was continuing. Inflation was running uncontrolled. The Communist Party was
showing increasing strength and belligerency. President
Sukarno took Indonesia out of the United Nations in January
1965 (Cooley, 1968:127). It was a period of political, economic and social unrest that had seldom been equaled.
     The political factor, however, was not the only nor
even the major factor in the slow down. Other factors were
in some ways related to the political unrest. The Mission in
1964 and 1965 showed a marked tendency toward consolidation.
This tendency is attested by the fact that only three congregations were planted in the period. The tendency toward
consolidation is most often encountered during periods of
stress, difficulty and even periods of rapid growth. Tippett
says, "It is easy for a Church to excuse herself from outreach
because of the 'necessity' for 'consolidation', but if intake
is stopped in order to consolidate, this tends to lead to
introversion rather than consolidation." Outreach is part of
the life of the Church (Tippett, 1967b:132).
     The problem of an overemphasis on consolidation is
squarely revealed by Sidney J. Clark who wrote:

If we stop in order that we may consolidate, we
shall find that we are in danger of exchanging
work which is spontaneous *in its growth for that*
which moves only in response to external *impulses...*
Life does not stop to consolidate; it either grows
or it dies. It is always so with living *things.*
Extension is *consolidation. When the Christian*
man stops to consolidate, he goes backward.
In the name of concentration and consolidation grave
injury is frequently done to the cause of missions.
The consequence of concentration always seems to be
more *concentration, just as expansion, because it is*
in harmony with a life principle, lends to further
expansion (1933:7).

Discussing Methodist growth in West Africa, Donald
McGavran challenges the conclusion of the historian, Southon,
who stated that the slow growth during one period was partially caused by the need for consolidation. McGavran disagrees
not in regard to the need for consolidation, a view with which
he agrees, but in the concept that expansion had to be followed
by consolidation which limited further expansion (see Tippett,
1967b:364). The most certain way to stop a Christward movement
is to limit further outreach in order to consolidate.
        It is possible, even probable, that responding to the
difficult and tense conditions, to lessened personnel and to
the extended outreach of the years before, the Baptists began
a policy of consolidation in 1964. Churches must always guard
against a policy of outreach that does not provide for the
care and growth of the new congregations. They must equally
guard against any tendency to reduce outreach and expansion
in order to consolidate.
        Had the events of 1965 and its aftermath not stimulated
the churches into a new thrust of outreach, this slowing tendency might have continued longer. The radical change in the
Indonesian political situation in 1965 brought fresh winds of
response. This new responsiveness opened the way for the
period of response among Baptists.

The Period of Responsiveness 1966-1969

        The sweeping growth that began in 1966 is attested by
reports of 798 baptisms, a number second only to the 821 reported in 1964. In 1967 the baptismal figure rose to 1,726
then to 2,381 in 1968 and on to 2,204 in 1969 (Minutes, 1969:
84). Total membership increased from the 3,965 of 1966 to
9,717 in 1969. The number of congregations rose from seventy
in 1966 to 153 in 1969. Sunday School renrollment reached
19,500. These were inspiring years of growth.
        A major factor, but not the only factor, in this period

of growth was the failure of the Communist Coup d'etat on
September 30,1965. This movement, already mentioned in chapter
one, left a void in the lives of the Indonesian people and a
new responsiveness to the Gospel. Around Indonesia came reports of unprecedented movements to Christ (at least during
modern times) (see Bradshaw, 1969:18).

This new responsiveness must be closely examined.
First, it must be seen that the movement into the churches did
not come without effort on the part of the Christians. Seeing
the tremendous possibilities of the times following the
Communist downfall, the massacre during the purges and the
generally unsettled conditions, the churches moved to fill the
vacuum. Witness was projected on every front. Thousands came
to the churches, some from disillusionment with their traditional religions; others out of fear of being branded atheist
(Communist); still others out of the awareness that in a time
of revolutionary change some firm direction and lasting values
were needed; some out of the recognition that salvation, joy
and hope are found only through what they had seen in Christians
(Cooley, 1968:113). These and other factors created in
Indonesia a new willingness to consider the Gospel.

It is a mistake to assume that these thousands came
into the churches only to seek protection. It is true that
many who have entered the churches have come from areas where
Communism was formerly strong. In addition, the families of
the victims of the purge also have come to the Church in great
numbers (Bradshaw, 1969:18-19). To assume that this is the
whole story would be simplistic. Cooley, it will be remembered,
contends that many of those who have been added to the churches
were "Nichodemuses" already attracted to Christianity but
afraid to openly confess Christ in the pre-1965 climate. The
new atmosphere allowed them to wait no longer (Cooley, 1968:90).

In examining this new responsiveness closely it is
apparent that while certain sectors of the population became
unusually responsive to the Gospel, other sectors remained as
resistant as ever. Thousands of Javanese Muslims have come
into the churches in Central and East Java. The Sundanese of
West Java, the Atjehenese and Minangkabau peoples of North
and West Sumatra, the Banjarese of South Borneo, the Makassarese
of Southern Celebes and the Maduranese of Madura and East Java
have on the other hand shown little change in their stance
within Islam and against Christianity. In Bali there had been
(before 1965) slight signs of an increasing interest in
Christianity coupled with a waning adherence to the Hindu-Bali
religion. In the aftermath of the Communist fall and the
purge of the Balinese Communists, a revival of Hinduism has
been experienced. The "Emerald Island" seems now less likely
than before to come to Christ (see Bradshaw, 1969:18-19).

Clearly, the responsiveness in Indonesia is not a
general phenomenon. Many of the churches of Central and East

Java have more than doubled in the four years following the
events of 1965. The new climate has resulted in the miracles
of northern Sumatra, Central and East Java and some of the
outer islands, notably Timor. It has not, however, broken
through to the great Islamic peoples. To say that Indonesia
is turning to Christ is to overstate what the Spirit has and
is doing. These statements are not to "play down" what has
and is happening. We are convinced greater victories are
coming--the best is yet to be.

The participation of the Baptist Churches in this
overall awakening came also in the wake of increased evangelistic activity. In addition to continuing an increasingly
productive local church evangelism, the Baptists promoted
several nation-wide projects. The Asian-wide Sunday School
Campaign and the GEHIBA Revival Campaign, that have been
mentioned, materially advanced the growth of the churches.
Both the Sunday School Campaign and the GEHIBA emphasized
the local church and the planting of new congregations. The
GEHIBA Campaign of 1966-1967 had as its goal, 1 + 1 = 80,
1 + 1 = 8,000. The goal meant that if each of the forty
Baptist Churches or Chapels should start one new congregation,
Baptist congregations would number eighty and if each of the
4,000 Baptist members should win one person, Baptists would
number 8,000. Had there not been the emphasis on planting
new congregations, the increase in membership could not have
been realized. In 1969 Baptists could point to 153 congregations and 9,779 members.

Village evangelism that produced churches among
Javanese peoples must be seen as a factor in the advance. In
Kediri among thirty-two congregations, six are definitely
located in the town areas, serve somewhat ethnically mixed
congregations and boast a membership of 1,113. Five other
congregations are listed as rural or village, but might be
considered semi-rural and have a membership of 418. The remaining nineteen congregations all are definitely in village
settings, serve totally Javanese constituencies and report
a total membership of 567. The town churches were started in
1955, 1962 and 1963. The village churches were mostly begun
between 1966 and 1969, yet they have over one half as many
members as the town churches and make up over one fourth of
the total membership in Kediri.

In Jogja out of 995 members 279 are in village congregations. Again the village churches are much younger than
the city churches. In Semarang in 1968, 579 of the 1,020
members reported were in the village or neighborhood congregations.

These statistics demonstrate that village and neighborhood areas have been unusually responsive during these years.
The indication would be that Baptists should devote increasingly active efforts in the villages and neighborhoods (kampungs).

In these areas families and kingroups are more likely to be won. Needless to say, this does not mean that urban churches should be neglected. Both avenues of service must be kept open. The growth of Baptist Churches has not been equal in every area. The next section of this chapter will study the rate of growth in each area. It will be readily seen that while nearly every region served by Baptists has produced growth, Central and East Java have grown more rapidly.

COMPARISON OF GROWTH BY AREAS

Baptist Churches are located in four major regions of Java. West Java, including the stations of Bandung, Djakarta and Bogor, are in the Sundanese region and the metropolitan center of Djakarta. Semarang, Solo, Jogja and Purwokerto are located in Central Java and serve largely Javanese peoples. Surabaja, Kediri and Madiun make up the East Java stations and likewise work in a primarily Javanese region. The opening of the stations in Djember and Probolinggo, East Java will bring Baptists not only into contact with millions of Javanese but also with Maduranese people who inhabit large areas in East Java.

Four regions in Sumatra are served. The Minangkabau peoples of West Sumatra are served in the cities of Bukittinggi and Padang. The city of Palembang in southern Sumatra is served by one Baptist Church. Baptists are also planting churches in northern Sumatra in the city of Medan and among the peoples of the Lampung area in southern Sumatra. The growth must be seen separately in each of the regions.

The study of growth in each area will be instructive in several regards. However, since it will primarily note the total membership figures, the area study tends to some degree to distort. This is because in this section little difference is made between kinds of churches and kinds of growth. This more detailed analysis will be taken up in the subsequent section. This section aims at helping the Baptists see the overall growth pattern in each area in order that they might better decide where emphasis should be placed.

Special Features in the Areas

Before examining membership and other features, it is necessary to clarify the basic differences that exist between the areas. These differences vitally relate to church growth. Without such understanding mistaken ideas would develop.

West Java (the Sundanese)

The Sundanese people of West Java have proved to be basically resistant to the Gospel. Historically, West Java

has been separate and distinct from Central and East Java. No
great kingdoms arose in the west. Hindu and Buddhist elements
were far less pronounced, consequently there was no great power
to oppose the advance of Islam. In addition Dutch influence
was felt both earlier and in more intense forms in western Java.
Islam in the west even more than in the east, became the alternative to bowing to the foreign Dutch rule by providing
better transportation and communications, resulted in more
Sundanese contact with the Moslem world. Historical factors
have therefore inclined West Java to a more pronounced Islamic
stand and had a part in rendering the region less responsive
to the Christian Message (Kraemer, 1958:102, 112-*114*).

The progress of the Gospel was likewise obstructed by
the Dutch refusal to undertake evangelistic efforts among the
peoples of Java. The first three Dutch missionaries to West
Java, who arrived in 1863, noted that although Dutch rule had
been established in 1596, no Dutch missionary had proclaimed
the Gospel outside the capital city (Kraemer, 1958:97). The
failure of the Dutch to introduce the Gospel in West Java
(indeed in all Java) during these critical two hundred years
must constitute one of history's most regrettable missionary
failures.

Ethnic factors have combined with the historical to
build barriers against Christianity in West Java. Economically
West Java has been more blessed than other parts of Java. West
Java has had a higher degree of material security (Cooley,
1968:93). Perhaps this security has given rise to the more
open, amiable and frank nature of the Sundanese when compared
to the more reticent Javanese. Sundanese demonstrate a pronounced family solidarity. They are even more collective than
other peoples of Java. Islam entered the Sundanese peoples
along family lines until now it is fused with the Sundanese
adat (customary law). This intensified the Sundanese attachment to Islam. Most Sundanese would consider abandoning Islam
as tantamount to abandoning their custom and nationality.
Their attachment is less to Islam than to their adat (Kraemer,
1958:112-115).

Faulty methods of missionary work have intensified
the general resistance in West Java. The missionaries failed
to understand anthropological and ethnological features of
Sundanese society. While the training of West Java missionaries
included study of the Sundanese language, there was little of
the study of culture. The missionaries made no attempt to
penetrate into the basic philosophy of life. Kraemer says:

>*Studying a language, mastering its grammar, acquiring
>a large vocabulary, all this is excellent and in-
>dispensable. Nevertheless, the gates of indigenous
>life remain shut, unless this knowledge of the lan-
>guage is placed in its true perspective: that it*

is a vehicle for the unravelling and inner under-
standing of the psychological and cultural reality
in which the speakers of the language stand. Hence,
the main emphasis in studying the language...should
be on the language as a means of penetrating into
an alien world, and of assimilating its literature,
either written or unwritten, with its underlying
philosophy of life (Kraemer, 1958:107).

Another missiologist, A. R. Tippett, also emphasized
the necessity for anthropological understanding. Tippett contends that with anthropological training a missionary can
reach the point of effectiveness in two years that sometimes
requires ten years experience without the anthropological
background. His conclusion is "Anthropology is a must"
(Tippett, 1968:8-9). Obviously, the penalty for overlooking
anthropology is foreignness and failure to adequately communicate the Gospel to the people.

Kraemer states that the greatest factor detracting
from the progress of the Gospel in West Java was the paternalism of the missionaries (Kraemer, 1958:120). Paternalism
is the imposition on the Church of the missionary's standards,
will, customary practices and plans with little regard for
the selfhood and feelings of the nationals. It is probably the
most serious sin of modern missions. Concerning the paternalism in West Java, Kraemer says:

The congregations should be guided in such a way
that it (sic) learns independently to accept the
Gospel as a gift and as a criterion to be applied
in its own situation; it should learn this as a
group and as a community (not just the missionary
or the guru-indjil nor the two together or elders
and deacons only), which means an acceptance of
the Gospel according to the measure of the living
insight which the group has attained. I wish to
stress this latter point in particular. For one
of the causes of our manifold failure lies in
the fact that we do not have the courage to allow
a group of Indigenous Christians to lead its own
life in accordance with the measure of living
insight which it has reached. This is the only
condition whereby a person or a group, whether
European or Indigenous, is able to live and grow.
Our method is that we wish them to live by the
measure of living insight that we have got. Thus
instead of arousing vital forces--which is our
aim--we tend to smother them (1958:120).

Missions must learn from Kraemer's assessment of the situation
in West Java and strive to overcome every vesture of paternalism.

All that Kraemer says about the faulty missionary
methods in early West Java is true and should be well considered by all who desire to communicate the Gospel in cross-cultural
situations. It must be stated however, that the Sundanese
have proved highly resistant to the Gospel. No matter what
methods had been employed, the growth would most likely have
been slow. Methods do not make response; they only aid in
the proper reaping of the ripening harvest. Faulty methods did
not alone cause the slow growth. The Sundanese are simply
resistant--in God's time the prayer is that resistance will
turn to response.

Central and East Java (the Javanese)

The resistance of West Java changes to responsiveness
in Central and East Java. Historical and ethnological factors
have also contributed to the Javanese religious climate. In
contrast to West Java, Central and East Java felt more extensive Hindu and Buddhist influences. The Sailendra and
Majapahit Empires brought increasing Indian influences. Due
partically to the Hindu-Buddhist influences and partly to the
basic Javanese philosophy, Islam, in Central and East Java, is
of a particular nature, sometimes referred to as Javanese
Islam (Fisher, 1964:250-251). Javanese Islam shows many
factors of orthodox Islamic faith, but beneath this religious
tradition lies a continuity of belief in the old spirits and
ancestral ghosts (Kennedy, 1942:105). This mixture of religious
traditions has resulted in the unique religious situation of
Central and East Java.

Javanese show a marked tendency to seek the mystic
and secret way of life that has even invaded their variation
of Islam. This characteristic, referred to as mentjari ngelmu
(seeking the Truth or Way), consists in searching for a way
to peace and fulfillment through mystical experience. It
provides a contact for the Gospel (Kraemer, 1958:74-75). Related to the search for ngelmu is the general Javanese tolerance that considers one religion as the same as another. The
fusion of animist, Hindu-Buddhist, Islamic and other religious
factors has brought about a religious situation unique among
Moslem peoples (Kennedy, 1937:297).

In chapter two of this study the relation of Javanese
family life and kinship patterns to church growth were set
forth. The social stratification into santri and abangan
groups also has great meaning for church growth. Obviously,
the abangan population constitutes the more fertile soil for
discipling. Since abangans are more numerous in the villages,
this may explain the response in the villages and mountain
regions.

Conclusion

The plain fact is that some peoples more readily accept the Gospel than others. Usually, the responsiveness or resistance is conditioned by cultural factors. The situation in West and East Java has been conditioned by historical, religious and ethnic factors.

Sumatra (the Minangkabau, Palembang, Batak and Lampung areas)

Baptist growth on Sumatra has been affected by the nature of the cultures in which the churches have been planted. The first Baptist Church on Sumatra, located in the West Sumatra city of Bukittinggi, lies in the heart of the Minangkabau society. The "Minang" people have strong national feelings springing partly from their legendary history that relates their ancestry to Rome or Mecca (which is not clear in the myths). Some myths even mention Alexander the Great! One set of myths contend that a great flood brought the first Minangkabau people to the mountains of West Sumatra where they have lived since (Cole, 1945:258).

It is established that the Minangkabau region early had contact with south India. However, only in certain high titles is Indian influence still seen in the culture (Cole, 1945:251). Though some contend that Islam came to the Minangkabau people from Atjeh, others contend that it was brought by traders from Persia and south India (Mansoer, 1960: 149). By whatever means it entered, Islam is now the dominant religion and no other has ever made the slightest impression on Minangkabau culture. There is, however, a strong animistic base beneath the Islamic superstructure which includes belief in the magic men (dukun), spirits, "rice mother" to whom sacrifices are given and other animistic practices (Cole, 1945: 263-265; H. Geertz, 1963:85).

The most striking feature of Minangkabau culture is its matrilineal kinship system. The husband comes to live at the home of the mother of his wife. The situation is complicated by the Moslem law allowing four wives. Divorce is relatively easy, which results in multiple marriages for many (Cole, 1945:265-266). Theoretically, all family members reside in one long house, but actually additional houses at times are constructed. The larger group, made up of all related houses, is called the parui gadang (big womb) and the individual houses the parui ketek (little womb). As the community grows it may attract others (friends, servants, former slaves, etc.) who will live on the land of the family but will have no voice in decisions. The interests of these friends, slaves, etc., are rigidly safeguarded by the family. Such a community is called a pajung and its head, kapella pajung or pungulu pajung. Several pajung make up a suku (tribe)

law). While marriage is allowed within the suku, those who
draw water from the same well are prohibited from marriage
even if from different suku (Cole, 1945:256-258).
      With the religious and cultural background of the
Minangkabau people it is not surprising that they have been
impervious to the Gospel. The only churches in Bukittinggi
are made up of Indonesians from other regions. The Baptist
Church in this region will continue as a probe, using medical
ministry to seek an entrance into the Minangkabau people.
      Baptist Churches have been planted in the city of
Palembang where Islam is less strong than in Atjeh or
Bukittinggi but still formidable. In Medan of North Sumatra,
while Islam is strong, there are many non-Moslem people who
can be evangelized. Of the two regions, the Medan church
should be expected to grow the faster. Some investigation
should be made to find what influence of the early Srivijaja
Empire (Buddhist) might still be operable.
      The Lampung area in southern Sumatra is a re-settlement
area for Javanese being moved from Java (Wertheim, 1965:106).
Both for this reason and because Islam is less intense among
the original peoples, the Gospel should win a hearing there.
It would be a mistake to attempt to plant a church there
among both the Javanese and the original Lampungese. In all
probability the more productive plan would be churches for
each ethnic group and any smaller homogeneous units within
these groups. To work among the various ethnic groups is to
follow valid mission methods. This is a general principle
relating to church growth.

Membership Growth in the Areas

      The discussion of the various regions should indicate
where churches would grow best. There is some surprise in the
facts of growth. The graph on page 163 shows membership figures
of the different areas (with Sumatra counted as one) for the
years 1958, 1962, 1965 and 1968.
      Surprisingly, until 1962 membership figures in West
Java were as large as East Java and larger than Central Java.
By 1965 both Central and East Java reported larger membership
figures than did West Java. Figures for 1968 show Central Java
to be far ahead in total membership with East Java still sub-
stantially above West Java. These facts reveal several interesting things about church growth.
      In light of the Sundanese resistance the position of
membership leadership of West Java during early periods demands
explanation. The answer partly lies in the fact that a majority
of the members of the churches in Bandung, Bogor and Djakarta
are either Indonesians of Chinese descent or are Indonesians
from other islands in the archipelago. This is not to detract
from the tremendously important opportunity to evangelize this

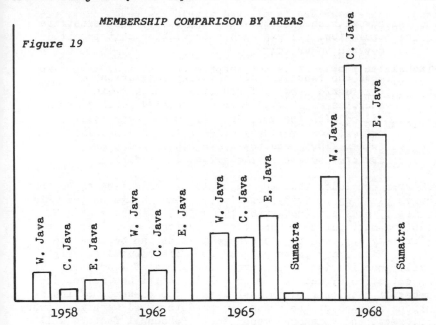

MEMBERSHIP COMPARISON BY AREAS

Figure 19

part of Indonesia's millions. However, it does substantiate basic resistance of the Sundanese. The churches are not growing among Sundanese.

Growth in West Java has been less aided by the institutions than have the other churches in Java. While the hospital in East Java and the seminary in Central Java have made notable contributions to church growth, publication ministry located in Bandung has influenced and helped all the churches. Publications has had little opportunity to greatly influence growth in Bandung except through the missionaries assigned to publication. The seminary students have actively participated in the evangelistic efforts in Central and East Java but have had only slight opportunity to aid West Java due to travel difficulties. The hospital evangelistic ministry has materially aided evangelism in the Kediri region. Publication, by the nature of the work, has aided the churches in other regions almost as much as Bandung churches.

Membership growth in the different areas is closely related to the number of congregations. In 1968 West Java reported sixteen congregations while East Java noted thirty-three and Central Java fifty-three. This church planting , which has been most actively pursued in the stations at Semarang, Solo, Jogja and Purwokerto, must be considered a major factor in the membership growth in the Central Java area. The same could be said of East Java, especially Kediri.

The only way to reach the millions of lost Indonesians is by a deliberate program of church planting that will cover

the islands with churchlets--reaching out to some substrata
of the population. It was such a conviction that prompted
Donald McGavran to write:

> *What the fantastically mounting populations of*
> *this world need is fantastically multiplying*
> *churches which will enable liberated populations,*
> *filled with the Holy Spirit, to generate their*
> *own Calvins, Wesleys, Wilberforces and Martin*
> *Luther Kings, and their own sober, godly and*
> *fruitful societies (McGavran, 1965a:457).*

McGavran concludes that the majority of Christians agree that
church planting activity constitutes what should be the main
thrust of missions (McGavran, 1968:337). Vigorous church
planting must put down hundreds of churches over Indonesia
before any approach to its evangelization can be expected.

Missionary personnel has been distributed on very
nearly equalitarian lines across the areas of Indonesia. The
concentration of medical personnel in Kediri has raised the
number of missionaries in East Java. The presence of institutions in each of the areas has predetermined much missionary
deployment and consummed much time. Personnel factors will
be discussed later. It is sufficient to see that disparagement
in growth was not caused by an imbalance of missionary staff.

Considered section by section membership figures demonstrate that the responsive regions of Central and East Java
have grown more rapidly. In addition to the obviously more
responsive nature of these areas, the aggressive church planting efforts, both on the part of missionaries and local churches
has played a part in the more rapid growth. The exact nature
of the growth of the Baptist Churches will become more clear
as attention is centered on each city and the churches in each
city.

GROWTH BY STATIONS

When growth is studied by stations and attention directed to the composition of individual congregations, the true
growth picture of the Baptist Churches within the Indonesian
mosaic is most clearly seen. In general, Baptists have two
types of churches. There are conglomerate churches composed
of members from many of the various ethnic peoples. The membership of these churches combines Javanese, Chinese, Minahasans,
Ambonese, Americans and occasionally other nationalities. In
some cases the leadership is mixed. In other cases the leadership is disproportionately from one ethnic group.

The second type of churches live almost exclusively
among one homogeneous unit of the Indonesian society. In many
cases these homogeneous churches are village and neighborhood

churches serving almost entirely Javanese peoples in Central
and East Java. However, some of the churches that are made
up almost entirely of Chinese Indonesians could also be viewed
as homogeneous churches.

Both types of churches are growing and should be continued. Facts will show that relatively more people are being
won in the homogeneous churches, especially among the Javanese.
Homogeneous units of the population are extremely important
to church growth thinking. The failure to understand and consider homogeneous units leads to many mistakes in missionary
work. The understanding of homogeneous units is essential for
good planning for church growth (see Shearer, 1966:80-142).

This section will allow the study of the various homogeneous units and the churches among them. The most accurate
picture of Baptist growth should be realized from this study.
The growth of the different types of churches will be analized.
The graphs of growth for each city should be carefully studied,
pages 166, 167 and 168.

The Churches in Bandung

Located in the heart of the Sundanese culture, the
churches in Bandung have grown almost exclusively among
Indonesians of Chinese descent and other non-Sundanese peoples.
Growth in recent years has not kept pace with the rate in
Central and East Java. Being located in the area where mission
work through the years has met with little response, the decision to work among the Indonesians of Chinese descent was
the only feasible procedure and should be aggressively continued. These churches among the Chinese should not, however,
expect or be expected to reach the Sundanese people. When the
Sundanese are reached for Christ, it will be through churches
that are planted solidly within the Sundanese culture, that
will allow the Gospel to flow naturally through the strong
family and kin ties in Sundanese society.

The fact that the Indonesian society is not built on
caste lines and uses primarily the national language, should
not blind us to the fact that basic and well defined differences
exist between the various peoples who make up the overall
Indonesian mosaic (See H. Geertz, 1963:24-96). Peoples become
Christians more easily when they do not have to cross cultural,
linguistic and class barriers to become part of the church.
They prefer to join churches in which they look like, think
like, live like and talk like the other members (McGavran, 1970:
198). This principle must be kept in mind in seeking to win
the peoples of Indonesia.

The per decade rate for the churches in Bandung, since
1956 is 640 (compared with 1,526 in Kediri). An important
factor and one that must be investigated further is the unusual
growth of the Bethlehem congregation in Bandung. In the past

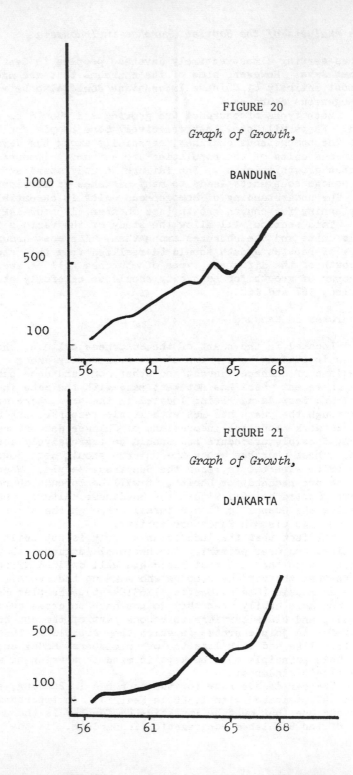

FIGURE 20

Graph of Growth,

BANDUNG

FIGURE 21

Graph of Growth,

DJAKARTA

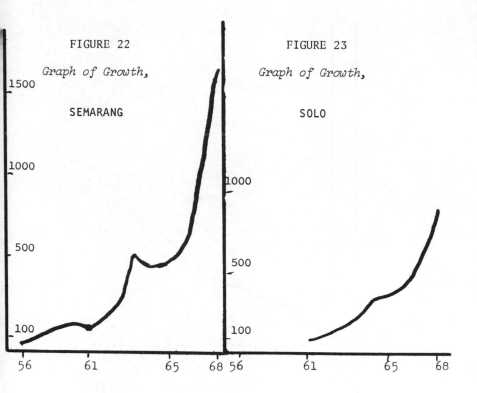

FIGURE 22

Graph of Growth,

SEMARANG

FIGURE 23

Graph of Growth,

SOLO

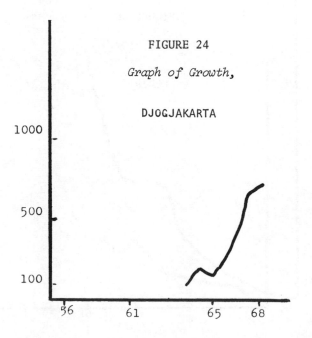

FIGURE 24

Graph of Growth,

DJOGJAKARTA

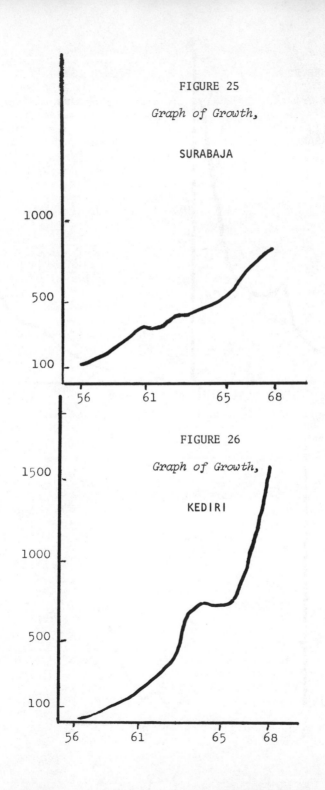

FIGURE 25

Graph of Growth,

SURABAJA

FIGURE 26

Graph of Growth,

KEDIRI

three years this one congregation with its two chapels has
reported forty-one percent of the baptisms of the Bandung
station. Moreover, in 1968 this church "...with its mission...
accounts for forty-eight percent of the baptisms and thirty-seven
percent of the Sunday School enrollment reported from Bandung..."
(Minutes, 1968:92).

The fact that this church, with a majority of Chinese
Indonesians, is no different from other churches in membership
and location, leads to the question of its extremely rapid
growth rate. It must be noted that the church was promoting
Sunday School work during these rapidly growing years. In 1968
the Bethlehem Church reported 275 enrolled in Sunday School
in the mother church and 250 at the two chapels (Minutes, 1968:
95a). The church was engaged in outreach, having opened the
two thriving chapels. This church is showing rapid growth
when the two older churches in Bandung are showing less advance
than in previous years (Minutes, 1968:93). Aggressive outreach
could be a large part of the reason for the growth of the church.

In conclusion, the churches of Bandung are growing
among Chinese Indonesians, who are for the most part of a
higher economic bracket than the Sundanese. The Bethlehem
Church indicates (as does the Efrata Church to a lesser degree)
that growth is possible. However, the churches of Bandung
must realize that Sundanese will seldom be drawn into the
Chinese led congregations. They will be reached when there
are Sundanese churches thoroughly immersed in Sundanese adat,
most likely using the Sundanese language. Even when such
methods are used, great growth will await the turning of the
Sundanese to God's will.

The Churches in Djakarta

The churches in Djakarta are conglomerate churches
with a high percentage of Chinese Indonesians together with
many Javanese, Ambonese, Batak and Minahasans who are living
in the capital city. The churches have resumed a growth rate
that had been interrupted before 1965. The total membership
in 1968 was 856 (Minutes, 1968:151). This would indicate a
growth of 660 per decade for the twelve years since 1956.
Since 1966 the churches have been growing at the rate of
2,470 per decade or more than forty-eight percent for these
two years.

The churches in Djakarta, like Bandung, have followed
the pattern of locating a building (mission provided) on a main
street or close to a main street and drawing people to it.
This has led to churches made up of people from many of the
various ethnic groups. The fact that Djakarta, the capital
city, is more cosmopolitan than other regions would indicate
such strategy would be more effective here than it might prove
in less integrated areas.

While the conglomerate churches of Djakarta are growing, they are not adequately reaching the four million persons who live in greater Djakarta. The existing churches, appealing across the mosaic population, can and still continue to reach people. I firmly believe that more rapid growth will be realized when churches are purposely planted with the idea of appealing to the various ethnic groups who are living in Djakarta. Such a plan would in no wise be viewed as divisive or destructive of brotherhood in Christ. It would provide a way for peoples to come to Christ in the manner most natural, that is by family, kinship, clan and ethnic lines.

Baptists in Djakarta should carefully consider the history of the Congregacao Crista No Brasil which has won something over 110,000 Italian immigrants in Brazil (see Read, 1965:23). While Djakarta would not provide such a large immigrant population, there are undoubtedly thousands of people who could be won into ethnic churches. The possibility of such movements must be investigated. It should be determined if there are existing pockets of ethnic groups where ethnic churches could be planted.

The Churches of Bogor and Sukabumi

The churches in Bogor and Sukabumi are also located solidly in the Sundanese region. They, like the churches in Bandung, contain a high percentage of Chinese Indonesians. The churches in Bogor, which began in 1965 are estimated as having seventy-one percent Chinese, eighteen percent Javanese and eleven percent other ethnic groups in their membership. Sukabumi divides its ninety-three members, ninety-six percent Chinese and four percent Sundanese (Trotter, 1969:1).

An opportunity exists for the churches in the Sukabumi area. Several plantations have at present large numbers of Javanese workers who can in all likelihood be evangelized. Since people uprooted from their homes are often open to change, this could well be the great opportunity in West Java. However, the evangelization of these peoples may well be made more difficult by the stronger adherence of the general Sundanese population to Islam. The strong Islam could also prove to be an aid in evangelizing the Javanese as they might reject it to show their independence. At any rate the churches must look toward this possibility.

The Churches in Semarang

Semarang churches have grown at a rate of 1,380 per decade since 1956. These churches represent several entirely different types. The Sion Baptist Church is a conglomerate church with eighteen percent Chinese, seventy-seven percent Javanese and five percent American and other island peoples.

It was for some five years pastored by missionaries and during these years has demonstrated remarkable growth. The leadership is largely Chinese with a strong Javanese outreach. The Iman Baptist Church on the other hand, has been under the leadership of a national pastor for a number of years but has had missionary co-workers. The membership is over ninety-six percent Javanese and the leadership solidly Javanese. The Tjandi Baptist Church is of a conglomerate type but still over ninety-five percent Javanese. This church, built in a wealthier area of town with the hope of attracting more well-to-do people, has only in a very small way achieved this goal. It has, however, in a remarkable way reached the masses. Then, the Semarang area has also a number of congregations located in the neighborhoods and villages, that are reaching almost exclusively Javanese peoples. The study of the churches in Semarang must note the growth pattern and the advance of these various types of churches.

Sion Baptist Church, with its history of missionary leadership, first as pastor, then as co-workers, has shown exceptional growth both in numbers of members and in qualitative and organic growth. It has the finest organization of any church in Indonesia. The church grew from 124 members in 1965 to 324 in 1969. It has for some years had the responsibility for the chapels at Ungaran and Kudus which were originally opened by the Seminary Extension Program. In addition two chapels have been opened by the church itself. One of these chapels points to a promising method. A number of members of Sion Church, all from the same neighborhood, were organized into a special fellowship and encouraged to jointly study evangelistic methods. Then this fellowship was planted as a congregation in their <u>kampung</u> (community). In this way a congregation, planted in and led by members of one <u>kampung</u> came into existence, drawing aid and encouragement from the mother church. This method is worthy of much attention as it attains the goal of establishing congregations in the <u>kampungs</u> under the leadership of people in that area.

The Iman and Tjandi Churches have shown a different type of development. Both churches have had a national pastor with close support of missionaries. Both churches show a membership growth even greater than Sion, Iman growing from eighty-nine in 1965 to 280 in 1969 and Tjandi from seventy in 1965 to 305 in 1969. Both Iman and Tjandi Churches have actively planted new congregations. Tjandi works with two chapels with a combined membership of fifty-nine. Iman Church has five chapels with a local member and a seminary student working in each. The other city church, Peterongan, has not grown to the extent the others have. Peterongan Church has a very conglomerate membership. It would be an instructive study to find why this church has grown more slowly while other churches are growing rapidly. Peterongan has a very healthy, indigenous, self-supporting chapel.

Other churches in the Semarang area were planted through the Seminary Evangelistic Extension Program. These churches, started by the evangelistic witnessing of the students, have generally followed the pattern of a student remaining as pastor of the resulting congregation. Twenty-five congregations have resulted from this program and reported a combined membership of 1,031 in 1969. From the standpoint of church planting this is a remarkable record. However, there are some definite weaknesses in the program. The churches formed have not shown sufficient organic growth, their stewardship is lagging (only three are self-supporting) and they have been pastored primarily from the outside, that is by seminary students. While the plan has been to provide places for students to gain experience in both soul-winning and pastoring, this is not the best way to achieve widespread growth. A better plan would be the use of unpaid leadership from each area. However, the purpose of providing experience for students would indicate that the program should continue.

An investigation of the membership and other data concerning these churches indicate that those churches that have been planted in the kampung areas have made rapid progress. Karang Aju Church was planted in 1962. By 1969 it had grown to 140 members and had achieved self-support in 1966. It grew from forty-two in 1965 to 140 in 1969. Puspowarno started in 1966 and had in 1969 a membership of ninety-five and was self-supporting Other churches in village areas have also prospered within the matrix of Javanese culture. Kilpantjur, started in 1968, has reached a membership of seventy-four and Malajudarat, planted in 1967 has grown to sixty-eight. The great needs of the Extension Program are a stronger emphasis on organic growth, stewardship and a determination to continue outreach.

The Churches in Solo

The churches in Solo show a similar history to other Baptist beginnings. The growth rate per decade is 1,090 since 1961. In most cases the churches were started with Mission funds providing places of worship. They also went through a period of "hot house" growth. However, the churches in Solo to a degree not excelled among Baptist Churches in Indonesia have been active in outreach through church planting. The Penumping Church, started in 1955, attained self-support in 1965. It grew from 188 in 1965 to 297 in 1969. However, this figure is a revised membership figure as the records were lost in a 1965 flood. Also, numbers of members have been "given" to the various chapels of this church--a highly significant factor in Baptist work in Solo. Penumping Church has four chapels that have a combined membership of 114. These

chapels are led by the pastor and laymen from the mother
church. As they progress the chapels have on two occasions
called seminary students as pastors.

In addition to the four existing chapels, Penumping
Church has been active in starting congregations in two other
towns and one area of Solo. These congregations are now independent of the mother church. The Arimathea Church grew
out of the Penumping Church from which it received a number
of its first members. It now has its own pastor (a seminary
student) and a membership of ninety-six. The church in the
city of Madiun (now a station with a resident missionary) was
started by the churches from Solo and now has twenty-one members. Two chapels from this church have already been opened
and great prospects are seen. The Penumping Church worked
with the missionary in Solo to plant a church in the city of
Sragen which now has a membership of around fifty-five.
Laymen from Sragen have been active in starting other chapels.

Another church, located in a sugar cane mill city,
Tjolomadu, near Solo, also has an unusual outreach program.
This church was originally begun by laymen from Penumping
but has been self-supporting since 1968. The present membership of 142 is an increase from the 1965 membership of only
forty-one. This church and its pastor promote fourteen chapels,
all but one meeting in homes. The church carries on its
program of outreach with no financial aid from the Mission
(Pennell, 1969:1-2).

The Solo area churches are to be commended for their
efforts in church planting. In the Solo area there are
eight churches and twenty-six chapels. These churches are
almost exclusively among Javanese, although some of the
churches in Solo have Chinese members. The Solo churches
have produced a large number of seminary students which is
some indication of qualitative growth. The churches should
work toward an even more indigenous nature, self-support
and education, but not it is hoped, at the expense of further
outreach. In such a rapidly growing area the tendency might
be to slow down outreach in order to seek consolidation. Such
a procedure would most likely fail to reach deeper growth
but would suceed in retarding outreach.

The Churches in Djogjakarta

The churches in Djogjakarta, who made their first
report of fifty-eight members in 1963, noted in 1968 a membership of 907 in eleven congregations. This produced a growth
rate of 1,860 per decade. In addition, the churches and
missionaries in Jogja were instrumental in planting a church
in Purwokerto, which is now a separate station. The witness
from Jogja has spread to nearby towns of Magelang, Klaten,
Sleman and to several areas in and around the city. Since 1966

the churches in Jogja have grown at the rate of 2,910 per
decade (J. Smith, 1969:1).

The aggressive outreach in the Jogja station has been
achieved through the efforts of the missionaries and national
Christians. As the churches have gained strength, lay people
have assumed leadership roles. The student center has provided an entry into the student population of the city. Since
Gadja Madah University in Jogja attracts students from many
areas, the center has been able to minister to and win many.
Students who have become Christians have been used to lead
services and plant congregations. This is an extremely productive venture in student ministry that deserves wide notice.

The churches in Jogja have consciously moved toward
planting churches in the kampung and village situations.
These congregations have been started by missionaries, by
laymen and by churches. Several continuing along indigenous
lined are noteworthy. The fine churches in Jogja are to be
commended for the aggressive church planting and outreach.
Additional efforts in the direction of qualitative growth
must be undertaken. A lay training program on a short-term
basis in 1969 should also be followed up that unpaid leaders
will be available for further outreach.

The Churches in Purwokerto

Outreach has been the main word in Purwokerto. The
church was planted by the Jogja station but since 1967,
missionaries have been stationed in Purwokerto and the church
has reached out to five nearby towns and three villages.
These congregations primarily serve Javanese people. They
depended largely on seminary students for leadership and as
yet have not achieved self-support. The work in this area
is still in the beginning stage. Keith Hamilton's advice
that this stage be passed through as rapidly as possible
should be heeded (Hamilton, 1962:139).

The Churches in Kediri

Since 1958 the churches in Kediri have been growing
at the rate of 1,526 per decade. From 1966 to 1968 the rate
of growth per decade was 4,160. The churches in Kediri are
of less conglomerate nature than those in the larger cities.
One church, Getsemani, reports a membership of thirty percent
Chinese and seventy percent Javanese. The other churches
are ninety percent or more Javanese. Getsemani has a number
of fine Chinese leaders, but the leadership of the other
Kediri churches is largely Javanese. Hence, the churches
in Kediri are not of the same pattern as those in Bandung
and Djakarta. The membership of the Setia Bakti Church increased from 240 in 1965 to 479 in 1969 while the Semampir

Church was growing from 142 to 242. The most rapid increase
was registered by Getsemani Church which grew from 100 in 1965
to 283 in 1969 (Rogers, 1969:1).

The churches in Kediri would do well to consider ways
to reach the Chinese Indonesian population, remembering that
people like to become Christian without crossing cultural
lines (McGavran, 1970:198). A definite plan to reach the
Chinese would strengthen the witness of the Kediri churches.
Churches primarily among one ethnic group constitute sound
mission strategy.

In addition to the growth in the churches in the town
of Kediri, the area has been most active in outreach, both
through local congregations and the Desa Program that has
been a cooperative effort of the association of churches. This
program has planted congregations in the villages. Five of
the churches in the villages have their own lay pastors and
receive no subsidy of any kind. Six others are helped only
in that transportation is provided for the lay pastor who comes
from town to the village (B. Lewis, 1969:2). These congregations in the villages are working solely in the Javanese
society. They are the most strictly indigenous situations
the Baptists have in Indonesia. The membership of the village
churches in 1969 stood at 574 as compared to 1,468 for the
older, town churches (Rogers, 1969:1). When it is noted that
most of the village churches were only planted in 1966-1969,
while the city churches have been in existence since 1955,
the growth of these homogeneous churches is the more striking.

Two dangers face the outreach program in Kediri: (1)
the ever-present tendency to begin some type of hidden subsidy,
(2) the even more present temptation to slow down outreach in
order to consolidate and teach. Recent reports of increasing
Moslem pressure and attempts to curb Christian outreach (B.
Lewis, 1969:2) show the necessity of continuing to expand
while the field is ripe. History proves that populations
become responsive for certain periods and then sometimes
lapse in less responsiveness after a time. We must work
while it is yet light.

The advice of mission strategists who point out the
time to reinforce growing churches is now must not be neglected
(see McGavran, 1955:142). To over-emphasize perfecting in
opposition to discipling is to lose the whole game. Both
must be done. However, "...during period of expansion when
the faith is surging forward in some population, if any part
of the task must suffer it should be perfecting. At such times
discipling has first priority" (McGavran, 1959:98). A. R.
Tippett notes, "The remarkable thing is that where the Church
is alive to its responsibility for outreach, it is usually also
found to be alive to the responsibility for inner quality
growth" (1967:132). Outreach through the active witnessing of
new converts is most likely the best method of perfecting.

The Churches in Surabaja

The churches of Surabaja grew at a rate of 690 per decade over the period of 1956-1968. Between 1966 and 1968 the
rate per decade was 1,510. These churches are more conglomerate
in membership as is general in urban areas.

The Surabaja churches are largely composed of Javanese
peoples, but the Immanuel Church shows a membership of fifty
percent Chinese and fifty percent Javanese. The Surabaja
churches have been almost exclusively started in a Mission
provided building. The Immanuel Church grew from 273 to 284
between 1965 and 1969, but this figure must be accepted in
light of an adjustment of membership figures that dropped in-
active members. The fact that the church reported fifty-one
baptisms in 1967 demonstrates that it was not standing still.
The Pengharapan Church with ninety-three percent Javanese
members grew from 169 to 376 in the 1965-1969 period. Gubang,
started in a kampung in 1957, increased to sixty-five members
by 1969. This fact goes against the general trend for kampung
churches to grow faster. Study as to the factors involved
in this situation should be made.

Five other congregations have been planted in the
Surabaja area by churches and missionaries in Surabaja. These
five congregations had a membership of 263 in 1969. A factor
to be noted is the achievement of self-support by six of
the eight congregations in Surabaja. Immanuel reached
self-support in 1957 but it was not until 1965 that Pengharapan
was able to support its own program. It required eleven years
for this church to reach self-support. Patemon, started in
1963, attained self-support three years later. Brongglan,
started by a church in 1968 and led by a lay pastor, was
self-supporting from the beginning. Self-support among so
many congregations points to good qualitative and organic
growth among these churches.

A feature of the growth in Surabaja has been the
steady increase (note graph on page 168). While Surabaja
churches have not increased to the numbers of Kediri, the
churches have the most consistent graph of growth of any city.
Surabaja has often shown a better than average relationship
between professions of faith and baptisms. The follow-up in
the Surabaja churches may well contain a needed lesson for
other Baptist Churches. This is not to say that spurts of
growth are not desirable but Surabaja churches have shown no
times of decline. It is to be hoped that further outreach
will be a major part of the ministry of the churches in
Surabaja in the years to come.

The Churches on Sumatra
Baptist witness on Sumatra has not had a long history.

The churches in Bukittinggi and Padang are located in the
midst of the strongly Islamic peoples of the Minangkabau.
Started in 1964 with the idea of giving an evangelistic
emphasis to the planned medical ministry, the church in
Bukittinggi has made little progress among the Minangkabau
people. This result is in line with the experience of all
churches in West Sumatra. Twenty-one members make up the
church in Bukittinggi, thirty-seven percent Chinese, seventeen
percent Javanese and forty-six percent other peoples. A part
of the last group is of course the missionary families who
make up almost one half the membership. The mission in Padang,
a port city, numbers about fifty percent of its twelve members
from Javanese people (Austin, 1969:1).

In such a resistant culture the church must maintain
a lighthouse ministry, attempting to win those winnable segments
of the society while keeping a watch for any movement among
Minang peoples. No people should be left without the witness
of the Gospel. In God's time response will come.

The church in Palembang has been a conglomerate church
made up of various peoples, but few if any from the indigenous
people of Palembang. The presence of a school that was able
to produce enough money to support the church has not stimulated
stewardship among the people of the church. Recent problems
in the church have left a rather confused situation. The
future of the church is at present unknown.

The year 1967 brought the Baptist witness to Medan in
northern Sumatra. The beginning of the church was significantly aided by the moving of a dedicated Baptist family from
Djakarta at about the same time the missionaries moved to
Medan (Minutes, 1968:108-109). The membership of the church
in 1968 reached twenty-two with fourteen having been baptized
(Minutes, 1968:151).

The new work in the Lampung area of Sumatra could prove
most fruitful. This station will make its first report in
1970. High hopes for the evangelization of this area among
resettlement peoples are held by Baptists.

PERSONNEL AND FUNDS

Important to any analysis of growth is the comparative
study of how personnel and funds have been employed. The
percentage of missionaries devoting themselves to various kinds
of ministries and the percentage of funds used in each type
of ministry will give some idea of the thrust and direction
of the mission and churches. This section studies how the
Baptists have used men and materials in their Indonesian
ministry.

Personnel Employment

The first consideration is the comparison of types
of work carried on by the missionaries. The types of work
done by Indonesian missionaries can be divided into seven
categories: church development, medical, seminary, student
evangelism, publication work, office staff and radio and
television. It must be understood that many of those engaged
in specialities are also actively involved in direct church
related ministries. The radio-TV personnel has doubled in
student evangelism, seminary personnel has led in church
planting and development, publication people have actively
served the local churches (at time as pastor of a church),
student workers have pastored churches and chapels and taught
in the seminary, medical personnel have actively served churches
and at times participated in church planting and evangelistic
personnel have helped at the seminary. Still, there is value
in noticing the major thrust of the missionaries in their
assignments.

For comparison, a couple working in any field will be
counted as two, even though the wife may not be actively
engaged in the service. A doctor's wife will be counted as
medical personnel even though she is unable to participate
directly in the medical service. Also, missionaries under
appointment but not yet to their assignments are treated as
missionaries in that type of work to which they are assigned.
On these terms, 40.8 percent of the Baptist missionaries
were assigned to church development work in 1959, 25.5 percent
to medical ministry, 12.1 percent to seminary education and
8.6 percent to each of publication and office ministry. At
the critical year of 1965, when the missionary staff had
increased to eighty-six, 45.3 percent were assigned to field
evangelism, 25.5 percent to medical services, 12.8 to seminary
education, 7.0 percent to publication, 5.6 percent to office
ministry and 4.5 percent to student evangelism. By 1968 the
staff had increased to ninety-nine of whom 49.4 percent were
engaged in field evangelism, 19.1 percent in medical work,
9.0 percent in both seminary and student work, 6.0 percent
in the mission office, 5.0 percent in publications and 2.0
percent in radio and television ministry. These years saw
an advance in the number of missionaries assigned to church
development from 23 to 49 percent while the medical staff was
expanding from 17 to 19 percent.

Almost one half the missionary staff engaged in direct
evangelism. This seems a noteworthy percentage. It should,
however, be pointed out that expansion to new cities has been
consistently delayed due to the lack of evangelistic workers.
Several factors have contributed to this state. First, there
simply have not been enough evangelistic workers to cover the

entire projected outreach. Second, there has not developed the kind of work that would allow missionaries to move on to other areas. It has been necessary to replace evangelistic missionaries who have moved or furloughed in almost every case. Although the Mission had a policy of not relieving furloughing evangelistic workers, implementation of this policy has generally been found impossible. Third, on several occasions, evangelistic workers have been forced to come to the aid of the institutions. This fact but emphasized the insatiable appetite of missionary institutions. On at least eight occasions, evangelistic workers or student evangelists have given at least part time to the seminary. Three times the Mission has been forced to transfer evangelistic workers to publication ministry. These problems partially explain the slow expansion of Baptist work into new centers.

Missions must always guard against the idea that the institutions must be staffed, even at the expense of outreach and evangelism. Institutions should not be allowed to rule the deployment of missionaries. Also, evangelistic missionaries must build such churches as can be left to plant others. These two correctives would free missionaries for greater church planting.

Comparison as to Areas of Work

Personnel should also be compared as to the areas in which the missionaries serve. Since institutions determine where the specialists will locate, the main factor to notice is the location of evangelistic workers. In 1959, there were twenty-three evangelistic workers under appointment to Indonesia. However, of that number, four had not yet arrived in Indonesia, four had not completed language school and four were on furlough. The remaining eleven missionaries were distributed as follows, two in Bandung, three in Surabaja, two in Solo, two in Semarang and two in Kediri.

The critical year of 1965 revealed the following deployment of the thirty-nine evangelistic missionaries. Three couples had not yet arrived in Indonesia and two were in language school. Two other couples were on furlough, leaving twenty-one actually on the field. Of these, two couples were working on Sumatra, four couples and one single lady in West Java, two couples and two single ladies in East Java and three couples in Central Java. This meant that 61.9 percent of the evangelistic force in 1964-1965 was laboring in the two least responsive areas of Baptist ministry. At this juncture, there were two evangelistic couples and a student couple in Jogja, while there was one evangelistic couple in Solo and none in Semarang. The Mission voted to open the new station in Bogor, thus by-passing the city of Purwokerto that has in recent years proved most fertile and neglecting Madiun, a city where foundations had already been laid.

The situation in 1964-1965, which was the period of
decline, must speak to the Mission. Response, not need, should
determine the deployment of missionaries and funds. The lion's
share of the resources of any Christian mission should be
planted firmly in the soil that promises the greatest harvest.
The Mission must continually face up to this fact. Roy Shearer
on this point writes:

> *We should concentrate our limited forces on areas*
> *where there is response. This will mean thinning*
> *our personnel for church extension in the unre-*
> *sponsive areas, since our missionary forces are*
> *limited, but the result will be more church growth*
> *in both areas. It is a sinful waste to keep two*
> *areas equally staffed just because there is the*
> *same number of citizens in each, when there is a*
> *great difference in potential for growth of the*
> *Church. If we say we must do our best to aid*
> *growth in the nonresponsive areas, thereby holding*
> *back resources from a church-growing area, we*
> *deceive ourselves (1966:220-221).*

The year of 1968 might be called the year of reinforcement. A total of fourteen newly arrived evangelistic workers
were in language school and six were on furlough, leaving
twenty-nine of forty-nine workers on the field. Of these,
nine were working in Central Java, seven in East Java, seven
in West Java and six in Sumatra. Thus, fifty-five percent
of the evangelistic force was working in the areas that were
at the time producing the greatest harvest. There would however
remain the question as to whether a greater reinforcement of
the responsive areas would not have produced even more substantial growth. Missionary strategy must give priority
to the rapidly growing segments of the Church. To fail to do
so may leave the ripe fields to be spoiled by changes in the
spiritual climate.

It should not be overlooked that during the periods
covered by the above statistics, missionaries other than
evangelistic workers were present and medical people were
actively participating in church planting and develpment.
Without the service of these "specialists", church development
would have indeed been neglected. The picture is not only
one of too few evangelistic missionaries but equally too many
sowing the seed in rocky ground while the fertile fields lay
beckoning, fallow, unplanted and thus fruitless.

The Baptists of Indonesia must take a close look at
the deployment of missionary strength in coming years. To
overlook the regions that promise rapid growth in order to
serve areas of resistance is to frustrate the main purpose
of the Mission as well as to reject the clear teaching of Jesus

in the parable of the soils (Matthew 13:3-8). While not be-
laboring the point, Jesus did say, "Life up your eyes and look
on the fields; for they are white to harvest..." (John 4:35).

The Use of Funds

No analysis of mission work is complete without a detailed look at the distribution of funds. Perhaps as clearly
as any other one factor, the use of funds shows the direction
a mission is taking. This section will study in depth the
use of money in the work of the Baptist Mission and the
churches of Indonesia

A Comparison of the Use of Budget and Capital Expenditures

Funds sent to the Indonesian Baptist Mission from
the Foreign Mission Board of the Southern Baptist Convention
are divided into two classifications. Current expenses are
termed budget appropriations and funds for buildings, major
equipment and the like are termed capital appropriations.
An analysis of the use of money must note both current and
capital funds.

The graph below shows the relative use of budget and
capital appropriations. It must be understood that these
figures are based on money appropriated and not on that
actually used. Some money granted may still be on the books.
The figures are composite for the years 1951-1968. They
indicate trends in spending.

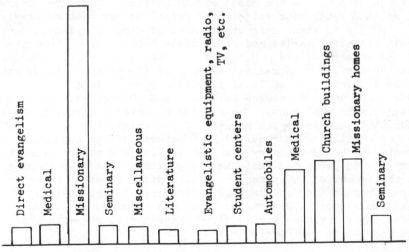

Figure 27   THE USE OF FUNDS, BUDGET AND CAPITAL   1953-1969

The most expensive item among the budget appropriations is the item "missionaries". The graph shows that since the beginning of the Indonesian Baptist Mission in Indonesia, 73.2 percent of the budget money has been spent on missionaries. Included in the budget item "missionaries" are such matters as salaries, child allowance, emergency compensation, medical charges, language study, children's school allowance, housing upkeep, mission travel, local leave, furlough travel to and from the field, refit allowance, furlough medical examination and various other expenses.

The item "direct evangelism" has third place in the budget, receiving 6.6 percent of the total. Included among the items covered by direct evangelism are property operating expenses, evangelistic work such as renting buildings and buying inexpensive equipment, conferences and promotion and audio visual materials. As will be note later, this is a dangerous item, involving as it does direct subsidy payments to the churches. While the item seems small, it is likely that it should not be larger.

Medical work required 6.8 percent of the Mission budget appropriations. This amount has operated both the hospital in Kediri and the out-patient clinic in Bukittinggi. This figure can be compared with the 4.8 percent budgeted for literature (including the publication ministry) and 4.2 percent for the operating expenses of the seminary. While the percentages have remained more or less stable over the years, the amounts rise as the work expands.

Some 4.4 percent of the budget is allocated for miscellaneous expenses. Items such as Mission committee expense, Mission Meeting and the needs of the Mission office are covered by this fund. The budget appropriations are granted yearly.

Eleven items make up the list of capital grants. Here again the missionaries and their needs took a large proportion of the appropriations. Missionary homes required 26.4 percent and automobiles required 6.5 percent of the total. Approximately 26.7 percent of the total capital appropriations since 1951 have gone into church buildings and .98 percent for evangelistic equipment. The Mission reserves a strategic land fund that amounts to .81 percent of the total.

Medical work required 23.8 percent of the capital grants while the seminary was granted 7.6 percent and student centers 4.3 percent. Radio and TV equipment has been granted to the amount of .52 percent of the capital grants. Other items include the headquarters building (1.5 percent) and language school (.32 percent) that have required small sums. These capital grants are in direct response to requests from the Mission to the Foreign Mission Board.

The Use of Funds in the Churches

The most important aspect of the use made of funds lies in direct payments to churches. Almost every church building used by Baptists in Indonesia has been constructed at least partly by mission funds. In Bandung there are five buildings, all built with Mission funds. Djakarta boasts four Mission built buildings. Although the Bogor station had purposed to not build a church building, eventually a house was purchased for the church. Semarang has six Mission built buildings in the city and several outside of town. Each church in Solo and Jogja has buildings provided by the Mission with one or two exceptions among the churches in village areas. Five churches in Surabaja and six in Kediri have Mission provided buildings.

The only congregations that have not been given buildings by the Mission are the churches in the Desa Program in Kediri, some few other home churches in Jogja, Semarang and other cities. Although the buildings have been built with Mission funds, the Mission has expressed its desire to turn over the ownership of the property to any church that meets the legal requirements of the Indonesian Government as a property holding body. At present the property is held by the government recognized Baptist Foundation (Jajasan Baptis Indonesia).

With the exception of certain of the churches in village and kampung areas, almost every Baptist Church in Indonesia has been subsidized in its early years. By 1967 twenty-seven churches had become self-supporting. This number of self-supporting churches had increased to forty-two in 1968. This increase is explained in part by the creation of numbers of self-supporting, indigenous churches in the villages (Minutes, 1968:151). The rate at which some churches became self-supporting shows great variation. One church in Surabaja, established in 1953 was self-supporting by 1957 while another started in 1954 did not attain self-support until 1965. Similar illustrations could easily be produced. Of course self-support is partially dependent on the income level of those who make up the congregation. The type of program projected also affects the attainment of self-support.

Baptists must take a long look at the entire matter of using funds in the churches. We must begin with the already mentioned fact that all use of Mission funds is not wrong. Melvin Hodges has taught that self-support—while it is the most discussed—is not necessarily the most important aspect of the indigenous church (Hodges, 1953:68).

Subsidy has been and will be used to good effect in missionary work. It provides for buildings, equipment and full-time pastors years before the congregation itself could

secure them. It is safe to say that most of the younger
churches of the world were started with at least a measure
of subsidy.

The problems of subsidy are as readily apparent as
are its values--perhaps even more apparent. The most obvious
weakness in the policy of outside support is that it is
difficult to terminate. By making the church dependent
subsidy tends to limit its outreach (see McGavran, 1955:135-
138). Tippett has further demonstrated that too much economic
support can and will hinder organic growth in the developing
church (Tippett, 1967b:346-347).

Much of the necessity for subsidization stems from
programs, procedure and equipment imposed by the missionaries
on the churches. This is what Roland Allen meant when he wrote:

> By importing and using and supplying to the natives
> buildings and ornaments which they cannot procure
> for themselves, we ten to pauperize the converts.
> They cannot supply what they think to be needful,
> and so they learn to accept the position of passive
> recipients. By supplying what they cannot supply
> we check them in the proper impulse to supply what
> they can supply (1962:56).

Sidney Clark indicated that the church can supply its indigenous needs. If things from the outside are imposed on the
church, these things must be supported by those who impose
them (Clark, 1928:30).

The idea is that often churches could support themselves on an indigenous level. But because the missionary,
with sincere motivation, teaches that many "Western" things
are necessary, the church comes to believe these things
necessary and turns to outside help to obtain them. The
trap of subsidy is thus sprung.

How then should subsidy be employed? Clark's suggestion is that it be used for evangelistic outreach but not
for local church needs (1933:4). This principle has merit.
It could, however, lead to the feeling that outreach is the
job of the mission rather than the local church.

The principle to be followed should be to employ
mission funds in such a way as to help the church to maturity
as soon as possible. This might at some times indicate not
employing all the equipment, literature and programs the
mission could give the churches. In this regard we should
listen to Hodges who says, "The future of the church should
not be sacrificed for the sake of temporary advantage" (1953:68)

It will be difficult for any one missionary alone to
go far toward solving the problem of subsidy. To make progress
there must be a basic policy. This policy should help and
not hinder. It should never stand in the way of the church's

growth. Subsidy is probably the most vital problem facing
most missions today.

DEVELOPMENTAL GROWTH

Church growth and church growth theory is not exhausted
with either the attainment or analysis of numerical increase
in church membership. Obviously, to determine and analize
the numerical growth of membership and congregations is easier
than to measure growth in grace and the ability to function
in the community as a church. Still, the measurement of the
development of the planted congregation as it progresses toward the ideal of God is an important and meaningful pursuit.

Tippett uses the term church growth in three ways. It
can be used in the sense of "conversion growth" which means
the change of heart and mind and the incorporation of the
changed man in the fellowship of the church. This meaning
of church growth has no direct bearing on the convert's
knowledge of Christianity but relates solely to his break
with the past and incorporation into the Christian community.

The term "organic growth" is used to mean the way
congregations emerge as the "church" in a community. It relates
to how the churches cease to be a part of the Mission and take
their place as a part of society, living naturally in the
matrix of their own culture. Organic growth cannot always be
registered statistically, but will become apparent in the life
of the churches through changing organizational patterns.
While organic growth is not numerical growth, it will, if valid,
enhance numerical conversion growth by providing new energies
and eliminating old obstructions.

Church growth can be used also as "quality growth".
By quality growth Tippett means internal growth. It is sometimes spoken of as growth in grace, perfection growth or
sanctification. It relates to the spiritual progress of the
members of the church. Such matters as theological understanding, piety, service and community participation would come under
the general heading of quality growth (Tippett, 1967b:30-32).

The latter two ways of speaking of church growth, organic and quality, we call "developmental growth". Church
planting is all important as no development can be realized
until the church is planted and converts have been reached.
All development will be a mere facade until churches multiply
and thousands, eventually entire communities and villages,
become baptized believers. After the saved have been brought
together in the church, there remains the important task of
helping the churches develop in the directions most likely to
produce a healthy, functioning church that continues to increase both in numbers and the Christian graces. Missiologists
of the "church growth" persuasion must continue to seek ways
both to measure, analized and enhance developmental church

growth.

There are several dangers inherent in considering developmental church growth. First, some may so major on this phase of ministry as to neglect outreach and the multiplication of churches. To so concentrate on building up one church-- bringing it to organizational and spiritual maturity--while neglecting the missions outside Grace, is to forfeit the game. The church must .continue to grow internally and must have a sense of external mission or outreach. As J. Waskom Pickett has taught, delinquent non-growing churches like delinquent parents, naturally produce delinquent children (1963:29).

A second danger in speaking of developmental church growth lies in the tendency to demand the same type of develop- ment for all churches. Different churches will be in different stages of development. All should not be required or expected to reach the same level. Even more important, different kinds of churches have different needs. The village congre- gations will not require all the organizational structure of the more formal, urban churches. The great danger is forcing unnecessary structures or programs upon congregations in the name of development.

A third point to remember in regard to developmental growth is the fact that nothing so clearly reveals the develop- ment of the church as the numbers of people being saved and incorporated into its life and the outreach it is attaining. Healthy organisms reproduce. Any program of development that hinders, limits or detracts from the continuous planting of missionary congregations among the various peoples of the world is a faulty program.

Having said this, we must return to the conviction that developmental church growth is important. It must be studied, analized, considered and bold plans made for its attainment. The question now facing us is, "How can organic and qualitative growth be measured and enhanced?"

Understanding Developmental Church Growth

In 1841 the Secretary of the Church Missionary Society, Henry Venn, called for the creation of a "native church" which would assume responsibility for pastoral duties thus leaving the missionaries free for pioneering evangelism. By 1851 Venn had established the concept of self-hood for the church. A decade later Venn set forth the three well known principles, self-support, self-governement and self-extension. The in- corporation of these elements, according to Venn, would lead to the healthy growth and expansion of the Church (Beyerhaus and Lefever, 1964:272).

The three "selfs" consummed the attention of missiolo- gists for years. J. L. Nevius, Roland Allen, Melvin Hodges and a host of others continued to clarify the meaning of the three "selfs" and formulate plans for their attainment. However, it remained for A. R. Tippett to materially expand the idea of these principles.

In his restatement of the doctrine of self-hood, Tippett sets out six "marks" of the indigenous church. The development of the church is best seen in the degree to which it has attained these six marks. Understanding developmental church growth is understanding these six "marks" of the church.

The first mark of an indigenous church, according to Tippett, is the self-image on the church's part, by which the church understands itself as the Church of Jesus Christ in its locality. Does the church see itself as the responsible body in all matters or does it look to the Mission or missionary to guide and support it through every emergency? Does the church see as its responsibility to minister to the community or does it see this responsibility as belonging to the missionary or the mission? The church must consider itself as the Church in its community. It must not see itself as a child under the fatherly mission.

Secondly, Tippett notes self-functioning as another mark of an indigenous church. The church must become an entity with its various parts participating together, each doing its own particular service in order to attain the goal of the whole body. The growth to self-functioning demands the development of the individual and the whole. As the church develops in self-functioning more and more local people will be involved in the work of the church and less reliance will be upon any one leader--either missionary or national. No church is self-functioning until it can from its own members provide for its worship services and other ministries. The churches connected with the Desa Program in Kediri and the Seminary Extension Program must take careful note of the principle of self-functioning.

The third mark of the indigenous church relates to its self-determining ability. Two elements are all important in the matter of self-determination. The church must have all decision-making solidly in its own hands and the decision-making patterns of the church must adhere to the patterns of the society rather than some foreign pattern. Here is an important factor in establishing an organically growing church. The church must be led to make its own decisions in the culturally acceptable way. The missionary should not impose upon the churches a foreign pattern of decision making, copied from his denominational structure.

Self-support is the fourth mark of the indigenous church. Here also Tippett notes two elements, one of which is often overlooked. Characteristically, missiologists recommend that the church provide its own financial needs. This principle is important. Often overlooked is the equally important matter of the church adequately financing its own service projects and

its own life. Self-support is one of the more easily ascertained and most important determinants of the organic growth of the
church.

The truly indigenous church is also self-propagating.
The matter of the spiritual condition of those outside the
Body of Christ must be a real concern for the church (Tippett,
1969:132-136). Hodges declares self-propagation is the vital
element and true objective of missionary endeavor (1953:35).
Self-propagation should be understood to mean not only winning
new members but planting new congregations as well. It is
an important factor in the development of the church.

Tippett's last mark of the indigenous church is its
devotion to self-giving. This is the mark of service and is
involved with facing and alleviating the social needs and
problems of the local situation which it faces. Service must
be rendered both to the members of the congregation and the
wider, secular world. The church has not attained its maturity
until it catches this vision (Tippett, 1969:132-136).

The best way to measure and analize the developmental
growth of a church is to find how it is progressing toward
these six principles. Several questions will reveal the
status of the church in regard to its developmental growth.
The student of church growth must devise plans and methods for
finding and evaluating the answers to the questions that follow.

There must be some understanding of self-support. Not
only must the fact of self-support be ascertained but also how
long did it take to attain it? Other important questions are:
"Does the church pay its pastor a living salary?" "Is the
church able to provide for its basic needs?" "What percentage
of the church's income is derived from mission funds?" "What
is the average economic level of the members?" "What plans
are in effect to achieve self-support?" Through these and
other questions, the church's progress in developmental growth
can be understood.

The self-functioning factor in church growth is equally
important. The student of developmental church growth must
ask: "How many different people are active in the various
activities of the church?" "To what extent are indigenous
elements used in the worship services and activities of the
church?" "Is the pastor a national or missionary?" "What
level of education has the pastor?" "What is the average
educational level of the members?" "Is the pastor the actual
leader of the church or is some other person or persons?"
"Does there seem to be any group who has more than proper
influence and power in the church?" Answers to such questions
as these point up the development of the church from the many
planted congregations to the mature churches that can fulfill
God's mission in its world.

In the realm of self-image several questions can aid
in determining the development of the church. Among these

questions are: "Does the church seek to meet its own emergency
needs or seek help from the mission?" "When crises arise in
the community (floods, volcanic eruptions, etc.), does the
church seek to meet them or does it ask the mission to meet
the need?" In some way the church's idea about itself must
be understood.

The degree to which the church is self-propagating
should be determined in seeking to understand its developmental
growth. Several questions would provide this information.
"How many chapels and/or preaching points does the church
operate?" "How were these chapels started?" "How are they
financed?" "Who brought each person to Christ?" (This question
would show how much the members are winning others). A detailed
family analysis would aid in understanding how the Gospel is
following family and kinship lines (McGavran, 1970:92-93).
Self-propagation, being one of the most important factors in
developmental church growth, must be measured and evaluated.

Any analysis of developmental church growth must take
into account the efforts of the church to serve its members
and the community. The study must seek: "What service programs
does the church promote?" "In what ways does the church seek
to influence its society?" "What does the church do for its
own members who are facing trials?" The service the church
renders to its fellowmen is a good indication of how it is
progressing toward the Will of God. It is a good index of
developmental growth.

In addition to the factors mentioned several other
items are imperative in measuring developmental growth. The
percentage of the membership who attend worship services
with regularity give some indication of piety. Tippett attempts
to formulate a tool for measuring the piety of a congregation
by studying the curve of attendance (1967b:308-318). Some such
device can be employed to measure the loyalty of the church
members to their church and to their Lord.

Some device for measuring the Bible knowledge of the
membership would be instructive in studying developmental
church growth. The number of full-time workers who have been
produced by the church would likewise indicate health. Further
indication of the development of the church could be indicated
by studying the numbers of lay members who are pursuing training
in religious subjects. These and other factors must be considered in striving to understand the developmental growth of
the church.

To get the truest ideas of developmental growth the
studies mentioned above should be made for several different
years. This procedure would show a gain or decline in the
various factors. Dr. A. R. Tippett uses the scale below for
visually showing the attainment of growth toward the six marks
(n. d.:32). The one making the study is forced to subjectively,
on the basis of questions such as noted above, decide where on

the scale the church's attainment should be marked. The church
lagging behind in a certain area would be given position one
or two on the scale. Those showing high attainment would be
marked four or five.

Figure 28   *Scale of Developmental Growth*

Level of Growth

1. *Self-image*   1   2   3   4   5

2. *Self-functioning*

3. *Self-determining*

4. *Self-supporting*

5. *Self-propagating*

6. *Self-giving*

        A comparison of developmental growth with other churches
of comparable size, type of membership and location would be
indispensable in gaining an understanding of the growth. As
more studies of these factors are made more valid comparisons
can be made and better understanding of developmental growth
attained. This type of study needs expanding and detailed
attention.

Developmental Growth of the Baptist Churches

        The study of developmental growth, like that of numeri-
cal growth, is most valid if formulated church by church. For
present purposes the study will be made on an overall and
station by station basis. In the future survey of the Indonesia
Mission the formulation of information on developmental growth
in each church should be a prime objective.
        From the overall viewpoint developmental growth among
the Baptist Churches shows substantial progress yet leaves much
to be desired. Indications are that Baptists must be concerned
with the important matter of planting and growing churches
that are more solidly indigenous. The methods of planting
churches has much to do with the direction in which they develop
There are, however, methods to develop churches in the correct
directions. Baptists must seek these methods.
        In 1959 the Baptist Churches of Indonesia boasted 967
members. The fact that the churches were served by seven
national pastors meant that the ratio of national pastors to
adherents was one to 138. In 1965 the number of churches had
increased to thirty-seven (fifteen in 1959), the number of

members to 3,391 and the number of national pastors to
thirty-nine. The ratio of pastors to adherents was just over
one to eighty-nine. The figures for 1968 showed eighty congregations with 8,086 members and sixty-four national pastors.
The ratio of pastors to adherents had fallen to one to 127,
only slightly better than 1959. The rapid multiplication of
the churches in the 1966-1968 period no doubt contributed to
the fall in percentage of national pastors to adherents. This
situation is not to be decried. However, the alternative of
hundreds of unpaid leaders was not attained and this is
regrettable. There should be, in addition to large churches,
hundreds of churchlets led by unpaid leaders.

    In self-support the Baptist Churches have shown increas-
ing maturity. This is some indication of developmental growth
of the churches as a whole. Of the total twenty-three congregations in 1959, six or about twenty-six percent had attained self-support. In 1964 the percentage of self-supporting
churches had risen to only 27.4 percent. The report for 1968
shows that forty percent of the 105 congregations were
self-supporting. This report shows progress. However, it must
be noted that in 1968 at least twenty-six of the self-supporting
congregations were the village congregations associated either
with the Desa Program in Kediri or with the Tjolamadu outreach
in Solo. These churches had been started indigenously from
their inception. Only sixteen of the city churches were
self-supporting. The lesson of these figures is too obvious
to need further comment.

    The Bible teaching function of the churches has con-
tinued to expand as the churches have matured. This is especially important as Baptist Churches have used the Sunday
School as a valuable evangelistic tool. Sunday School enrollment has increased from 2,642 pupils in twenty-three Sunday
Schools in 1959 to 3,828 pupils in fifty-four schools in 1965
and on to 9,699 pupils in ninety-six schools in 1968. The
Baptist practice of holding Bible study classes for all age
groups has proved its effectiveness. New converts classes
also contribute to Bible study emphasis.

    Some interesting features come to light when one
studies the same group of figures that have just been noted
from a station-to-station viewpoint. It becomes apparent that
in 1959 West Java showed a ration of one to 424 adherents and
national pastors. Central Java reported a ration of one to
175 and East Java a ratio of one to 194. In the year 1964 the
percentages were respectively one to ninety-one, one to
seventy-four and one to 121. The report of 1968 shows the
ratio of national pastors to members in West Java as one to
304, Central Java as one to eighty-six and East Java one to 132.
The larger use of lay pastors in the Kediri area and the
seminary students who serve as pastors in Central Java contribute
to this difference. Also, notable is the fact that Central Java

reports almost twice the number of Sunday Schools and pupils
enrolled as West and East Java. Central Java reported in 1968
forty-seven schools to twenty-one in West and twenty-three in
East Java and 4,248 enrolled members to 2,476 and 2,573 in
West and East Java respectively. The large number of chapels
that are not self-supporting in Central Java, where only thirteen congregations are self-supporting while forty-four are
not, is explained by the Seminary Extension Program that has
planted many congregations but has not yet brought many of
these to self-support. Clearly, this is an area where developmental church growth needs to be stressed. On the other hand,
the presence of only seventeen congregations in West Java
points to the need of wide outreach and church planting in
these three large cities and their surrounding villages.
Church planting even in unresponsive areas can be accomplished
among pockets of people who will believe.

        In general terms of developmental church growth,
Baptists of Indonesia need to pay attention to several areas.
First, church government must be considered. To be truly
indigenous the church must be self-determining and seek the
answer to its own problems in its own way that is in keeping
with the culture in which it lives. Two primary problems exist
in almost every church started by a mission in regard to
self-government. The first is the all to familiar pattern of
missionary paternalism that refuses to trust the governing of
the church to the national constituency. History has proved
that paternalism keeps the church tied to the missionaries
and is a barrier to the development of a strong, thriving
church. The dean of writers on mission history, Latourette,
notes that post World War II conditions in Indonesia prevented
both Dutch and German missionaries from free access to the
country. Still, both Protestant and Roman Catholic Churches
registered substantial gains (Latourette, 1953:1444-1445).

        Other writers have also indicated that the Churches
in Indonesia grew stronger during the war period when missionary
aid had been withdrawn. These facts indicate not that missionaries are not needed, but rather that missionaries should allow
the church to develop its own life and govern its own affairs.
Speaking of the general missionary tendency to hold on to the
governing power in the churches, A. R. Tippett says, "This
pernicious doctrine (paternalism) fits both mission paternalism
and commercial colonialism, prolongs the dependence of the
islander, and generally retards progress because all decisions
are made _for_ the people instead of _by_ the people" (1967b:89).
The first threat to self-determination is the missionary's
refusal or delay in leading the church to self-government or in
failing to completely relinquish the reins. Changing to
self-government in the church requires an act of faith on the
part of both the missionary and the national church.

        The second threat to true self-determination is the

tendency of the denominational machine to impose its own
pattern of church government on the younger church with no
regard to the social structure to which the church belongs.
Tippett says, "...the decision-making should be carried out
within a structure which is culturally appropriate. It should
reflect in some way the accepted decision-making mechanism of
the tribe; that is, it should be something they can feel is
their own" (1969:134). The New Testament Churches employed
the democratic, congregational form of church government because that was the type of government in the world in which
it originated. In planting churches in other cultures with
different structures, following the New Testament principle
does not involve imposing the exact form of government of New
Testament mode but rather the form of government most in harmony with the culture in which the church is living. The
congregational government of the Baptists is for the most
part compatable with Javanese culture. Perhaps greater recognition should be accorded the older men. Church government
should make full use of the Indonesian genius for "musjiwarah"
(discussion until consensus is reached). This form of business
meetings will be more productive in Javanese churches than the
more precise majority rule and structured procedure of Robert's
Rules of Order.
      Another area that needs improvement in Indonesian
churches is the whole idea of missions. While a rather strong
program of outreach is being promoted by many churches, there
is not sufficient consciousness of a world-wide responsibility.
Mission is indispensable to a developing church. The churches
need a vision of the next kampung, the next village, the other
islands and the rest of the world as their evangelistic responsibility.
      To study, analize and enhance developmental church
growth is one of the great frontiers of missionary thinking
today. The Baptists of Indonesia (and indeed every church
everywhere) must give serious consideration to the principles
and plans that will bring the Church toward the status of a
living, functioning organism, firmly planted in, serving and
living in its own cultural matrix and at the same time bring
men to real faith in Christ and obedience to His Will.

CONCLUSION

      As stated in the beginning this analysis is both pre-
liminary and interim. The facts and conclusions are subject
to correction by other studies—indeed, the very purpose of this
work is the provision of a point of reference for the fuller
study that is to come. These pages should be read in this light.
As future study leans against this paper, the purpose of the
present work will be realized.

6

Recommendations

The facts of Baptist growth amid the Indonesian religious situation drive irresistibly to several conclusions.
These will be stated in the form of recommendations to the
Baptists of Indonesia. The recommendations are purely personal
and do not represent the feelings of the survey committee.

*1. Formulate and Implement Firm Plans for Seventy
Thousand New Members by 1980*

Baptist Churches in Indonesia will report in excess
of ten thousand members in 1970. To plan for eighty thousand
in the next decade is not overly optimistic. To attain this
growth, Baptists must engage in unprecedented church planting.
Should the 149 churches reported in 1969 triple their membership
before 1980 the total membership would reach only 29,300. To
reach the goal of eighty thousand, which is in every way possible, will require planting no less than fifty new congregations
yearly. The key to God-pleasing growth is extensive and expanding church planting. McGavran says, "The only way in which
the Good News of Jesus Christ can possibly reach the myriads
of earth is for fantastic church planting to take place..."
(McGavran, 1970:357).

2. Make Full Use of Survey Materials and Insights

The Baptist Churches and missionaries must make full
use of the opportunity to take a long, dispassionate, objective
look at the work that has been done, the results of that work
and the analysis of that work which is made available through
the survey. Cal Guy says, "Conducting a survey is worthless
unless churches and missions are prepared to act on the information" (Guy, 1965:143). The survey can, if allowed, lead Baptists
to new approaches, corrections for faulty methods or unproductive
policies and better plans for discipling the millions in
Indonesia. Only as the survey results in action is the survey

justified (McGavran, n. d.:9).

3. Win the Winnable Now

The principle "win the winnable now" must be engraved upon the heart of every Baptist. The major thrust of men and material must be aimed at those who show signs of response. Response, rather than need, must constitute the determinant for the deployment of resources. While a "lighthouse" ministry will continue in areas not showing a ready response, the emphasis and stress must always be on the winnable. In their main effort Baptists must be as ruthless as a battlefield surgeon (who centers his efforts on those most likely to live) in choosing to center their efforts on those showing the greatest promise of believing.

This principle will not involve withdrawal from existing places of witness. It will involve seeking the responsive regions for further mission efforts. It may well mean eschewing romantic ventures for the more humble and sweaty work of reaping promising fields where the harvest is waiting. No effort should be spared to find where men are believing and to move in force to disciple these thousands.

4. Plant Churches in Homogeneous Units

The statistics have demonstrated that unusual growth is taking place in those churches planted among the homogeneous units of Indonesian population. Each village and kampung church will grow rapidly as it lives the Christian Way in its own social setting. Movements to Christ can start along family, neighborhood or friendship lines. These "Web Movements" are one type of people movements and can help bring thousands into faith in Christ without displacing them socially. Baptists should consider churches among the ethnic groups in the large cities, among recent immigrants and anywhere there are found groups with a strong feeling of solidarity.

5. Accept the Idea of Home Churches and Unpaid Pastors

The Baptist image does not require large church buildings and highly trained pastors. Indeed, the feeling that such are needed could well be the result of "cultural overhang" (see McGavran, 1955:85-92). Baptists cannot provide places of worship and trained pastors for fifty new congregations each year for the next ten years. However, it is easily possible that house churches, led by unpaid pastors, planted solidly in the matrix of their own communities could be planted in the forthcoming years. Baptists must recognize the validity of such churches and such pastors. Unpaid or slightly paid non-seminary trained pastors should be recognized and allowed to

function fully as pastors, leading their congregations with
full freedom, drawing their authority from the Lord and the
congregation they lead.

6. Design Theological Education to Meet the Demands of Growth

Obviously, the remendous need for unpaid leaders for
local congregations cannot be met with one central seminary,
however important this institution is and however efficiently
it is administered. There must be developed some form of
extension training that can equip the pastors in their own
locality to better lead their people and disciple their neighbors. Pastors so trained should be accorded full benefits
and respect by all Baptists.

The existing pastor training program in the seminary
should be continued and expanded as resources allow. The
faculty would as rapidly as possible add still more national
members. In addition, the present curriculum should be enriched
to include courses on church growth and development.

7. Use Heart Languages

Baptists will continue to major on the use of the
national language, <u>Bahasa Indonesia</u>. In addition, more churches
in the village and neighborhood areas should be encouraged to
make use of the regional languages that still speak to the
hearts of many of the people. Some missionaries should make
the effort to learn the heart languages in the various areas.
A procedure such as outlined will in no way interfere with
the Government's drive to make the national language even
more solidly the language of the nation. It will only enable
men to become Christians more easily and more naturally as
they hear the Message in the language of their youth.

8. Encourage Local Church Outreach

The major outreach and expansion should come through
the efforts of the local churches, both by means of their
own church planting activities and by means of their cooperative
ventures in associational mission action. Baptist Churches
must learn missions. They must see their "Jerusalem" but as
clearly must perceive their "Judea", their "Samaria" and their
"uttermost parts". Churches should stand ready to commission
a part of their members to break off from the mother church and
constitute themselves as a congregation in their own neighborhood. The lack of mission consciousness could well be one of
the most neglected areas of Baptist development.

9. *Produce Indigenous Literature*

Christian literature is an indispensable factor in church growth. The production of literature, designed exactly to fit the situation of the churches in Indonesia, should receive top priority. While translated materials are of value, the materials produced from within and specifically for the Indonesian culture will be of even greater use. This principle must include the hymns. An indigenous literature and hymnody will enhance church growth.

In addition, the production of simple Bible lessons that could serve to aid in opening a new church would be invaluable. These lessons should certainly be made available in the regional languages. Further study toward the production of indigenous literature should be undertaken.

10. *Come to Grips with Subsidization*

The problem of subsidy must come in for close scrutiny by the Baptists not only in Indonesia but in other parts of the world. All subsidy is not wrong. Even Nevius, the champion of self-support, used mission funds for his month-long training courses (Nevius, 1958:39-40). The great danger of subsidy is that the churches will continue to be dependent on mission funds for their day-to-day needs. To plant a church that for ten years continues to require mission subsidy is to miss the reason for subsidy which is to excelerate the development of the church. The great danger is that the missionaries will teach the churches to feel the need for programs and equipment which the churches themselves can never afford. The principle in regard to subsidy is that it marks a first stage that should be rapidly passed through.

If subsidy is given, growth must be demanded and encouragement to growth must be provided. No doubt, Baptists will continue to build some buildings and provide some equipment for the churches from Mission funds. One thing must be clearly understood. The only churches capable of unlimited multiplication are those that can and will provide their own meeting places and raise and support their own leaders. The program of subsidy and the provision of church buildings carries with it the likelihood of self-limitation. For this reason, the entire matter of subsidy must be carefully studied and kinds of churches which require no subsidy must be discovered.

11. *Seek Service Opportunities*

The natural result of genuine revival and true church growth is an increasing social awareness. Baptists must be ever involved in meeting and alleviating the pressing social problems faced by the people and the country. Social service must be

done, but in proportion to propagating the faith. Discipling
is basic to serving. As thunder naturally and inevitably
follows lightening so social service naturally and inevitably
follows true revival and church growth. However, to attempt
to substitute social work for discipling is to attempt to
create thunder without lightening.

Both as churches and as individuals, Baptists need to
be active in the social arena. Individual Christians must
show the fruit of the Spirit in their relations to the world
and to others. Churches must do all in their power to meet
the problems faced by the society, both by programs and by
providing men with a determination and ability to overcome
social injustice. The social needs of the nation constitute
a frontier for Baptist Churches in Indonesia.

12. Nurture Churches in Developmental Growth

As Baptists multiply new churches by ever increasing
numbers they must not neglect the nurture of the congregations
already planted. Each church must gauge its development
against the six principles of an indigenous church set forth
by Tippett. Definite plans must be laid from the beginning
for each church to develop to the fullest in each of these
areas. Self-support should not be accorded such an important
place that the other factors are neglected. Churches must be
led to see the necessity of growing in the areas of organic
and qualitative growth just as they seek to progress in numerical fashion. Members must be aided in their own "growth in
grace". Let it not be forgotten that one of the best ways of
measuring the growth in grace of any church is to notice the
evangelistic activity both of the church as a whole and its
individual members.

13. Adjust Church Polity to Indonesian Life

Church life in Indonesian Baptist Churches should be
thoroughly Indonesian. There has been too much transplanting
of the Baptist pattern from American church life into the
Indonesian setting. Baptist Churches in Indonesia must become
thoroughly Indonesian and rather than opposing such development,
missionaries should foster and welcome it. Luzbetak has said:

> One of the most basic natural rights of a society
> is its right to its own culture, its right to its
> own national distinctiveness, its own character....
> To deprive a people of this right would be a flagrant
> violation of justice, whether it be done by a selfish
> capitalist, a fanatical Communist, or a well-meaning
> missionary (1970:342).

Baptist missionaries in Indonesia must ask if the churches are
truly Indonesian churches or if they have been led toward the
denominational policies and methods of American churches.

Baptist Churches must seek out ways to make their
worship and polity as thoroughly palatable to the Indonesian
way of life as possible. This would involve using Javanese
music, dance, ways of government, methods of interpersonal
relationship and other cultural features that would "Javanize"
the Church. This of course would be done only in Javanese
districts. Other regions would adapt to the custom of their
area. The churches should live and reproduce naturally in the
matrix of their own culture. They must be thoroughly Indonesian
without sacrificing the essential marks of Christianity.

**14. *Find Valid Contact with the Animistically Oriented
Peoples of Indonesia.***

It has been seen that the Indonesian religious scene
is at least in major respects animistically oriented, even
among followers of one of the great religions. Baptists must
come to grips with the animistic way of looking at life. The
Gospel is most effective when presented as meeting some felt
need or needs in the culture (Luzbetak, 1970:67,68). Realizing
that the animist has the fear of the unseen spirits and ghosts
of ancestors, the Gospel should be presented as the power that
can overcome all other powers. The peace that Jesus can and
does give should be a major element in the message. Nida says,
"Without a doubt a great deal of the success of Christian
missions among predominantly animistic people is related to
the lack of security found in animistic beliefs" (Nida, 1954:
18,19). Here is one of the great approaches to animistic
peoples.

Closely allied with the foregoing principle is the need
of animists to feel the assurance of a personal God. Most
animists have the concept that God or the gods created the
world and then left it alone to run itself. Their idea of
God is an absentee deity who cannot help in the everyday affairs.
The truth of a personal God who is interested in and willing
to accept any who come to Him in faith is ever an open door to
the hearts of animists. Again, Nida says, "Accordingly, it is
not strange that a religion which explains life in terms of the
love of God and order in the universe has a great appeal to
him (an animist)" (Nida, 1954:19).

In approaching animistically oriented peoples the
missionary must keep in mind the need for functional substitutes.
To reject cutural ways of providing peace in the face of felt
needs is to leave a cultural void and invite relapses to
pre-Christian ways and/or syncretistic adaptations of the
Christian Message. Functional substitutes supply the felt needs
of the people without non-Christian meanings. They not only

satisfy the felt need but also bring about a closer congregational involvement in the act of worship itself. In the case of
offerings to the rice goddess, prevalent in Indonesia, the
churches should devise some Christian worship act that would
call upon God to bless the essential rice crop. In this way
the former non-Christian rite has been turned into a confession
of faith in God as the Provider (see Tippett, 1967b:269-275).
Some Christian ceremony such as the ceremony of "First Fruits"
could answer the need presently met with the <u>selamatan</u> and at
the same time point the people to a greater faith in God.
Baptists should seek to form functional substitutes for many
Indonesian practices that now have either animistic or Moslem
meanings and convert the needs expressed in these rites to
Christian meanings.

15. *Continue Toward a Convention*

The Baptists will continue to work toward a genuine,
responsible national convention in which the churches will
assume the load of evangelism and service. In time the institutions will more and more be under the responsibility of
the churches. In the establishment of the convention, care
must be exercised that no one is prohibited from evangelizing.
Both nationals, churches <u>and</u> missionaries must be free to
disciple the peoples as the Holy Spirit leads them.

16. *Face the Future with Optimism*

Baptists face the coming decade with full assurance
that the best is yet to be. By 1980 Baptists can and should
have eighty thousand members. The advance from 1953 to 1969
is only the foundation for the growth that should begin now.
The necessary growth will take place only if churches are
multiplied fantastically, thousands are discipled and brought
into worshipping, serving, witnessing missionary congregations
that themselves reach out to the lost world. It can be done
and Baptists must go forth believing that it can be.

Bibliography

ALLEN, Roland
    1962   Missionary Methods: St. Paul's or Ours? Grand
            Rapids, William B. Eerdman's Publishing Company.

AUSTIN, Ruth
    1969   Questionaire on Bukittinggi

BAKKER, D.
    1968   "Active Islam," SEAJT., 9,3:44-50

BARNETT, H. G.
    1953   Innovation: The Basis of Cultural Change. New York,
            McGraw-Hill Book Company, Inc.

BAVINCK, J. H.
    1960   An Introduction to the Science of Missions.
            Philadelphia, The Presbyterian and Reformed Publishing
            Company. (Translated from the Dutch by D. H. Freeman)

BENDA, Harry J.
    1958   The Crescent and the Rising Star. The Hague,
            W. van Hoeve, Ltd.

BENTLEY-TAYLOR, David
    1967   The Weathercock's Reward. London, Overseas
            Missionary Fellowship.

BERG, C. C.
    1932   "Indonesia," in H. A. R. Gibb (ed.)

BEYERHAUS, Peter and LEFEVER, Harry
    1964   The Responsible Church and Foreign Missions. Grand
            Rapids, William B. Eerdman's Publishing Company.

BOSCH, F. D. K.
    1951   Selected Studies in Indonesian Archaeology.
            The Hague, Martinus Nighoff.

BRACKMAN, Arnold G.
    1963   Indonesian Communism: A History. New York,
            Fredrick A. Praeger.

BRADEN, Charles S.
    1945   "Hinduism," An Encyclopedia of Religion, ed. Virgilius
            Ferm. New York, Philosophical Library.

BRADSHAW, Mac
    1967   "A Hand Moving in Indonesia," East Asia's Millions,
           75, 6:81-83.

    1969   Church Growth Through Evangelism-in-Depth. Pasadena,
           William Carey Library.

BRIGGS, Lawrence Palmer
    1951   "The Syncretism of Religions in Southeast Asia,
           Especially in the Khymer Empire," Journal of the
           American Oriental Society, LXXI:230-249.

BRYAN, Gainer
    1967   "Indonesia: Turmoil Amid Revival," Christianity
           Today, 12:312-313.

    1968   "The Pacific: Scene of Miracles Today," Christian
           Life, 29, 12:47-49.

CADY, John F.
    1964   Southeast Asia: Its Historical Development.
           New York, McGraw-Hill Book Company, Inc.

CLARK, Sidney J.
    1928   The Indigenous Church. London, World Dominion Press.

    1933   Indigenous Fruit. London, World Dominion Press.

COEDES, G.
    1968   The Indianized States of Southeast Asia. Honolulu,
           East-West Center Press (Trans. Susan Brown Cowing)

COLE, Fay-Cooper
    1945   The Peoples of Malysia. New York, D. van Nostrands
           Co., Inc.

COOLEY, Frank L.
    1962   "A Church Reformed and Reforming," IRM., 51:26-32.

    1966   "Altar and Throne in Central Moluccan Society."
           A Ph. D. dissertation, Yale University (m/f used).

    1968   Indonesia: Church and Society. New York, Friendship
           Press.

    1970   Letter to Author.

CRAIG, Charles W.
    1963   "Short Outline of People and Work of A. B. M. S.,
           West Irian," in a letter to Buford L. Nichols.

CRAWLEY, J. Winston
1958   Into A New World. Nashville, Convention Press.

CROMMELIN, D.
1934   "The Growth of the Native Church in the East Indian
       Archipelago and the Development of Christian
       Character," IRM., 23:367-377.

CROOKE, W.
1920   "Hinduism," The Encyclopaedia of Religion and Ethics,
       ed. James Hastings. Edinbrugh, T. & T. Clark.

DAVIS, J. Merle
1938   The Batak Church: An Account of the Organization,
       Policies and Growth of the Christian Community of
       the Bataks of Northern Sumatra. International
       Missionary Council, Department of Social and
       Industrial Research.

DEPARTMENT OF STATE
1969   "The Republic of Indonesia," United States Department
       of State Publication 7786.

DERKACH, Nadia
1965   The Soviet Policy Towards Indonesia in the West Irian
       and Malaysian Disputes. Santa Monica, The Rand Corp.

DEWAARD, Nellie
n.d.   Pioneer in Sumatra. London, China Inland Mission.

DJAJADINIAGRAT, P. A. Hoegien
1958   "Islam in Indonesia," in Kenneth W. Morgan (ed.).

DU BOIS, Cora
1949   Social Forces in Southeast Asia. St. Paul,
       University of Minnesota Press.

DUBE, A. C.
n.d.   The Story of A. B. M. S. Work in West Irian.
       Melbourne, The Australian Baptist Missionary Society
       (memeographed).

1970   Letter to Author.

ENS, Adolf
1970   Letter to Author

FEITH, Herbert
1963   "Dynamics of Guided Democracy," in Ruth T. McVey (ed.).

1964   The Decline of Constitutional Democracy in Indonesia.
        New York, Cornell University Press.

FISHER, Charles A.
    1964   South-East Asia: A Social, Economic and Political
            Geography. London, Methuen and Co., Ltd.

FRAZER, R. W.
    1920   "Saivism," The Encyclopaedia of Religion and Ethics,
            ed. James Hastings. Edinburgh, T. & T. Clark.

GEERTZ, Clifford
    1960   The Religion of Java. New York, The Free Press of
            Glencoe, Inc.

GEERTZ, Hildred.
    1961   The Javanese Family. New York, The Free Press of
            Glencoe, In.

    1963   "Indonesian Cultures and Communities," in Ruth T.
            McVey, (ed.).

GENTRY, Melvin
    1967   Report on Village Worship Program, Kediri. (memeograph)

GIBB, H. A. R. (ed.)
    1953   Mohammedanism: An Historical Survey. London, Oxford
            University Press.

GRAMBURG, B. W. G.
    1942   "The Batak Church in Fiery Trials," IRM., 31:322-328.

GUY, Robert Calvin
    1965   "Eliminating the Underbrush," in Donald A. McGavran,
            (ed.).

HALL, D. G. E.
    1964   A History of South-East Asia. London, Macmillian
            Company.

HAMILTON, Keith E.
    1962   Church Growth in the High Andes. Lucknow, India,
            Lucknow Publishing House.

HODGES, Melvin L.
    1953   The Indigenous Church. Springfield, Illinois,
            Gospel Publishing Company.

HUGHES, John
    1967   Indonesian Upheaval. New York, David McKay Co, Inc.

HUMBLE, Arnold
    1968   "Dyaks Attack Chinese and Destroy Food," Conservative
            Baptist Impact, 25, 1:11.

HURGRONJE, C. Snouck
    1906   The Achenese. Leyden, E. J. Brill. (Translated by
            A. W. S. O'Sullivan from the original Dutch).

INDONESIAN BIBLE SOCIETY
    1968   Indonesian Bible Society Newsletter, No. 5 (September),
            Djakarta, Indonesia.

INGOUF, John
    1969   Questionaire on Surabaja.

IRM
    1938   "Survey of the Year," 27:10-29.

    1941   "Survey of the Year," 30:9-31.

    1968   "Survey of the Year," 57:10-30.

JAY, Robert R.
    1963   Religion and Politics in Rural Central Java, Yale
            University, Cultural Report Series, Southeast Asia
            Studies.

KAHIN, George McT. (ed.)
    1958   Major Governments of Asia. Ithaca, Cornell
            University Press.

KAHIN, George McT.
    1958   "Indonesia," in George McT. Kahin (ed.).

KENNEDY, Raymond
    1937   "A Survey of Indonesian Civilization," in George
            Pater Murdock (ed.).

    1942   The Ageless Indies. New York, The John Day Company.

    1943   Islands and Peoples of the Indies. Washington,
            Smithsonian Institute.

    1962   Bibliography of Indonesian Peoples and Cultures,
            Revised Edition. New Haven, Yale University Press.

KERN, H.
   1920   "Hinduism" <u>The encyclopaedia of Religion and Ethics</u>,
           ed. James Hastings. Edinburgh, T. & T. Clark.

KOENTJARANINGRAT, R. N.
   1960   "The Javanese of South Central Java," in George P.
           Murdock (ed.).

KRAEMER, Hendrick
   1952   <u>Agama Islam</u>. Djakarta, Badan Penerbitan Kristen.

   1958   <u>From Missionfield to Independent Church</u>. The Hague,
           Boekencentrum.

KRIELE, Ed
   1927   "Nias Revival," <u>IRM</u>, 16:91-102.

KRUYT, A. C.
   1915   "The Presentation of Christianity to Primitive
           People: the Toradja Tribes of Central Celebes,"
           <u>IRM</u>., 4:81-95.

   1924   "The Appropriation of Christianity by Primitive
           Heathen in Central Celebes," <u>IRM</u>., 13:276-275.

KEESING, Felix M.
   1958   <u>Cultural Anthropology</u>. New York, Holt, Rinehart and
           Weriston.

LANDON, Kenneth Perry
   1947   <u>Southeast Asia: Crossroads of Religion</u>. Chicago,
           University of Chicago Press.

LATOURETTE, Kenneth Scott
   1953   <u>A History of Christianity</u>. New York, Harper and
           Row, Publishers.

   1965   <u>Christianity Through the Ages</u>. New York, Harper
           and Row, Publishers.

LEE, Carl
   1969   Questionaire on Purwokerto.

LEGGE, J. D.
   1964   <u>Indonesia</u>. Englewood Cliffs, New Jersey,
           Prentice-Hall, Inc.

LEWIS, Beverly
   1969   <u>Annual Report of Indonesian Baptist Mission</u>, 1968-1969.
           (typeset).

LEWIS, Frank
    1969   Questionaire on Semarang.

LIE, Beng Tjoan
    1953   "The Christian Approach to the Chinese Community in
            Indonesia for the Church's Witness," Unpublished
            Th. M. Thesis, Union Theological Seminary, New York.

LUZBETAK, Louis J.
    1970   The Church and Cultures, (reprint). Techny, Illinois,
            Divine Word Publications.

McGAVRAN, Donald A.
    1955   The Bridges of God. New York, Friendship Press.

    1959   How Churches Grow. New York, Friendship Press.

    1963   Church Growth in Mexico. New York, Harper and Row,
            Publishers.

    1964   "Is 'Little Growth' Cultural Overhand?" CGB., 1,2:4-5.

    1965a   "Wrong Strategy: The Real Crisis in Missions,"
           IRM., 54:451-461.

    1965b   "Homogeneous Populations and Church Growth," in
           Donald A. McGavran (ed.).

    1965c   "Knowing Each Variety of Church Growth," in Donald
           A. McGavran (ed.).

    1966   "Why Neglect Gospel-Ready Masses," Christianity Today,
            10:769-771.

    1968   "Church Growth Strategy Continued," IRM., 57:335-343.

    1970   Understanding Church Growth. Grand Rapids, William
            B. Eerdmans Publishing Company.

    n.d.   How to Do A Survey of Church Growth. Pasadena,
            School of World Mission and Institute of Church Growth.

McGRATTY, Arthur R.
    1952   Fire of Francis Xavier: the Story of An Apostle,
            New York, Bruce Publishers.

McVEY, Ruth T. (ed.)
    1963   Indonesia. New Haven, Yale University Press.

MANSOER, M. D.
    1960   "Some Aspects of Traditional Culture in Indonesia,"
           Cultures in Southeast Asia. Bombay, Longman's

MARTIN, Gerald
    1970   Letter to Author.

MASTRA, J. W.
    1967   "The Impact of the Gospel and the Balinese Culture:
           An Approach to Making an Indigenous Church,"
           Unpublished Th. M. Thesis, University of Dubuque.

MIDDELKOOP, Pieter
    1960   Curse--Retribution--Enmity. Amsterdam, Jacob van
           Campen.

MINUTES OF THE INDONESIAN BAPTIST MISSION OF THE SOUTHERN
       BAPTIST CONVENTION, 1953-1969.

MOODY MONTHLY
    1968   "Opposition in Indonesia," June:6-8.

MORGAN, Kenneth W. (ed.)
    1958   Islam--The Straight Path, New York, The Ronald Press.

MURDOCK, George Peter (ed.)
    1937   Studies in the Science of Society. New Haven,
           Yale University Press.

    1960   Social Structure in South East Asia. New Haven,
           Yale University Press.

MULLER-KRÜGER, Th.
    1959   Sedjarah Geredja di Indonesia. Djakarta, Badan
           Penerbitan Kristen.

NANCE, John Irvin
    1969   "A History of the Indonesian Baptist Mission:
           1950-1960." Unpublished M. A. Thesis, Baylor
           University, Waco, Texas.

NEVIUS, John L.
    1958   The Planting and Development of Missionary Churches.
           The Reformed and Presbyterian Publishing Company.

NICHOLS, Buford L.
    1958   Echoes from Indonesia. Nashville, Convention Press.

    1969   "Seminari Kita", Address delivered in Semarang, Java.

NIDA, Eugene A.
 1954   Customs and Cultures. New York, Harper and Brothers.

 1960   Message and Mission. New York, Harper and Row,
        Publishers.

 1965   "Culture and Church Growth," in Donald A. McGavran (ed).

NIEUWENHUIJZE, C. A. O.
 1958   Aspects of Islam in Post-Colonial Indonesia. The
        Hague, W. van Hoeve, Ltd.

NOLDEKE, Th.
 1920   "Arabs, Ancient," Encyclopaedia of Religion and
        Ethics, ed. James Hastings. Edinburg, T. & T. Clark.

NYHUS, Edward
 1968   "The Encounter of Christianity and Animism Among
        the Toba Bataks of North Sumatra," SEAJT. 10,2-3:
        33-53.

NORTH AMERICAN PROTESTANT MINISTRIES OVERSEAS
 1968   North American Protestant Ministries Overseas.
        Missionary Research Library.

PALMEIR, Leslie H.
 1960   Social Status and Power in Java. London, Athlone
        Press.

PAUKER, Guy J.
 1967a Towards a New Order in Indonesia. Santa Monica,
        The Rand Corporation.

 1967b Indonesia in 1966:The Year of Transition. Santa
        Monica, The Rand Corporation.

 1967c Indonesia's Convalescence. Santa Monica, The
        Rand Corporation.

 1968   Indonesia: The Age of Reason. Santa Monica,
        The Rand Corporation.

PAYNE, Ernest A.
 1945   South-East from Serampore. London: The Carey Press.

PELZER, Karl J.
 1963   "Physical and Human Resource Patterns," in Ruth
        T. McVey (ed.).

PENNELL, Wayne
    1969   Questionaire on Solo.

PICKETT, J. Waskom
    1963   The Dynamics of Church Growth. Nashville, Abingdon
           Press.

PITT, Malcolm
    1955   Introducing Hinduism. New York, Friendship Press.

PLANHOL, Xavier de
    1959   The World of Islam. New York, Cornell University
           Press.

PONDER, H. W.
    n.d.   Javanese Panorama. London, Seeley, Service and
           Company, Ltd.

RAUWS, John, VAN HASSELT, F. J. F., KRAEMER, H. deBRUINE, S.
    1935   The Netherlands Indies. New York, World Dominion
           Press.

READ, William R.
    1965   New Patterns of Church Growth in Brazil. Grand
    Rapids, William B. Eerdmans Publishing Company.

REPORT OF THE FOREIGN DEPARTMENT OF THE CHRISTIAN AND
           MISSIONARY ALLIANCE
    1930, 1935, 1940, 1945, 1950, 1955, 1960, 1961, 1962,
    1963, 1964, 1965, 1966, 1967, 1968

ROGERS, Ray
    1969   Questionaire on Kediri.

SARGINSON, Charles R.
    1970   Letter to Author.

SCHENNEMANN, Detmar
    1969   "Our God is Marching On," Thrust, 6, 5:1-3.

SCHILLER, A. Arthur
    1955   The Formation of Federal Indonesia, 1945-1949.
           The Hague, W. van Hoeve, Ltd.

SCHRIEKE, B.
    1957   Indonesian Sociological Studies, Part Two. The

    1966   Indonesian Sociological Studies, Part One. The
           Hague, W. van Hoeve, Ltd.

SIMATUPANG, T. B.
    1969   "The Situation and Challenge of the Christian
            Mission in Indonesia Today," SEAJT., 11:10-27.

SIMON, Gottfried
    1912   The Progress and Arrest of Islam in Sumatra. New
            York, Marshall Brothers, Ltd.

SHEARER, Roy E.
    1966   Wildfire: The Growth of the Church in Korea.
            Grand Rapids, William B. Eerdmans Publishing
            Company.

SKINNER, T. William
    1963   "The Chinese Minority," in Ruth T. McVey (ed.).

SMITH, Datus C.
    1961   The Land and People of Indonesia. Philadelphia,
            J. B. Lippincott Company.

SMITH, Ebbie C.
    n.d.   Perkembangan Geredja-Geredja Baptis. Semarang,
            Seminari Theologia Baptis di Indonesia.

SMITH, John
    1969   Questionaire on Jogja.

SOEDJATMOKO, Mohammad Ali, RESERIK, S. J. and KAHIN, George
    1965   An Introduction to Indonesian Historiography.
            Ithaca, Cornell University Press.

STERLING, M. W.
    1943   The Native Peoples of New Guines. Washington,
            Smithsonian Institution.

STUCKEY, Bob
    1970   Letter to Author.

SUNDA, James
    1963   Church Growth in the Central Highlands of West
            New Guinea. Lucknow, India, Lucknow Publishing
            House.

SUNDSTROM, H. W.
    1957   Indonesia: Its People and Politics. Tokyo, The
            Hokuseido Press.

SUMARDI, Timothy
    1969   Questionaire on Semarang.

TANUTAMA
    1969   "Geredja Isa Almasih" (typeset).

TASDIK
    1969   "New Congregations in Indonesia," SEAJT., 11:1-9.

TER HARR, B.
    1962   Adat Law in Indonesia. Djakarta, Bhratara.

THOMAS, Winburn T.
    1953   "The Protestant Movement in Indonesia," IRM.,
            42:297-305.

THOMSON, Alan
    1968   "The Churches of Java in the Aftermath of the
            Thirtieth of September Movement," SEAJT., 9, 3:7-20.

TIPPETT, A. R.
    n.d.   "A Non-technical Testing and Grading Scale for
            Church Growth Analysis Among Second Generation
            Christians." Unpublished typescript.

    1965   "Numbering: Right or Wrong?" Church Growth
            Bulletin, 1, 3:1-2.

    1967a   Religious, Group Conversion in Non-Western
            Society. Research-in-Progress, Number 11.
            School of World Mission, Pasadena, California.

    1967b   Solomon Island Christianity. London, Lutterworth
            Press.

    1968   "Anthropology: Luxury or Necessity for Missions,"
            Evangelical Mission Quarterly, 1:7-19.

    1969   Verdict Theology in Missionary Theory. Lincoln,
            Illinois, Lincoln College Press.

TROTTER, George
    1969   Questionaire on Bogor and Sukabumi

UNITED STATES ARMY HANDBOOK
    1964   United States Army Handbook for Indonesia.
            Washington, American University, Foreign Area
            Studies Division. Department of the Army
            Pamphlet, No. 550-39.

VAN CAPELLEVEEN, J.
    1968   "A Special Report," Moody Monthly, June:27-29.

VAN DER KROEF, Justus M.
　　1951　"The Hinduization of Indonesia Reconsidered,"
　　　　　Far East Quarterly, XI:17-30.

　　1962　"Recent Trends in Indonesian Islam," The Muslim
　　　　　World, 52:48-58.

VAN LEUR, Jacob C.
　　1955　Indonesian Trade and Society: Essays in Asian
　　　　　Social and Economic History. The Hague, W. Van Hoeve.

VAN NIEL, Robert
　　1963　"The Course of Indonesian History," in Ruth T.
　　　　　McVey (ed.).

VANDENBOSCH, Amy
　　1942　The Dutch East Indies, Berkeley, University of
　　　　　California Press.

VERHOEVEN, F. R. J.
　　1962　Islam: Its Origin and Spread in Words, Maps and
　　　　　Pictures. Amsterdam, Djambatan.

VLEKKE, Bernard H. M.
　　1943　Nusantara: A History of Indonesia. Cambridge,
　　　　　Harvard University Press.

　　1945　The Story of the Dutch East Indies. Cambridge,
　　　　　Harvard University Press.

WARNECK, G.
　　1912　"The Growth of the Church Among the Bataks,"
　　　　　IRM., 1:20-43.

WARNECK, John
　　n.d.　The Living Christ and Dying Heathenism. New York,
　　　　　Fleming H. Revell Company. (Translated by Neil
　　　　　Buchanan).

WERTHEIM, W. F.
　　1956　Indonesian Society in Transition. Bandung,
　　　　　Sumur Bandung.

　　1965　East-West Parallels. Chicago, Quadrangle Books.

WILLIS, Avery
　　1964　"First Family," The Commission, XXXI:10-14.

WILSON, J. Christy
　　1959　Introducing Islam. New York, Friendship Press.

WOLD, Joseph Conrad
    1968   God's Impatience in Liberia.   Grand Rapids,
            William B. Eerdman Publishing Company.

WOODMAN, Dorothy
    1955   The Republic of Indonesia.   London, The Cresset
            Press.

WORLD CHRISTIAN HANDBOOK
    1952   World Christian Handbook, Grubb, Kenneth and
            Bingle, E. J. (eds.).

    1953   World Christian Handbook, Grubb, Kenneth and
            Bingle, E. J. (eds.).

    1962   World Christian Handbook, Caxill, H. Wakelin and
            Grubb, Kenneth, (eds.).

ZWEMER, Samual M.
    1920   The Influence of Animism on Islam.   London,
            Central Board of Missions.

Index

William Carey Library
PUBLICATIONS

Africa

PEOPLES OF SOUTHWEST ETHIOPIA, by A. R. Tippett,Ph.D.
A recent, penetrating evaluation by a professional anthropologist of the cultural complexities faced by Peace Corps workers and missionaries in a rapidly changing intersection of African states.
1970: 320 pp, $3.95. ISBN 0-87808-103-8

PROFILE FOR VICTORY: NEW PROPOSALS FOR MISSIONS IN ZAMBIA, by Max Ward Randall.
"In a remarkably objective manner the author has analyzed contemporary political, social educational and religious trends, which demand a re-examination of traditional missionary methods and the creation of daring new strategies...his conclusions constitute a challenge for the future of Christian missions, not only in Zambia, but around the world."
1970: 224 pp, Cloth, $3.95. ISBN 0-87808-403-7

THE CHURCH OF THE UNITED BRETHREN OF CHRIST IN SIERRA LEONE, by Emmett D. Cox, Executive Secretary, United Brethren in Christ Board of Missions.
A readable account of the relevant historical, demographic and anthropological data as they relate to the development of the United Brethren in Christ Church in the Mende and Creole communities. Includes a reformation of objectives.
1970: 184 pp, $2.95. ISBN 0-87808-301-4

APPROACHING THE NUER OF AFRICA THROUGH THE OLD TESTAMENT, by Ernest A. McFall.
The author examines in detail the similarities between the Nuer and the Hebrews of the Old Testament and suggests a novel Christian approach that does not make initial use of the New Testament.
1970: 104 pp, 8 1/2 x 11, $1.95.
ISBN 0-87808-310-3

Asia

TAIWAN: MAINLINE VERSUS INDEPENDENT CHURCH GROWTH,
A STUDY IN CONTRASTS, by Allen J. Swanson.

A provocative comparison between the older,
historical Protestant churches in Taiwan and the
new indigenous Chinese churches; suggests stag-
gering implications for missions everywhere that
intend to promote the development of truly indigenous expressions of Christianity.

1970: 216 pp, $2.95. ISBN 0-87808-404-5

NEW PATTERNS FOR DISCIPLING HINDUS: THE NEXT
STEP IN ANDHRA PRADESH, INDIA, by B.V. Subbamma.

Proposes the development of a Christian movement that is as well adapted culturally to the
Hindu tradition as the present movement is to the
Harijan tradition. Nothing could be more crucial
for the future of 400 million Hindus in India
today.

1970: 212 pp, $3.45. ISBN 0-87808-306-5

GOD'S MIRACLES: INDONESIAN CHURCH GROWTH, by Ebbie
C. Smith, Th.D.

The fascinating details of the penetration of
Christianity into the Indonesian archipelago make
for intensely interesting reading, as the anthropological context and the growth of the Christian
movement are highlighted.

1970: 224 pp, $3.45. ISBN 0-87808-302-2

NOTES ON CHRISTIAN OUTREACH IN A PHILIPPINE
COMMUNITY, by Marvin K. Mayers, Ph.D.

The fresh observations of an anthropologist
coming from the outside provide a valuable, however
preliminary, check list of social and historical
factors in the context of missionary endeavors in a
Tagalog province.

1970: 71 pp, 8 1/2 x 11, $1.45. ISBN 0-87808-104-6

Latin America

THE PROTESTANT MOVEMENT IN BOLIVIA, by C. Peter
Wagner.

An excitingly-told account of the gradual
build-up and present vitality of Protestantism.
A cogent analysis of the various subcultures
and the organizations working most effectively,
including a striking evaluation of Bolivia's
momentous Evangelism-in-Depth year and the possibilities of Evangelism-in-Depth for other parts
of the world.

1970: 264 pp, $3.95. ISBN 0-87808-402-9

LA SERPIENTE Y LA PALOMA, by Manuel Gaxiola.
    The impressive success story of the Apostolic
Church of Mexico, (an indigenous denomination
that never had the help of any foreign missionary),
told by a professional scholar now the director
of research for that church. (Spanish)
    1970: 200 pp, $2.95. ISBN 0-87808-802-4

THE EMERGENCE OF A MEXICAN CHURCH: THE ASSOCIATE
REFORMED PRESBYTERIAN CHURCH OF MEXICO, by James
Erskine Mitchell.
    Tells the ninety-year story of the Associate
Reformed Presbyterian Mission in Mexico, the trials
and hardships as well as the bright side of the
work. Eminently practical and helpful regarding
the changing relationship of mission and church in
the next decade.
    1970: 184 pp, $2.95. ISBN 0-87808-303-0

FRIENDS IN CENTRAL AMERICA, by Paul C. Enyart.
    This book describes the results of faithful and
effective labors of the California Friends Yearly
Meeting, giving an analysis of the growth of one of
the most virile, national evangelical churches in
Central America, comparing its growth to other evangelical churches in Guatemala, Honduras, and El
Salvador.
    1970: 224 pp, $3.45. ISBN 0-87808-405-3

Europe

THE CHALLENGE FOR EVANGELICAL MISSIONS TO EUROPE:
A SCANDINAVIAN CASE STUDY, by Hilkka Malaska.
    Graphically presents the state of Christianity
in Scandinavia with an evaluation of the pros and
cons and possible contributions that existing or
additional Evangelical missions can make in Europe
today.
    1970: 192 pp, $2.95. ISBN 0-87808-308-1

THE PROTESTANT MOVEMENT IN ITALY: ITS PROGRESS,
PROBLEMS, AND PROSPECTS, by Roger Hedlund.
    A carefully wrought summary of preliminary
data; perceptively develops issues faced by Evangelical Protestants in all Roman Catholic areas of
Europe. Excellent graphs.
    1970: 266 pp, $3.95. ISBN 0-87808-307-3

U.S.A.

THE YOUNG LIFE CAMPAIGN AND THE CHURCH, by Warren
Simandle.

If 70 per cent of young people drop out of the
church between the ages of 12 and 20, is there room
for a nationwide Christian organization working on
high school campuses? After a quarter of a century,
what is the record of Young Life and how has its
work with teens affected the church? *"A careful
analysis based on a statistical survey; full of
insight and challenging proposals for both Young
Life and the church."*

1970: 216 pp, $3.45. ISBN 0-87808-304-9

THE RELIGIOUS DIMENSION IN SPANISH LOS ANGELES:
A PROTESTANT CASE STUDY, by Clifton L. Holland.

A through analysis of the origin, development and present extent of this vital, often un-
noticed element in Southern California.

1970: 304 pp, $3.95. ISBN 0-87808-309-X

General

THEOLOGICAL EDUCATION BY EXTENSION, edited by
Ralph D. Winter, Ph.D.

A husky handbook on a new approach to the education of pastoral leadership for the church.
Gives both theory and practice and the exciting
historical development in Latin America of the
*"Largest non-governmental voluntary educational
development project in the world today."* Ted Ward,
Prof. of Education, Michigan State University.

1969: 648 pp, Library Buckram $7.95, Kivar
$4.95. ISBN 0-87808-101-1

THE CHURCH GROWTH BULLETIN, VOL. I-V, edited by
Donald A. McGavran, Ph.D.

The first five years of issues of a now-famous
bulletin which probes past foibles and present opportunities facing the 100,000 Protestant and Catholic missionaries in the world today. No perio-
dical edited for this audience has a larger reader-
ship.

1969: 408 pp, Library Buckram $6.95, Kivar
$4.45. ISBN 0-87808-701-X

CHURCH GROWTH THROUGH EVANGELISM-IN-DEPTH, by
Malcolm R. Bradshaw.
   *"Examines the history of Evangelism-in-Depth
and other total mobilization approaches to evangelism. Also presents concisely the 'Church
Growth' approach to mission and proposes a
wedding between the two...a great blessing to the
church at work in the world." WORLD VISION
MAGAZINE.*
   1969: 152 pp, $2.45. ISBN 0-87808-401-0

THE TWENTY FIVE UNBELIEVABLE YEARS, 1945-1969, by
Ralph D. Winter, Ph.D.
   A terse, exciting analysis of the most significant transition in human history in this millenium
and its impact upon the Christian movement. *"Packed
with insight and otherwise unobtainable statistical
data...a brilliant piece of work."* C. Peter Wagner.
   1970: 120 pp, $1.95. ISBN 0-87808-102-X

EL SEMINARIO DE EXTENSION: UN MANUAL, by James H.
Emery, F. Ross Kinsler, Louise J. Walker, Ralph D.
Winter.
   Gives the reasons for the extension approach to
the training of ministers, as well as the concrete,
practical details of establishing and operating
such a program. A Spanish translation of the third
section of *THEOLOGICAL EDUCATION BY EXTENSION*.
   1969: 256 pp, $3.45. ISBN 0-87808-801-6

ABOUT THE WILLIAM CAREY LIBRARY

William Carey is widely considered the "Father of Modern Missions" partly because many people think he was the first Protestant missionary. Even though there was a trickle of others before him, he deserves very special honor for many valiant accomplishments in his heroic career, but most particularly because of three things he did before he ever left England, things no one else in history before him had combined together:

1) he had an authentic, personal, evangelical passion to serve God and acknowledged this as obligating him to fulfill God's interests in the redemption of all men on the face of the earth.

2) he actually proposed a structure for the accomplishment of that aim - he did indeed, more than anyone else, set off the movement among Protestants for the creation of "voluntary societies" for foreign missions, and

3) he added to all of this a strategic literary and research achievement: shaky those statistics may have been, but he put together the very best possible estimate of the number of unreached peoples in every part of the globe, and summarized previous, relatively ineffective attempts to reach them. His burning conclusion was that existing efforts were not proportional to the opportunities and the scope of Christian obligation in Mission.

Today, a little over 150 years later, the situation is not wholly different. In the past five years, for example, experienced missionaries from all corners of the earth (53 countries) have brought to the Fuller School of World Mission and Institute of Church Growth well over 800 years of missionary experience. Twenty-six scholarly books have resulted from the research of faculty and students. The best statistics available have at times been shaky -though far superior to Carey's - but vision has been clear and the mandate is as urgent as ever. The printing press is still the right arm of Christians active in the Christian world mission.

The William Carey Library is a new publishing house dedicated to books related to this mission. There are many publishers, both secular and religious, that occasionally publish books of this kind. We believe there is no other devoted exclusively to the production and distribution of books for career missionaries and their home churches.

ABOUT THE AUTHOR

Ebbie C. Smith is a native of the state of Texas. He received the B.A. from Hardin-Simmons University in 1954, the B.D. and Th.D. from Southwestern Baptist Theological Seminary in 1957 and 1961. Dr. Smith worked toward the M.A. in mission at the School of World Mission and Institute of Church Growth, Fuller Theological Seminary, in 1970.

In 1960 Dr. and Mrs. Smith were appointed for service in Indonesia by the Foreign Mission Board of the Southern Baptist Convention. He served two terms as teacher in the Baptist Theological Seminary in Semarang, Indonesia. In 1970, the Indonesian Baptist Mission requested Mr. Smith to establish an Extension Bible School in East Java. This school will attempt to provide pastoral leadership for small and mostly rural congregations in East Java.